WHAT CAN TRIBES DO?
STRATEGIES AND INSTITUTIONS IN AMERICAN INDIAN ECONOMIC DEVELOPMENT

Edited by
STEPHEN CORNELL and JOSEPH P. KALT

American Indian Studies Center
3220 Campbell Hall
405 Hilgard Avenue
University of California
Los Angeles, CA 90024-1548

American Indian Manual and Handbook Series No. 4

Library of Congress Catalog Card No. 92–054417
ISBN No. 0–935626–37–9
©1992, The Regents of the University of California

This publication was made possible by a grant from the
Ford Foundation to the American Indian Studies Center,
University of California, Los Angeles

American Indian Studies Center
University of California
Los Angeles, CA 90024-1548
USA

CONTENTS

PREFACE

The last decade of the twentieth century is rapidly emerging as a time of critical importance for American Indian nations. Having overcome the threat of the termination policy of the 1950s and 1960s, having succeeded in the 1960s and 1970s in wresting from the federal government increased control over their own affairs, those nations today face the task of converting their limited but significant powers into lasting benefits for their peoples.

The challenges they face are imposing. The historical legacy of land dispossession, federal control, and poverty has had often devastating effects on Native American societies. Their newly invigorated sovereignty is being threatened once again by faltering federal policies, negative court decisions, and the political mobilization of non-Indian constituencies wishing to gain greater access to the resources Indian nations still possess. Yet there is opportunity as well. While still tenuous and frequently at risk, the hard-won era of self-determination has presented Indian nations—for the first time in a century—with the realistic possibility of shaping their own futures through their own actions.

Nowhere is this more apparent than in the area of economic development. The poverty of Native American populations has long been of great concern to Indian leaders. It has been of concern to federal policymakers as well, but their answer often has been to impose federally designed solutions or to invite the private sector of the United States economy to step in and take over the reservation development process. Seldom have Indian nations had the opportunity to propose their own solutions, the power to implement them, or the information necessary to design solutions that can work on tribal terms and in highly diverse tribal contexts. Today—at least for a time—the opportunity is there, and the power, while limited, is there as well. Informational resources, however, remain scarce.

This collection is part of an ongoing effort to address this scarcity. For the last five years, the Harvard Project on American Indian Economic Development has been carrying out extended study of the conditions under which self-determined economic development can be successful on Indian reservations. The core research method has been the comparative analysis of development efforts on selected reservations: What works where, and why? A central objective of this research has been to develop information and insights that can be used by tribes themselves as they wrestle with the unique combination of opportunities and obstacles confronting them today.

This volume includes some of the products of that research. While some Project findings have been published elsewhere,* the purpose of this collection is to make more widely available the work of Project researchers that may be directly useful to tribal leaders and policymakers. The focus of the collection is on the institutional bases of economic development and on the institutional and development strategies most likely to lead to success on tribal terms.

A number of these papers were commissioned originally by Indian tribes and national Indian organizations. Thanks to our funders, the Harvard Project has been able to offer a number of tribes and organizations *pro bono* research services using the energy and analytical skills of graduate students at Harvard University's John F. Kennedy School of Government. Over a four-year period, the Project has carried out more than fifty such research projects.** These efforts have sought answers to development-related problems that Indian tribes or organizations had identified, but which, for lack of time, money, or in some cases, necessary research skills, they were unable to pursue on their own. The chapters by Michael Cameron, Andrea Skari, Paul Nissenbaum and Paul Shadle, and Margaret Hargreaves and Hedy Chang are revised versions of their reports completed under this program while the authors were students in the

---

* See, for example, Stephen Cornell and Joseph P. Kalt, "Pathways from Poverty: Economic Development and Institution-Building on American Indian Reservations," *American Indian Culture and Research Journal* 14, no. 1 (1990); and Stephen Cornell and Joseph P. Kalt, "Where's the Glue? Institutional Bases of American Indian Economic Development," Working Paper Series, Malcolm Wiener Center for Social Policy, John F. Kennedy School of Government, Harvard University, 1991.

** A number of the reports on these projects have been published in the Harvard Project Report Series. For a complete list, write to the Harvard Project on American Indian Economic Development, John F. Kennedy School of Government, Harvard University, 79 JFK Street, Cambridge, Massachusetts 02138.

Masters in Public Policy program at the Kennedy School. The chapters by Eduardo Cordeiro and Matthew Krepps are revised versions of the authors' recent B.A. theses in Harvard's Department of Economics. The opening chapter by the editors and the concluding chapter by Ronald Trosper were written especially for this volume.

We would like to thank the Ford Foundation and the Northwest Area Foundation for their support of Harvard Project research, and the Ford Foundation for its support of the effort by the American Indian Studies Center at UCLA to make the results of that research more widely available to Indian tribes and other interested readers. Our thanks also to Duane Champagne, Director of the Center and Associate Professor of Sociology at UCLA, for the assistance and encouragement that made this publication possible, and to Judith St. George, Boyd Nelson, and Janet Coulon for their assistance in preparing the manuscript for publication. Finally, we wish to thank those Indian tribes and organizations whose willingness to participate in this research has made it possible to enhance the informational resources available to Indian nations as they confront the tasks and dilemmas of economic and institutional development.

Stephen Cornell
University of California, San Diego

Joseph P. Kalt
Harvard University

1

RELOADING THE DICE: IMPROVING THE CHANCES FOR ECONOMIC DEVELOPMENT ON AMERICAN INDIAN RESERVATIONS[1]

Stephen Cornell and Joseph P. Kalt

The experiences of a wide array of societies around the world amply demonstrate that achieving sustained, self-determined economic development is a complex and difficult task. Certainly this is the case on the Indian reservations of the United States, where numerous obstacles face tribal leaders, managers, and other individuals concerned about the economic well-being of their peoples.

In the introductory chapter, the editors of this volume review the specific obstacles that Indian nations face as they pursue their own development goals, outline the critical role that institutions of tribal governance play in the development process, and suggest ways that newly empowered tribal governments can improve tribes' own chances of achieving self-determined development success.

I. INTRODUCTION

American Indian societies are phenomenally resilient. In the last several centuries, they have faced winds of economic, political, and cultural change that have blown as fiercely over them as over any people in history. These winds have brought military violence and subjugation, epidemics of disease, seizures of land and property, vicious racism, and economic deprivation. Yet, as the twenty-first century approaches, hundreds of distinct Indian nations built upon dozens of cultural lineages still persevere and grow, variously bound together by ties of family, language, history, and culture. The lesson from Indian Country is a lesson of strength.

This strength is still being tested. Among the most formidable challenges facing native peoples today are those rooted in economic conditions. American Indians living on the nation's nearly 300 reservations are among the poorest people in the United States. On most reservations, sustained economic development, while much discussed, has yet to make a significant dent in a long history of poverty and powerlessness. Despite the many federal programs and the large sums of federal and philanthropic money that have been used over the years, many Indian reservations continue to experience extremely high unemployment rates; high dependency on welfare, government jobs, and other transfer payments; discouraging social problems; and an almost complete absence of sustainable, productive economic activity.

At the same time, in the last two decades some reservations have made significant progress. The examples are relatively few, but tribes as diverse as the Confederated Salish and Kootenai of the Flathead Reservation, the White Mountain Apaches, the Mescalero Apaches, Cochiti Pueblo, the Mississippi Choctaws, the Muckleshoots, and various others have shown that economic development can take place on Indian reservations, under Indian auspices, and serving Indian goals.[2] (Table 1 provides summary data on fifteen tribes whose development situations illustrate the range now apparent in Indian Country.) Still, the task of sparking and fueling development is enormous and complex. The challenge facing tribal leaders and policymakers remains immense.

For the last five years, the Harvard Project on American Indian Economic Development has been studying economic development on

TABLE 1

Economic Conditions
On Selected American Indian Reservations

	Change in Income 1977–1989	Adults with 1989 Income >$7000	1989 BLS Unemployment	1989 Total Unemployment
Flathead	16%	39%	20%	41%
White Mountain Apache	12%	33%	11%	21%
Cochiti Pueblo	10%	43%	10%	22%
Mescalero Apache	9%	18%	52%	58%
Mississippi Choctaw	9%	36%	26%	27%
Muckleshoot	6%	16%	50%	57%
Pine Ridge Sioux	-1%	21%	61%	73%
Passamaquoddy	-3%	19%	56%	66%
San Carlos Apache	-7%	16%	51%	66%
Rosebud Sioux	-10%	4%	90%	93%
Lummi	-11%	19%	46%	58%
Hualapai	-11%	11%	45%	74%
Yakima	-12%	20%	61%	63%
Crow	-12%	11%	67%	78%
Northern Cheyenne	-15%	29%	48%	55%
All Reservation Indians	-1%	24%	40%	48%

Note: "Change in Income" refers to the change in the percentage of adults with incomes in excess of BIA poverty levels ($5000 in 1977 and $7000 in 1989). "BLS Unemployment" measures adults looking for employment but not finding it. "Total Unemployment" measures the percent of the tribal workforce not working.

Source: U.S. Department of the Interior, Bureau of Indian Affairs, "Indian Service Population and Labor Force Estimates," January 1989.

Indian reservations. Our research has been prompted by two developments:

- Beginning in the 1970s, there has been a federal policy shift toward tribal self-determination. While this shift is tenuous and under constant attack, it has made it possible for tribes to exert increased control over their own development goals and programs.

- In the era of self-determination, tribes have begun to take different development paths, often with very different results. Some tribes are moving forward, under their own definitions of "forward." Others appear to be stuck in place.

Our research objectives have been to explain why tribes differ in their economic development strategies and in the outcomes of those strategies, and to discover what it takes for *self-determined economic development*—development that meets tribal goals—to be successful. We make no assumption that all tribes share the same development goals, nor do we assume that they should embrace non-Indian definitions of development success. On the contrary, we think success itself ultimately must be evaluated on the basis of the tribes' own criteria. It seems clear, however, that most tribes are deeply committed to improving the economic welfare of their peoples. At the same time, they are concerned that this be accomplished without losing political or social sovereignty, i.e., control over their own affairs and over the quality and nature of reservation life.

Much of our research has involved talking to and working with selected tribes—some successful, some not—on their development policies, projects, and programs. We also have looked in depth at the available numerical data on sixty-seven reservations around the country. This is a large and comprehensive research effort. It is not yet completed, but certain findings have become clear.

The purpose of this chapter is to outline our findings in a way that may help tribes make choices that improve their chances for sustainable, *self-determined* development. We begin by looking at the major obstacles Indian tribes face in the development arena. We then discuss those development factors that appear, from our research, to be most important *and that tribes can actually do something about* as they try to expand tribal sovereignty and improve the economic welfare of their peoples. Our focus is on what *tribes* can do to promote their economic, political, and social well-being. In no sense does this mean that federal and state policies play only minor roles in the course that reservation economies take. Indeed, we conclude this study with a discussion of the implications of our findings for federal and state policy.

II. THE DEVELOPMENT GAMBLE

Economic development is a difficult task anywhere in the world. In Indian Country, however, self-determined economic development is a major gamble: the odds are hardly promising; the effort required is tremendous; the results are at best uncertain. A few tribes—for the time being, at least—have won. Many continue to lose. In fact, the dice are heavily loaded against economic development on Indian reservations.

A. OBSTACLES TO DEVELOPMENT

The obstacles are daunting. Tribes face a host of problems. Some of these problems are shared with other would-be developers—countries, cities, states—while some are specific to Indian tribes. Among the obstacles often listed in reports and studies or mentioned in Indian Country as explanations of continuing reservation poverty are these:

- Tribes and individuals lack access to financial capital.
- Tribes and individuals lack human capital (education, skills, technical expertise) and the means to develop it.
- Reservations lack effective planning.
- Reservations are subject to too much planning and not enough action.
- Reservations are poor in natural resources.
- Reservations have natural resources, but lack sufficient control over them.
- Reservations are disadvantaged by their distance from markets and the high costs of transportation.

- Tribes cannot persuade investors to locate on reservations because of intense competition from non-Indian communities.
- Federal and state policies are counterproductive and/or discriminatory.
- The Bureau of Indian Affairs is inept, corrupt, and/or uninterested in reservation development.
- Non-Indian outsiders control or confound tribal decision making.
- Tribes have unworkable and/or externally imposed systems of government.
- Tribal politicians and bureaucrats are inept or corrupt.
- On-reservation factionalism destroys stability in tribal decisions.
- The instability of tribal government keeps outsiders from investing.
- Reservation savings rates are low.
- Entrepreneurial skills and experience are scarce.
- Non-Indian management techniques won't work on the reservation.
- Non-Indian management techniques will work, but are absent.
- Tribal cultures get in the way.
- The long-term effects of racism have undermined tribal self-confidence.
- Alcoholism and other social problems are destroying tribes' human capital.

These explanations are not necessarily wrong. Most of them are right somewhere or other in Indian Country. But some are far more important than others, and some are either insignificant, misleading, or mistaken. Whatever the case, the sheer magnitude and variety of such a list makes it virtually useless as a guide to tribal or federal policy and action. If all we know is that virtually everything is working against development progress, then we have no clear idea of where to begin in the effort to improve the chances of success.

A more useful approach is to identify the key ingredients of successful economic development, determine which of these ingredients are most important, and identify which ones tribes actually can do something about. This approach can give tribes a better sense of where to devote time and energy so as to have the greatest impact; of how, in effect, they can "reload the dice" so as to increase the chances of success in the development gamble.

B. KEY DEVELOPMENT INGREDIENTS

The key ingredients of development can be divided into three categories: external opportunity, internal assets, and development strategy.

1. EXTERNAL OPPORTUNITY

External opportunity refers to the political, economic, and geographic settings that reservations find themselves in and by which they are linked to the surrounding society. These settings can limit or enhance tribes' opportunities to accomplish their development goals, and are part of the reality they must deal with. The critical factors are:

(1) *Political sovereignty*: the extent to which a tribe has genuine control over reservation decision-making, the use of reservation resources, and relations with the outside world. As discussed more fully below, the evidence is clear that as sovereignty rises, so do the chances of successful development.

(2) *Market opportunity*: unique economic niches or opportunities in local, regional, or national markets. These opportunities can come from particular assets or attributes (minerals, tourist attractions, distinctive artistic or craft traditions), or from supportive federal policies (as in gaming, wildlife, and favorable tax treatment). As such opportunities increase, so do the chances of successful development.

(3) *Access to financial capital*: the tribe's ability to obtain investment dollars from private, governmental, or philanthropic sources. Access depends on such factors as federal tax policy, tribal reputation, private sector knowledge and experience, and public funding. As access to capital improves, so do the chances of successful development.

(4) *Distance from markets*: the distance tribes are from the markets for their products. The greater the distance, the more difficult and costly it is

to serve those markets, reducing the chances of successful development.

2. INTERNAL ASSETS

Internal assets refer to characteristics of tribes themselves and the resources they control that can be committed to development. The critical factors are:

(1) *Natural resources*: minerals, water, timber, fish, wildlife, scenery, fertile land, etc. As natural resource endowments rise, so do the chances of success. It is worth noting, however, that such resources are not necessarily the key to successful development. A number of tribes with substantial natural resource endowments have been unable—despite major efforts—to turn them into productive economic activity, while some tribes almost completely lacking in natural resources have done quite well. Matthew Snipp has shown that reservations with significant energy resources, taken together, "are somewhat better off than other reservations but not by a large margin."[3]

(2) *Human capital*: the skills, knowledge, and expertise of the labor force. These are acquired largely through education or work experience. As human capital rises, so do the chances of successful development.

(3) *Institutions of governance*: the laws and organization of tribal government, from constitutions to legal or business codes to the tribal bureaucracy. As these institutions become more effective at maintaining a stable environment in which investors feel secure and effort is rewarded, the odds of successful development improve.

(4) *Culture*: conceptions of normal and proper ways of doing things and relating to other people, and the behavior that embodies those conceptions. Such conceptions and behavior vary widely, with significant implications for development strategy. For example, the hierarchical "boss-worker" relationship that characterizes industrial factories may be acceptable in some tribes and abhorrent in others, while a strong central government may be viewed as proper in one tribal culture and as grossly inappropriate in another.

The role of culture in development is complex and cannot easily be reduced to simple "if this, then that" statements that apply universally to all tribes. We will have more to say about this below, but, in general, our research keeps pointing to the conclusion that culture and the institutions of governance are a crucial pair of factors in development.[4] Economic development can take hold in the face of a wide range of cultural attitudes on such matters as the sanctity of natural resources or the propriety of individuals trying to make themselves wealthier. However, unless there is a fit between the culture of the community and the structure and powers of its governing institutions, those institutions may be seen as illegitimate, their ability to regulate and organize the development process will be undermined, and development will be blocked. Without a match between culture and governing institutions, tribal government cannot consistently do its basic job: creating and sustaining the "rules of the game" that development in any society requires.

3. DEVELOPMENT STRATEGY

Development strategy refers to the decisions tribes make regarding their plans and approaches to economic development. The important choices are:

(1) *Overall economic system*: the organization of the reservation economy itself. Will it be a system consisting primarily of tribal enterprises, individual or family entrepreneurship, non-Indian investment or entrepreneurship, federally sponsored and controlled activity, or some combination of these? Again, we will have more to say about this below, but in general, where there is a match between the approach a tribe pursues and the social organization and culture of the tribe, the odds of successful development increase.

(2) *Choice of development activity*: the selection of specific development projects (e.g., a convenience store, a gaming operation, a motel, a timber enterprise, commercial hunting of wildlife, a manufacturing plant, etc.). Activities and projects that take advantage of tribes' market opportunities, allow tribes to specialize in using the natural and/or human resources most available to them, and are consistent with tribes' cultures are more likely to be successful.

It is important to note several things about these lists of external opportunities, internal assets, and development strategies. First, weakness in one or even several of the internal or external factors does not spell doom for development efforts. Distance from markets, for example, may not be a problem if the commodity a tribe is selling is rare, less expensive than alternatives, or easy to transport. The market, in effect, moves closer as it becomes more difficult or costly for buyers to obtain the product from someone else. Thus Navajo uranium, for example, while mined in areas remote from major markets, has been saleable in part because it is scarce. Similarly, human capital may be less important if a tribe's primary product is cut timber sold as logs to a broker. Producing it is fairly simple, and a relatively unskilled work force can be productive.[5] Or, to use another example, natural resources may not be important to a tribe with skilled labor and good access to markets, as the Mississippi Choctaw case shows. A surplus of one factor may compensate for a shortage of another.

Second, the contributions of some of these factors clearly depend upon the presence of other factors. The best example, perhaps, is access to financial capital. The primary problem tribes face in obtaining investment capital is real or perceived instability in tribal governments and policies. Thus, capital access is first and foremost a problem of political development: the establishment of an institutional environment in which investors feel secure. This holds true whether the investors are banks, corporations, venture capitalists, or tribal members. With declines in federal funding over the last decade and poor prospects for significant increases in the near future, attention to the institutions-of-governance factor can be the best way to overcome the access-to-capital obstacle.

Finally, which of these factors can tribes do something about? Not all of them are equally easy to change. On certain factors, tribes essentially are stuck with what they've got; on others, they can alter the situation. Table 2 lists key development ingredients and indicates the degree to which they can be changed directly by tribes.

Tribes can do little, for example, to improve their natural resource endowments or their distance from markets. Similarly, a reservation's market opportunity is largely a matter of economic forces that are outside tribal control. Tribes can invest in human capital via education and training, but the payoffs can take a long time to appear. Tribes may thus be compelled to "import" managers and skilled workers from outside, as tribes such as the Mississippi Choctaw and White Mountain Apaches have done while they wait for the training of their own people to take hold. However, whether it takes place by investment or importing, improving human capital requires money. As for changes in tribal culture, even if tribes were willing to make significant changes—a highly questionable assumption— cultures cannot simply be fine-tuned to meet a set of predetermined criteria.

TABLE 2
How Much Control Do Tribes Have over the Keys to Development?

	Degree of Control		
	Low	Moderate	High
External Opportunities			
Political Sovereignty		X	
Market Opportunity	X		
Distance from Markets	X		
Access to Capital		X	
Internal Assets			
Natural Resources	X		
Human Capital		X	
Governing Institutions			X
Tribal Culture		X	
Development Strategy			
Economic Policy			X
Development Activity			X

Cultural changes that do occur often take a long time to accomplish, and changes that enhance well-being require leadership and vision that are themselves scarce in most societies.

Political sovereignty can be changed, but an individual tribe cannot easily change it. The central determinant of political sovereignty is federal Indian policy, itself a product of interactions among the executive branch, the Congress, the federal courts, and various public and private constituencies, of whom tribes are only one. These interactions can be influenced through lobbying, public relations, and litigation, but such efforts require time and money, and the ultimate payoffs—especially in the courts—are hard to predict[6] Sovereignty, therefore, while critical to success, is only partially and unpredictably subject to the control of the individual tribe.

This is hardly an argument for complacency. Expansions in tribal sovereignty since the 1960s have come about largely as a result of the political activities of tribes and national Indian organizations. Those expansions have been key components in making self-determined economic development possible. Presumably, further improvements in tribal sovereignty—and preservation of the gains already made—will similarly depend on what Indians do, and the future of economic development in Indian Country will depend to some extent at least on Indian success in this battle to sustain and expand existing tribal sovereignty. The question here, however, has to do with where individual tribes can most productively focus their energy in the development arena so that what has been made possible by expansions in tribal sovereignty is realized in real development gains. This depends increasingly on the ability of tribes to effectively *exercise* the sovereignty they now command.

As Table 2 indicates, three factors stand out as major candidates for tribal action. The first is institutions. Tribes can alter their own institutions of self-governance, with major impacts on their chances of development success. The second and third come under development strategies: Tribes also can exercise control over development policy and over the specific development projects they pursue. What can tribes do in these areas?

III. WHAT CAN TRIBES DO?

For many Indian nations and their leaders, the problem of economic development has been defined as one of picking the right projects. Tribal governments often devote much of their development-related time and energy to considering whether or not to pursue specific projects: a factory, a mine, an agricultural enterprise, a motel, and so on. Some of these are proposed by outsiders, some by tribal members; others are simply whatever is currently fundable under federal programs. Using their own judgment and whatever information they can assemble, tribal councils and tribal planners try to pick winners.

Picking winners is important, but it is also rare. In fact, Indian Country is dotted with failed projects that turned sour as investors' promises evaporated, or enterprises failed to attract customers, or managers found themselves overwhelmed by market forces and political instability. In fact, many tribes pursue development backwards, concentrating first on picking the next winning project at the expense of attention to political and economic institutions and broader development strategies. Development success is marked, in part, by the sustainability of projects. Generally speaking, only when sound political and economic institutions and overall development strategies are in place do projects—public or private— become sustainable on reservations. Much of the development success we have seen has occurred where tribes have paid prior and ongoing attention to the structure and powers of their political and economic systems.

Indeed, in our research two factors more than any others distinguish successful tribes from unsuccessful ones: *de facto* sovereignty and effective institutions of self-governance. The strategic issues, while important, follow on these.

A. THE ROLE OF SOVEREIGNTY

By "de facto" sovereignty we mean genuine decision-making control over the running of tribal affairs and the use of tribal resources. While the legal status of Indian sovereignty waxes and wanes with federal court decisions and legislation, it is still the case that an assertive and capable tribe can take primary control of many economic decisions away from the leading contender for such power—the Bureau of Indian Affairs (BIA). In case after case where we see sustained economic development, from the Flathead and Mescalero Apache reservations to Cochiti Pueblo and Mississippi Choctaw, tribal decision-making has effectively replaced BIA (as well as other "outside") decision-making. While the resulting relationships between tribe and BIA range from the cooperative to the contentious, they are characterized by a demotion of the BIA's role from decision-maker to advisor and provider of technical assistance.

The reason why tribal sovereignty is so crucial to successful development is clear. As long as the BIA or some other outside organization carries primary responsibility for economic conditions on Indian reservations, development decisions will tend to reflect outsiders' agendas. In the case of the BIA, for example, bureaucratic standards of success (protecting a budget, expanding authority) will tend to be given more weight than tribal standards of success. But when BIA or other federal decisions lead to lost opportunities or wasted resources, the costs are borne most directly by the affected tribe, not by the federal bureaucracy.

Transferring control over decisions to tribes does not guarantee success, but it tightens the link between decision-making and its consequences. Tribes have stronger incentives to make appropriate development decisions than the BIA because they are the ones who more directly bear the costs and reap the benefits of those decisions. This is evident in comparisons of tribes' overall development efforts.[7] It is also borne out in specific sectors of the economy, such as forestry, where transferring significant control from the BIA to tribes has spurred productivity (see the chapter by Matthew Krepps in this volume).

The legal and de facto sovereignty of tribes has been subject to constant challenge, and it is frequently asserted that if tribes wish to be sovereign, they must first establish sound, nondependent economies. Our research indicates that, for two basic reasons, this reasoning is backwards. First, as we have said, sovereignty brings with it accountability. Those whose resources and well-being are at stake are the ones in charge. Without this accountability, as in the years before self-determination became established federal policy in the 1970s, sustainable development on reservations was virtually nonexistent. Second, the sovereign status of tribes offers distinct legal and economic market opportunities, from reduced tax and regulatory burdens for industry to unique niches for gaming and the commercial use of wildlife. Sovereignty is one of the primary development resources tribes now have, and the reinforcement of tribal sovereignty under self-determination should be the central thrust of Indian policy. One of the quickest ways to bring development to a halt and prolong the impoverished conditions of reservations would be to undermine the sovereignty of Indian tribes.

Having said this, the fact is that the formal boundaries of tribal sovereignty are not easy for the individual tribe to change. Tribes may not be able to do very much, at least in the short run, to alter the legal position they occupy within the larger society. What tribes can do is be more or less aggressive in asserting the sovereignty they possess. As we have noted, the successful tribes we have studied are uniformly marked by aggressive assumptions of authority over tribal development decisions.

B. THE ROLE OF INSTITUTIONS

Assertions of sovereignty, however, are not enough. Once established, sovereignty must be put to effective use. This requires more than simply aggressive decision-making. A tribe laying claim to the right of self-determination must be armed with capable institutions of self-governance. In Indian Country, as in developing societies around the world, such institutions are essential not only to the successful exercise of sovereignty, but to successful economic development as well.

Institutions can be thought of as the formal and informal mechanisms by which groups of people act together. Formal institutions include constitutions, charters, laws, and other formal rules that regulate what people do. Informal institutions include culturally supported standards of right and wrong, proper and improper, normal and abnormal. These standards likewise regulate what individuals and groups do, but through the values, rules of behavior, and ideas we all learn from growing up and living in a particular community. They are communicated to us as part of a society's culture, enforced by the approval and disapproval of our parents, peers, elders, and other authority figures.

As tribes set about achieving genuine self-government, the need is to put in place formal governing institutions that can perform three basic tasks: (1) mobilize and sustain the tribal community's support for its institutions and for particular development strategies; (2) efficiently make and carry out strategic choices; and (3) provide a political environment in which investors—large or small, tribal members or nonmembers—feel secure. These institutions of self-governance have to work both at the level of policy and group action (for example, the design of the reservation economic system and the making of rules and laws) and at the level of day-to-day bureaucratic functions (for example, program administration and law enforcement).

TASK 1:
MOBILIZE AND SUSTAIN SUPPORT FOR
INSTITUTIONS AND STRATEGIES

The power of self-governance in and of itself is no guarantee of economic development. Such power can be the key to creating an environment in which self-determined economic development succeeds, or it can create an environment in which self-determined economic development becomes impossible. Societies in Eastern Europe, Asia, Africa, and Latin America are repeating these lessons on a daily basis. To perform beneficially, self-government—governing institutions and their decisions—ultimately must have the support of the community. Without this support, the results are likely to be instability, stagnation, and a government that serves only the temporary interests of the faction currently in power.

But where does sustainable support for the institutions and policies of self-government come from? Our research indicates that such support depends critically on achieving a match between the formal institutions of governance on the one hand and the culture of the society on the other.

For example, among the things we learn as part of our experience in a community are certain political standards. These constitute answers to such questions as: Who should rightly wield governmental power? What are the legitimate rights of citizens and leaders? How should we resolve disputes among ourselves? and so on. These culturally shared political standards ideally form the foundations of the formal institutions of self-government. Without such cultural foundations, the formal government of a society is likely to lack legitimacy and respect in the community it is supposed to govern.[8] It is then more likely to be an engine of conflict and a vehicle for the pursuit of personal gain, and less likely to be able to resolve conflict, articulate and support the public interest, and create an environment in which social and economic development can take place.[9]

For many American Indian tribes, there is a very real possibility of a mismatch between their formal governments and the standards of political legitimacy found in their cultures. Tribal constitutions often have been written and, if not imposed, at least promoted by outsiders. Most of the constitutions adopted under the Indian Reorganization Act (IRA) of 1934, for example, under which many tribes operate, were drafted by the Department of the Interior with minimal attention either to indigenous forms of government or to the broad diversity among Indian tribes.[10] Tribes had the opportunity both to accept or reject, via tribal referenda, the IRA itself, and to adopt tribal constitutions designed under its provisions. In some of the early tribal referenda on the IRA, member abstentions were counted as favorable votes, and both the IRA and some constitutions were adopted in some tribes despite the abstentions of significant majorities of eligible voters.[11] Especially in the early years of the IRA, outsiders and their objectives often dominated tribal bureaucracies. The bureaucratic functions of most reservation governments were designed to fit BIA and other federal programs and needs, and to serve as channels through which resources could be transferred back and forth between the reservations and external governments. In few cases were the structures of tribal government effectively designed to assist tribes in making and implementing their own policy decisions. As Vine Deloria and Clifford Lytle point out, in the original conception of tribal governments on which the IRA was based, "the intent of tribal governments [was] to manage Indian resources, not to act in a national capacity."[12]

Nonetheless, certain tribes appear to have done relatively well under the IRA. IRA constitutions—and those modeled on them—typically created a system of centralized tribal government with a single chief executive (the tribal chair or president), a one-house legislature (the tribal council), and a weak or absent judiciary.[13] This system appears to match certain tribes' traditions and norms regarding the legitimate structure and powers of government, and these tribes may function effectively under these provisions.

The relatively successful Apache tribes (Table 1), for example, carry a tradition of often popularly selected, strong chief executives with significant administrative and judicial powers at the local group and band levels, and with considerable moral authority and symbolic significance in group affairs. Notwithstanding the range of authority conferred on Apache executives, ascendancy to leadership depended upon a form of the "consent of the governed" citizens. Leaders who abused their positions were simply deserted. The indigenous Apache term for leader is "he who convinces us," suggesting limits on executive powers that might otherwise be turned to the pursuit of private interests over public interests.[14]

These historic foundations of Apache governance share some common ground with the IRA system, i.e., in both indigenous Apache governance and the IRA we find few and relatively undifferentiated branches of government.[15] Our research repeatedly finds that this kind of common ground—this match between cultural standards of governmental legitimacy and the formal structure of tribes' current governments—is a key to creating an environment conducive to economic development.

By the same token, it comes as no surprise that where tribes' governments are not backed up by accepted cultural standards of propriety, tribal governments can become destabilizing forces that discourage not only the effective exercise of political and social sovereignty, but economic development as well. Imposition of the IRA constitution on some Sioux societies, for example, where economic and social problems are marked (e.g., Table 1), serves as a case in point.

Historic Sioux societies had fairly fluid but highly developed political systems. Oglala bands, for example, were governed by a council, or legislature, known as the Big Bellies or *naca*, composed of headmen, medicine men, warriors, and other men of stature. This council selected from among its number an executive council of four chiefs or councilors, who bore primary responsibility for the welfare of the group. They were ultimately responsible for camp policy, dispute resolution, and for advising the people on issues of significance to the community as a whole. They in turn delegated authority to four younger men, known as "shirt wearers," who served as the executives of the tribe and the voice of the chiefs, responsible for carrying out their policies. These then appointed marshals or *akicita* who were responsible for the maintenance of order, for seeing to it that the decisions of the chiefs and the laws of the society were observed by all the members of the camp—including the Big Bellies and the chiefs themselves—and for disciplining violators.[16]

Political organization above the band level apparently was rare and fleeting, but according to Royal Hassrick, something resembling a national assembly met yearly prior to the mid-nineteenth century. In these gatherings hundreds of delegates from the Oglala, Miniconjou, Brulé, and other Sioux tribes selected four "Supreme Owners" who served as chief executives of the nation.[17] At the same time, it seems clear that collective identity was most prominently focused at the band or *tiyospaye* level, where there was a high degree of group autonomy.

This intricate governmental structure—with its strong legislature, executives selected by the legislature in a parliamentary fashion, articulated judicial authorities, and perhaps a federalist national system of some sort—apparently served the Sioux well during their rise to dominance on the northern plains. Eventually, sustained warfare with the United States and the loss of the buffalo overwhelmed it, while reservation administrators actively suppressed indigenous Sioux government. When the new tribal government was established at Pine Ridge under the IRA in the 1930s, the old *tiyospayes*—still apparent in the settlement pattern on the reservation—as well as the complex and multilayered structure of Sioux government were largely ignored. As it turned out, however, the cultural standards that supported traditional Sioux government had not been entirely eradicated, nor had localized allegiances and identity.[18] At Pine Ridge, citizens continue to spontaneously create subnational district governments and organizations that take over functions that might otherwise be performed by the central IRA tribal government. The United States, meanwhile, continues to treat the centralized tribal government (with its one-house legislature and popularly elected single president) as the legitimate government of the tribe.

Under these circumstances, it is no wonder that the IRA government at Pine Ridge is subject to turmoil and experiences great difficulty in exercising stable, sovereign authority or in winning the allegiance of the community. In such an environment, tribally sponsored economic development has difficulty taking root.

In short, the Apache-Sioux contrast illustrates the point: Some IRA tribes have indigenous traditions and structures that "fit" better than others the IRA model of centralized government operating under a single chief executive and a one-house legislature without an independent judiciary. Where this kind of match holds, tribes have relative success in moving forward under self-determination. Other tribes' traditions may include decentralized authority and identity, regional or clan-based government, or political power founded on religious belief. These tribes have greater difficulty governing themselves under IRA-style constitutions. What this suggests is that, for many tribes, constitutional reform is the appropriate first step toward sustainable economic development.

TASK 2:
IMPLEMENT STRATEGIC CHOICES

Task 2 requires laws, rules, and procedures that can get things done. Several dimensions of this stand out in Indian Country.

(1) *Formalized Decision Rules and Procedures.* No society of significant size can count solely on the goodwill of its leaders and citizens or their spontaneous loyalty to shared cultural values to hold the society together, especially across activities as diverse as investing public monies in schools, roads, or resource development; litigating, lobbying, or negotiating with other nations; or regulating, prohibiting, or penalizing various behaviors by the society's own members. Conflicts of interest and opportunities for private advantage inherent in these activities cannot consistently be controlled simply by appeals to conscience or to essential or traditional "Japanese" or "American" or "German" or "Cherokee" or "Arapahoe" or "Sioux" values. Sharing such values can be important in helping people to understand, sympathize, and identify with each other, and to recognize that there is, indeed, a public interest to be served, particularly in times of fundamental change (as, for example, during constitutional reform). But sustaining public spiritedness during the long, hard battles over defining and implementing the will of the people is a nearly impossible task.

For this reason, among others, human societies devise rules and procedures that delegate and delimit authority. From the orally transmitted laws of the Iroquois Confederacy to Robert's Rules of Order to the fish and game code of the White Mountain Apaches, formalized rules and procedures serve to *empower* a people by allowing them to carry forward the public's interest. In promoting government by law, such rules and procedures help to insulate the public interest from the possibility that individuals interested only in their own advantage on occasion will end up in positions of power.

The need for such systems of formalized rules and procedures in Indian Country is amply evident. Business codes that regulate on-reservation permit procedures can prevent every new enterprise proposal from turning into a political fight. Similarly, environmental codes governing land use, wildlife, and resource extraction can streamline decisions on individual projects while still embodying the people's views on the proper use of reservation assets (see, for example, the chapter by Nissenbaum and Shadle in this volume).

Codes themselves, however, must be implemented through a process that clearly defines the rights and responsibilities of all affected parties: When can the tribal council overrule the land-use office? When can public debate be cut off? What right of appeal do applicants have, and to whom? What is the power of the tribal council vis-à-vis the judiciary? and so forth. The tribe that fails to answer these kinds of questions with clear and hard-to-change rules and laws invites the kind of conflict and instability that raises roadblocks to development.

(2) *Professional Financial, Personnel, and Record Systems.* Many tribal governments encounter repeated difficulty as a consequence of their inability to maintain close control over tribal finances or of the failure to keep day-to-day operations running smoothly. Development will be discouraged if the paperwork on the new business permit is lost, or if tribal records are cleared out each time the leadership changes hands, or if the building contractor's bill goes unpaid until funds can be shuffled around departments, or if each firing of a tribal employee turns into a political crisis. Good financial controls and record systems prevent abuses, improve performance monitoring, increase accountability, and enhance the tribe's ability to make informed, knowledgeable decisions regarding tribal assets and opportunities.

Similarly, professional personnel standards and grievance procedures (such as a personnel appeals board that has genuine authority) allow the tribal bureaucracy to weather political storms and can insulate tribal politicians from petty factionalism (for example, the disgruntled worker can be directed to a personnel grievance process instead of to the tribal chair). Where resolving grievances on the part of tribal employees depends less on who is tribal chair or on who sits on the tribal council and more on a formalized, fair, and dependable grievance process, the tribe enhances its political stability and increases its ability to effectively manage its own affairs.

In short, the ability to get things done, typically through a professional and capable bureaucracy, is a critical element in translating tribal policy choices into results. Such a bureaucracy need be neither large nor elaborate, as the relatively effective bureaucracies at Cochiti Pueblo and Muckleshoot illustrate. The revenue office at Rosebud Sioux consists of a director and one assistant; when collections need to be made, it is likely to be the director who gets in her pickup truck and drives across the reservation to pick up the check. The point is not to build up some complicated set of bureaucratic offices or elaborate staff, but to establish rules that consistently govern the way tribal affairs are handled, and to make certain those rules survive changes in leadership or other personnel.

This bureaucratic capability appears to be a significant factor in relative development success at reservations such as Flathead, Mescalero, and Mississippi Choctaw, and of selected operations at White Mountain Apache and Cochiti Pueblo. It also is important in recent improvements in the development situation at Muckleshoot.

TASK 3:
ESTABLISH A POLITICAL ENVIRONMENT
SAFE FOR DEVELOPMENT

American Indian reservations compete with other localities to attract economic activity, including not only the activity of outside investors, but that of their own citizens. To be successful in this competition, reservations generally must be able to offer the opportunity to earn economic returns commensurate with, or better than, the returns people and assets might earn somewhere else. Financial capital can readily migrate away from the reservation, and tribal labor can look for work off the reservation or, in a bad regional labor market, move away altogether. While personal ties and commitments may help to retain labor on the reservation, the greater the employment opportunities, the more likely people are to stay.

Even when labor is settled and available on the reservation, financial assets are also necessary for economic development. Investment dollars have to come from somewhere in order to provide people with the tools and materials needed to make them productive and competitive. The $10,000 needed to stock an auto parts store, the $8,000 needed to buy used agricultural equipment, the $2,000 to expand an arts and crafts cooperative, or the millions needed for a tribal sawmill all depend on individuals' or private or public entities' willingness to invest.

Throughout the world, countries' economic policies and governmental systems eat into the returns that investors can expect in two primary ways: by raising risks and by raising production costs. Investors' risks are raised, for example, by uncertainty in tax and/or regulatory policy, and by insecurity in the enforcement of contracts and agreements. Investors' costs can be raised by governmental actions such as hiring policies designed to shield certain workers from competition, inadequate provision of public services (roads, water systems, and waste disposal facilities, etc.), high taxes, or rules that change with every new administration. More subtly, investors' returns can be squeezed by delays, legal hurdles, and political infighting.

This is not to say that tribes should never tax, should never encourage hiring certain kinds of workers, or should provide every public service an enterprise demands. Nevertheless, it must be recognized that the power to govern can be the power to transfer wealth, at investors' expense, to those who govern. Insisting on employment for the chair's supporters, dipping into the cash reserves of the tribal enterprise to fund a popular project, or changing lease or royalty terms in midstream—these kinds of actions can discourage investment and effort to the point that they shrink the reservation economic pie. They thus work unambiguously against the tribal public's interest in a healthy economy.

The results are doubly destructive when the prospect of being on the lucrative receiving end of such actions encourages individuals to invest their time, effort, and capital in wealth-destroying governmental activities. We have only to look at the staggering economies of Eastern Europe to see how development is blocked when the goal of a country's hardest working and most capable individuals is to become a bureaucrat, when enterprise managers' incentives are to keep themselves in the good graces of politicians, and investment capital flees at the first opportunity.

The central problem is to create an environment in which investors—whether tribal members or outsiders—feel secure, and therefore are willing to put energy, time, and capital into the tribal economy. The successful tribes we see have solved, in one way or another, two critical aspects of this problem.

(1) *The Separation and Limitation of Powers: Who Controls What?* As the foregoing suggests, all societies face the problem of preventing

those who exercise the legitimate powers of government from using that power to transfer wealth—or additional power—to themselves. The use of government for personal gain can take place either through direct (though often hidden) taking of funds or authority, or through the biasing of laws, rules, and regulations so as to favor the interests of those in authority. This activity is socially destructive. Where government is viewed largely as a source of power or wealth, many of a society's best and brightest people will devote their energy and talent to seeking government favors. But such investments of energy and talent add nothing to a society's productive output. In fact, they discourage productive investment: Investors will not step forward with their dollars or their energy if they suspect that their investment is going largely to the enrichment of other people.

The problem is to limit the role of those in power to that of "third party" enforcer—the third party that referees and enforces the rules of the game—rather than a self-interested primary party in disputes and decisions over the use of a society's resources. Around the world, from the United States to Korea to the Philippines to Zaire, success at this task stands out as a make-or-break characteristic distinguishing those sovereign nations that have been able to develop economically from those that have not.[19]

This is as true in Indian Country as it is anywhere else. Too often, for example, those with claims against either the tribe as a whole or other tribal members can appeal only to the tribal council. Without constitutional checks and balances, such as an independent judiciary of some sort, tribal politicians are in a position to turn authority into personal power or gain. Such conditions discourage investment because potential claimants see little chance of fair adjudication of their claims.

The range of attempted tribal solutions to the problem of limiting and allocating governmental power is broad. While many tribes have weak judicial branches in which judges serve largely at the pleasure of the tribal council and their decisions are subject to council or even chair reversal, several tribes have formed strong, effectively independent judiciaries (see the chapter by Andrea Skari in this volume). In such cases judges typically are appointed by the tribal council but are not subject to direct council control, have terms of office longer than those of council members, can be removed only for gross improprieties, and have the power to resolve disputes. The Flathead Reservation has such a system, with the further twist that appeals of tribal court decisions are made not to the tribal council but to an independent intertribal judicial board.

Both Yakima and Rosebud have experimented with tribal ethics boards empowered to review grievances against politician and bureaucrat behavior. At Rosebud, board members—usually elders—are chosen by the tribal council on the basis of their "wisdom, integrity, and knowledge of Lakota culture."[20] Those with grievances can appeal to the board, which hears cases in confidence and then makes recommendations to the council. The board has little formal power beyond its carefully guarded reputation for disinterested action, but that has been sufficient to give it decisive impact in a number of cases.

A third solution is the submission of claims to outside adjudication through limited waivers of sovereign immunity or, since many tribes are reluctant to make such waivers, third-party arbitration. Finally, tribes can depend on strict constitutional delineations of powers or, in rare cases such as Cochiti Pueblo, on informal, culturally based, but powerful rules to control what those in power do. But whatever the mechanism a tribe employs, its effectiveness requires the support of sufficient, and sufficiently influential, tribal members.

At Mescalero Apache and White Mountain Apache, for example, there are strong chief executive forms of tribal government supported by a mixture of the rule of law and the rule of custom. Single, often charismatic individuals effectively hold and exercise much of the power in the governing system, but within limits that, to one degree or another, restrict self-serving behavior. These limits come from the formal (constitutional) organization of government, backed up by the kinds of culturally rooted standards and expectations regarding the appropriate behavior of leaders and the legitimate powers of centralized government that we have discussed above.[21]

We find a sharp contrast at Crow, which operates under a constitutionally based, general council form of government. The general council—the legislature—consists of all voting-age tribal members (and thereby has a membership in the thousands). This council is virtually unlimited in its authority over the structure and powers of tribal government, and bears little resemblance to prereservation forms of Crow governance, in which authority was minimally organized through kinship relations, particularly the clan system, the policing powers of warrior societies, and relatively weak executives.[22] At Crow today there are no formal separations of power, no checks and balances. The result is "winner take all" politics in which the power to control a quarterly council meeting is the power to command virtually all disposable resources (e.g., tribal government jobs and budgets in a setting that effectively lacks any private sector alternatives). Individual leaders have little incentive to invest in other than the patronage of their own political factions, at the expense of longer-term tribal interests in economic well-being and social and political sovereignty. The consequence is an environment in which the tribe has extreme difficulty in attracting and keeping investment and employment opportunities, has a governmental bureaucracy that is paralyzed in its ability to carry out day-to-day administration, and has experienced occasionally dramatic social and political breakdown.

The Flathead case illustrates a more successful approach to the problem of effectively allocating and limiting governmental power. The reservation is home to an amalgam of tribes with weak prereservation histories of political association. It operates under a constitutional parliamentary system with a strong legislature (the tribal council) and a relatively weak chief executive. The chair is selected by the popularly elected parliamentary representatives (the council) from among their members, rather than being elected by the tribal membership. In this way power is shared among people with no tradition of consolidating power in a single authority. As noted, Flathead also has an effectively separate (i.e., professional and legislatively protected) judiciary. The result is a system of formal separations of powers, complete with "checks and balances."

Both this reliance on formal control of governmental power at Flathead and the general council at Crow are in sharp contrast to the theocracy of Cochiti Pueblo. Cochiti has no written constitution or legal codes, but relies instead on culture-based, religious limits on self-interested behavior on the part of political leaders, and a well-defined separation of powers. These are embodied in the formal institution of the *cacique*, the chief religious leader of the tribe, who selects the primary tribal executive officials each year, including the governor of the pueblo, but has no direct authority in day-to-day tribal operations.[23] Cochiti's relative economic success (see Table 1) and the apparent sustainability of its major development efforts indicate that this approach works, at least for Cochiti. Indeed, the contrast with Flathead's government illustrates the crucial point that all tribes face the same problem of limiting self-serving behavior on the part of tribal leaders,

TABLE 3
Contributions of Alternative Governmental Forms to Reservation Employment Levels

	General Council	Parliamentary System	Strong Chief Executive
No Independent Judiciary	—	10.8%	14.9%
Independent Judiciary	5.0%	15.8%	19.9%

Notes: 1. *General Council* places all voting tribal members on the tribal council (legislature). *Parliamentary System* has a representative tribal council which itself elects the tribal chair from among its members. *Strong Chief Executive* has a representative tribal council and a tribal chair with a term of more than 2 years, elected by all voting members of the tribe.

2. Reported measures of contribution to employment are for an otherwise average tribe (i.e., with average resource endowment, educational attainment, economic conditions in surrounding off-reservation locale, etc.), after taking into account the effects of such factors on employment levels.

3. Data are for 1989 for a sample of 67 tribes with populations greater than 600.

Source: Stephen Cornell and Joseph P. Kalt, "Where's the Glue? Institutional Bases of American Indian Economic Development," Harvard Project on American Indian Economic Development, Project Report Series, February 1991.

but that formal solutions may be very different from tribe to tribe.

On the other hand, not just any solution will do. The solutions tribes turn to not only have to be appropriate to tribal cultures, they also have to work. Solutions that fit with indigenous culture but fail to constrain the power of those who govern will only further undermine the possibilities of politically, socially, and economically successful development.

The importance of governmental structures is borne out by available systematic evidence. In our study of sixty-seven tribes for which comparable data are available, we found that tribes with constitutionally based, strong chief executive (i. e., directly elected, typically to four-year terms of office) and strong (parliamentary) legislature governments consistently outperform general council governments. Moreover, independent judiciaries promote economic well-being under all types of tribal executive and legislative systems. As shown in Table 3, after accounting for the influence of other factors that can affect development (such as natural resources, educational attainment, and local market conditions), strong chief executive governments outperform, to some degree, strong legislature governments. Both forms of government account for at least a 10 percent improvement over general council systems. Independent judiciaries generally improve tribal employment by an additional 5 percent.[24]

(2) *The Separation of Electoral Politics from Day-to-Day Management of Business Enterprises.* A second, related problem has to do with the direct role of tribal government in development projects. Tribal governments play—and should play—a critical role in tribes' strategic decision-making. It is appropriate that strategic decisions regarding the disposition of reservation resources and the character of reservation life be brought into the political arena. Turning a reservation mountainside into a ski resort or a mine, inviting IBM or the Department of Defense onto the reservation— these decisions rightly are topics for political debate.

This does not mean, however, that tribal governments should make all or even a significant number of the day-to-day business decisions on reservations. This is not always an easy pill for tribal governments—or any other governments—to swallow, particularly on reservations with tribally owned businesses. After all, the enterprises are the property of the people; shouldn't the people's representatives—the politicians—have a direct say in how business is run? Unfortunately, although this argument has some appeal, the reality is that it can only be made in the short run. In the long run, inserting politics into day-to-day business decisions invariably undermines efficiency and productivity, saps the resources of the organizations, and runs tribal enterprises into the ground.

The primary economic task of a nation's government is not to make day-to-day business decisions, but to create and sustain an appropriate economic environment for that nation, to lay in place the rules of the game that economic players then follow, and to make *strategic decisions* about the overall direction development should take. This is true from the United States to Poland or Japan, and from the Passamaquoddy Reservation to the Northern Cheyenne.

For the tribe seeking economic development, however, *day-to-day decisions on how to run a business* are another matter: whom to hire at the tribal store, how many elk to take in the fall hunt, how to manage the payroll at the manufacturing plant. In fact, keeping tribal governments focused on strategic issues and out of the day-to-day affairs of reservation businesses is one of the keys to sustainable development. A staple of storytelling in Indian Country has to do with political interference in business activity. Over and over one hears of voided leases, hired or fired cousins, politicized management, and enterprises drained of funds by tribal council interference. Such problems are not unique to Indian Country—witness Chicago or Boston, or the Philippines or Mexico, where the politics of patronage and personal aggrandizement have memorable histories. While the details vary across reservations and other societies, their consequences are depressingly similar: costs are raised and competitiveness reduced; earnings are dissipated and capital is not replenished; investors fear being held hostage to politics and turn away. In a highly competitive world, there simply is no cushion to absorb costs that are higher than they have to be, production that is less efficient than it can be, or quality that is lower than customers can find elsewhere.

Successful business enterprises in Indian Country, whether private or tribally owned, are typically distinguished by the insulation of their day-to-day affairs from political interference. In those cases where there is a strong private sector on the reservation (such as at Flathead) one of the keys is a capable, independent tribal judicial system that can uphold contracts, enforce stable business codes, settle disputes, and, in effect, protect businesses from politics. In some cases where tribes have attracted large outside investors to the reservation, enterprises are effectively insulated from political interference by formal agreements between the investors and the tribes, backed up by provisions for third-party arbitration and/or limited waivers of sovereign immunity (i. e., subjection to an outside court).

Where businesses are tribally owned, it is more difficult to separate day-to-day enterprise management from politics, but the problem can—and must—be solved. Table 4 shows the results of a survey of the tribally owned businesses of eighteen tribes. As of 1990, these tribes owned a combined total of seventy-three enterprises, covering a wide range of sizes and activities, from agriculture to manufacturing. A total of thirty-nine of these enterprises were identified by their respective tribal leaders as being insulated formally from tribal politics, typically by a managing board of directors and corporate charter beyond the direct control of individual council members and the tribal chair. Some of these enterprises were operating profitably; others were losing money. However, the odds that an independently managed tribal enterprise was profitable were almost seven to one. On the other hand, the odds that a tribal enterprise that was not insulated from tribal politics was profitable were only 1.4 to one (see Table 4).

The ways that tribally owned enterprises can be insulated effectively from politics vary. Those now apparent in Indian Country range from culture-based separations of powers and limits on self-interested behavior, as at Cochiti Pueblo, to constitutional or legal limits, as at Mescalero Apache. In recent years a number of tribes—for example, Salish-Kootenai, Lummi, Cochiti—have put together their own development corporations to manage tribal enterprises. The successful ones place such management in the hands of appointed boards of directors that are accountable to the tribal council in the long run, but are genuinely independent of it in the day-to-day management of business operations. Certainly the success of such operations still depends on a host of other factors, such as skilled personnel and adequate markets, but through such corporations tribes can insulate their enterprises from politics and allow them to go about the business of creating wealth and opportunity. (A prototypical tribal development corporation is described in detail in Michael Cameron's chapter in this volume.)

As these examples illustrate, and as we stressed above, the solution lies in effective institutions. These institutions need not all be alike—they almost certainly will not be—but each tribe has to find ways to minimize the impact of politics on day-to-day business affairs. Of course, designing effective institutions is not easy. Tribal councils are reluctant to give up

TABLE 4
Profitability of Tribal Enterprises in 18 Tribes:
Independent v. Council-Controlled Management

	Independent	Council-controlled
Profitable	34	20
Not Profitable	5	14
Odds of Profitability	6.8 to 1	1.4 to 1

Source: Self-reported survey of 18 tribal chairs, Senior Executive Education Program for Tribal Leaders, College of Business, Northern Arizona University, Flagstaff, Arizona, June 1990.

direct supervision of tribal enterprises or direct control of the investment environment. This is understandable. Such control gives council members a great deal of power. Outstanding individuals may exercise that power wisely, but in fact it weakens the tribe over the long run by creating a situation in which development success depends on the character of individual leaders. Who knows whether the next individual chosen for that position will be as good? If the society could count on *always* choosing leaders with sufficient integrity and wisdom to manage tribal businesses in ways that ultimately serve both the public interest and the interests of investors, this would hardly be a problem. But few—if any—societies in the world have managed to put together such a record. Given the diversity of individuals in the world and the unpredictability of free citizen selection of leaders, institutions become the necessary insurance that the tribal interest will be protected.

Traditionally, most Indian tribes had institutional solutions to these problems. In many tribes, for example, war or hunt leaders and peace leaders were not the same. Responsibility for the day-to-day management of food procurement or warfare lay in the hands of persons specially chosen and qualified for those tasks, and vested with adequate authority to carry them out. Interference in their decisions, even by individuals with substantial status and power, was not tolerated. On the other hand, longer-term decision-making about the society's welfare—essentially strategic management—lay in the hands of often more senior individuals who, because of their accumulated wisdom, were trusted to interpret and protect the collective interest over the long run. While the variation among tribes was substantial, many displayed little of the concentration of power across diverse activities that we see in many tribal governments today.[25] But whatever their specific form, these were formal institutional solutions to management and leadership problems, even if they were never written down in constitutions and the like. Today the details of the problems have changed and the institutional solutions may be different, but the fundamental issue—how to create an environment in which investors, including tribal members, feel secure—is essentially the same.

By developing institutional solutions that can effectively solve problems and that fit each tribe's cultural standards, tribes can create an environment in which development has the support of the institutions themselves and is less dependent simply on the quality of the people currently in office. In doing so, tribes in fact increase their power: the power to attract investment, to pursue distinctive tribal goals, and to exercise their sovereignty in meaningful ways.

C. CHOOSING EFFECTIVE DEVELOPMENT STRATEGIES

Once armed with effective institutions of self-government, the strategic decision-making that tribes must engage in takes two primary forms. First, it is most prominently tribal governments that make key decisions regarding such matters as the extent of public and private ownership on the reservation, the type and form of business law, regulation and taxation, and the provision of basic social services such as education and law enforcement. These decisions constitute a tribe's economic development policy and establish its basic *economic system.*

Second, as a primary arbitrator of public opinion, it falls on tribal government to make and implement key choices regarding investment of a reservation's land, water, and environmental resources: Should we offer this lease to a non-Indian manufacturer? Should we turn that mountain into a ski resort? Is a gambling casino right for this tribe? Should we offer commercial hunting of our wildlife? and so on. In answering these kinds of questions, whether thoughtfully or by default, tribal government controls a reservation's economic *development activity.*

A tribe's choices over economic system and development activity are *strategic* choices in the sense that they determine the overall kind of development that the reservation will try to initiate and sustain. They set the development direction for the tribe.

1. ECONOMIC SYSTEM

The kinds of institutions we have described—constitutions, courts, capable bureaucracies, management boards—provide a base on which to build toward successful development. But what kind of development policy should these institutions support? What kind of economic system should a tribe adopt? Who should be the primary actors on the development stage?

Four major models are emerging in Indian Country in answer to these questions. The critical issue is: How well does each model fit the particular set of internal and external conditions (of the type presented in Table 2) that a tribe faces?

(1) *Federal control.* Federal control is the default mode of tribal economic organization and historically the most common. This is what happens if tribes are unable to assert control over development. In other words, this is what happens in the absence of sovereignty and the institutions needed to back it up. The federal control model typically means that the BIA is the real decision-maker when it comes to deciding what investments to undertake and what activities to pursue. It also means the BIA usually has to pick up the pieces when enterprises fail. In fact, this is what makes it occasionally attractive to tribes.

Federal control can also be attractive to tribes because of the immediacy of their needs for income and employment. In the case of a relatively small tribe such as the Hualapai of Arizona (population just over 1,000), federal projects and monies may be enough to employ a large fraction of the tribe. But the result is that the Hualapai are unusually dependent on government employment; according to the last available United States census data (1980), 89 percent of the civilian jobs at Hualapai are in the public sector. Tribal members and officials repeatedly express their dissatisfaction with this dependence.

Given tribal goals of political and social sovereignty, the federal control model is almost always radically inappropriate. It also is typically unproductive in economic terms: The historical lack of progress in reservation economies is in part at least a direct consequence of nontribal control. This is true at both the level of individual programs and of tribes' overall development efforts. At the program level, for example, Matthew Krepps reports in his chapter in this volume that shifting 10 percent of the forestry labor force from BIA control to tribal control under Public Law 638 could increase the average timber tribe's revenues by $60,000 per year. Shifting from the current average level of tribal control (about 20–40 percent) of the workforce to total tribal control could increase the productivity of reservation forests by as much as 45 percent. At the overall tribal level, the history of sustained development at White Mountain Apache, Flathead, Mescalero, Mississippi Choctaw, Passamaquoddy, and Cochiti can be traced directly to, among other things, the emergence of non-BIA leadership able and willing to take real control of tribal economic affairs.[26]

The story of the White Mountain Apaches is representative. As on many reservations, for decades the BIA was, in effect, the reservation government. The local BIA superintendent routinely sat beside the tribal chairman during tribal council meetings, and the council looked to the superintendent for direction on the most important decisions. The sale, lease, and disposal of tribal resources was largely in the hands of federal officials. The impressive recent development history of White Mountain Apache had its beginnings in the late 1960s when the tribe took control of its own affairs, excluded the BIA superintendent from council meetings, and precipitated an armed showdown in which the tribe took control of important reservation land leases away from the federal government.

The federal government itself has begun to push tribes away from the federal control model. The transfer of economic control to tribes (through, for example, Public Law 638 contracting) is paying net positive dividends.[27] The BIA has launched a tribal self-governance project intended to transfer virtually all former BIA management functions to tribes under what amounts to a block grant to tribal governments. A block grant approach to federal assistance is a much needed step in Indian affairs, replacing federal determination of what types of projects tribes should pursue with tribal determination, backed by federal investment. Systematic block grants to tribes would allow tribal control without pulling the plug on assistance dollars. Block grants of base funding would allow tribes to stabilize their own tribal bureaucracies and the provision of basic infrastructure and government services. They also would promote better decision-making by bringing the opportunity costs of tribal government actions to bear more directly on tribal politicians. A dollar from the block grant spent on, for example, hiring more administrative personnel would mean one less dollar available to invest in the tribal forest. When the grants that tribes pursue are program specific (a housing grant, a capital investment grant, etc.), this discipline is weakened.

(2) *Tribal enterprise.* In this model the tribe itself is the developer. It owns and operates a set of tribal enterprises and manages the development of its own resources. One of the strengths of this model is that it takes full advantage of the economic payoffs to tribes' legal status. Tribes are exempt from state and federal income taxes, empowered to levy their own taxes and devise their own business codes, and often exempt from federal and/or state economic regulation.

On the other hand, both inside and outside Indian Country, it is difficult to make government ownership of business work. Two basic problems stand out. First is the problem of motivating top management. Under private ownership, business profits go to stockholders who, in turn, can pay high salaries and bonuses to hardworking and successful managers. While it is hardly uncommon in various parts of the world for government officials to enrich themselves through the management of government-owned businesses, this has more often happened through corruption than rewards for honest labor. It generally has not been politically acceptable for government officials to gain significantly off the operations of businesses that are, in effect, publicly owned. Second, government ownership makes the necessary separation of politics from day-to-day business management, discussed above, difficult to achieve.

These problems can be solved. As far as tribally owned businesses are concerned, the voting-age members of a tribe are the effective stockholders in tribal enterprises. For most tribes, the number of these stockholders is small (compared to the number of stockholders in a major corporation), and the access to tribal politicians is notably personal. As a result, tribal politicians can be made to feel the heat and become motivated to serve stockholders' interests. Generously compensating top management so as to keep motivation high between elections, on the other hand, can be more difficult, particularly in tribes where cultural values fail to support a system in which individual members, even those with top management responsibility, can get personally wealthy off of tribal resources. When top management and a high level of motivation can only be had at a high price, some tribes have solved this problem by turning to nontribal members (Indian or non-Indian) to fill key positions.

But the number one problem for tribal enterprises is separating politics from day-to-day business affairs. As we look at cases where tribal ownership of enterprises appears to work well, we find that at least one of two conditions usually has been met. Either the tribe has set up independent boards (of the kind described above) to manage tribal enterprises, and/or the tribe has a strong chief executive form of government.

Independent management boards, as noted above, insulate top management decisions from political pressure. They also provide cover for tribal leaders, who are frequently under pressure from constituents to redistribute tribal resources such as jobs and profits. It is much easier for a tribal leader to resist such pressures, particularly those that involve direct kinship relations, if he or she is prevented constitutionally from compliance. For example: "I can't help you get a job at the tribe's factory because I'm a tribal council member, not a manager at the factory, and have no control over hiring. You'll have to apply at the personnel office along with everyone else."

The strong chief executive fits tribal ownership best because it concentrates accountability and streamlines decision-making. In Indian Country as elsewhere, decision-making by committee, whether of a relatively few persons (as in a parliamentary council) or by literally hundreds or even thousands (as in the general council) is a poor way to run an enterprise on a day-to-day basis.

Of course neither the strong chief executive form of government nor independent management boards guarantee that tribally owned businesses will be either free of politics (or successful as businesses). These governing institutions have to have the support of the "stockholders." They have to be backed up by cultural standards that make them legitimate in the eyes of the people; otherwise, they are as likely as any others to be corrupted over time.

What cultural standards would make a tribe a good candidate for tribal ownership of enterprises and for the institutions that are needed to make it work? It appears that one requirement is support for centralized forms of political authority. Is the typical tribal member's primary loyalty to the tribe? Or is it to some subdivision within the tribe, such as a local community, a district organization, or a clan? The difference appears to be part of the explanation for why tribal ownership has been relatively more successful at Cochiti, White Mountain Apache, Mescalero, and Muckleshoot, and relatively less successful at San Carlos Apache, Pine Ridge, and Rosebud. The contrast between San Carlos on the one hand and Mescalero and White Mountain Apache on the other illustrates the point. It is striking how the central tribal government and, in particular, the tribal chair, appear to represent focal points and even embodiments of Apache ideals and identity at Mescalero and White Mountain Apache. In contrast, at San Carlos a history of tribal mixing and of extreme military and administrative subjugation by federal authorities appears to have resulted in much less cohesion at the tribal level, and much less success with the tribal enterprise model.[28]

Further evidence comes from the Pine Ridge and Rosebud Sioux reservations. Both groups show strong adherence to Sioux values that continue to support the long historical traditions of local authority and independence rooted in kinship units (*tiyospayes*) and in the original band-based settlement patterns on these reservations. Despite the fact that the IRA constitutions under which both tribes operate closely parallel the White Mountain and Mescalero constitutions, centralized tribal government is relatively ineffectual for reasons discussed above. This is particularly true when it comes to owning and operating businesses and making decisions about tribal resources. Both tribes are candidates for an economic system based on something other than tribal enterprise.

Even in tribes with strong cultural support for centralized government, the institutions of a strong chief executive and/or independent management boards have to be seen by the people as legitimate. Independent management boards, for example, require cultural acceptance of the delegation of authority. A tribe in which it is every citizen's right to intervene in every tribal decision, including the business decisions of tribal enterprises, is unlikely to be able to set up and maintain independent management boards. An effective, strong chief executive (tribal chair or president), meanwhile, must have the ability to make tough decisions and the authority to make them stick. This will not happen if his or her right to make such decisions is constantly questioned, or if each decision becomes a political crisis.

Of course, the downside of centralized authority is the risk of corruption, or the possibility that decisions can be turned somehow to the personal benefit of the chief executive. Therefore, an effective chief executive system is one in which the office carries a great deal of authority to make decisions *that are in the interests of the tribe's citizens*, but no authority to make decisions that only promote the executive's interests. This kind of cultural "contract" between citizens and leaders holds the chief executive to a high standard: lots of power, but power that is easily lost at the first sign of corruption or pettiness.

(3) *Private (Micro) Enterprise with Tribal Member Ownership.* This strategy sets up an economic system based on the individual, family, or small group entrepreneurship of tribal members. In the face of the scarcity of capital in Indian hands, it envisions a reservation economy consisting primarily of small businesses ("microenterprises") that are started, owned, and operated as private businesses, serving either local or export markets, or both. A reservation microenterprise system looks a great deal like the economy of much of the rural and small town United States, other than

large-scale agriculture. It recognizes that raising large amounts of capital is inconsistent with the generally low levels of savings in Indian Country and with the generally poor track record in borrowing funds for reservation business. It calls on the marketplace to provide motivation and accountability to private tribal members.

The microenterprise strategy is particularly appropriate where cultural norms support individual accumulations of at least modest wealth; where individual achievement is honored and not cause for personal rejection; where there is cultural resistance to the importation of nonmember management that might otherwise be needed, at least for a time, to run large enterprises; where larger businesses that require "bosses and workers" hierarchies are incompatible with cultural standards regarding who can tell whom what to do; and where people's political allegiances may not be fixed on central tribal authorities.

Microenterprise is best suited to retail services and small-scale manufacturing. It is generally not well suited to situations in which the primary economic opportunities are in such natural resource areas as mining, forestry (except for small-scale cutting), and even much of agriculture (where competition increasingly demands large-scale enterprises). Recent work by organizations such as the First Nations Financial Project and the Seventh Generation Fund suggest that economic systems based primarily on private microenterprises are well suited to certain reservations. An example is Pine Ridge, where the lack of support for a powerful centralized government hinders tribal enterprise, and where research indicates that entrepreneurial and other productive talents are exercised extensively in the informal sector of the economy, including both money and barter transactions. According to a 1988 study, despite reported unemployment rates on the order of 70 percent, as of 1987, 83 percent of Pine Ridge reservation households participated in the "self-initiated, home-based . . . income-generating" activities of the informal sector; 30 percent of households received more than half of their income from the informal sector; and 24 percent of the median household income at Pine Ridge came from the informal sector.[29]

Of course, even in hospitable cultural settings, an economic system based on private microenterprise depends on political institutions capable of protecting investors and entrepreneurs from political interference with their capital commitments, and capable of enforcing workable business codes and the law of contract. Without courts and judges—or some effective equivalent—that can resolve disputes in ways that keep the rules of the game stable and free of politics, investors will refuse to launch enterprises. It is no accident that the reservation in our sample that probably has the most successful formal private sector of microenterprises— Flathead—is also the reservation with arguably the most fully developed, independent, and professional judicial system. At the same time, it is no accident that the tribal judge at San Carlos Apache reports (as of 1990) being suspended more than a dozen times by the tribal council in preceding years, and even tribal-member microenterprise efforts commonly migrate to towns just outside the reservation.

(4) *Private Enterprise with Nontribal Member Control.* This model involves the promotion of non-Indian businesses on Indian lands, and/or the management of Indian resources by non-Indian companies, usually through joint ventures or royalty arrangements. The tribe's primary task is to construct an environment which, with tax breaks, labor costs, regulatory relief, or other incentives, will attract non-Indian enterprises to the reservation. In recent years the Navajo, for example, have vigorously pursued this strategy, while the Rosebud Sioux have had an office dedicated to finding outside businesses willing to locate on the reservation.

This strategy is most commonly used in the manufacturing and resource processing sectors, involving large-scale investment projects with workers organized in a factory setting. Culturally, an economic system based largely on big private investment is best suited to a tribe whose self-confidence and cultural standards can support extended cooperation with outsiders, and in which hierarchical "bosses and workers" systems are not seen as personally demeaning by tribal workers.[30]

Encouraging the non-Indian private investor to come to the reservation offers a solution to the often pressing problems of access to financial and human capital. On the other hand, it brings onto the reservation significant outside actors whose interests and culture may diverge radically from those of the tribe. Whether or not this is seen as a threat to a tribe's political and/ or social sovereignty depends in part on the strength of the tribe's formal and informal institutions of social control. A tribe with capable institutions, able to solve the tasks of governance discussed above, is less likely to have its economic and social systems upset by a large outside business investor or partner. For example, a tribe with an effective land-use policy and bureaucracy is less likely to be taken to the cleaners by a real estate developer. A tribe with a constitution that fits with its own cultural standards of authority and legitimacy will be better able to weather changing tribal administrations or an instance of corruption without ruining its reputation in the eyes of investors. Tribal members will be more likely to stand by tribal institutions in a crisis if they view those institutions as culturally legitimate.

The pursuit of economic development, particularly when it involves large outside investors, is often debated in terms of modern or mainstream versus traditional or tribal values. To the extent that these terms reflect fears that development will destroy a tribe's culture or change reservation life in ways that destroy the society, they frequently miscast the choices tribes face. Every society faces pressures to change, from the Detroit auto workers concerned that they will have to behave more like Japanese in order to compete, to the South Dakota farmers trying to keep pace with technology that alters the ways they learned to farm.

At least in Indian Country, the extent to which pressures of this kind are socially destructive or constructive appears to depend on the degree to which tribes themselves control the ways they adapt. In some cases, as at Muckleshoot and Passamaquoddy, the combination of large-scale investment by outsiders and vigorous assertions of control by tribes themselves appears to have been a force bringing tribal members together with an enhanced sense of cohesion and power. On the other hand, it is certainly the case that the introduction of a large enterprise that directly challenges indigenous cultural standards or tribal objectives can have seriously disruptive effects on the tribal community, while outside enterprises that bring with them large numbers of outsiders may have difficult-to-control impacts on the nature of community life. These possibilities raise major issues in the area of social sovereignty which tribal communities facing such opportunities will have to confront.

As with the private microenterprise strategy, an economic system built on large-scale investment by outsiders requires an institutional structure that assures investors that their investment will be safe from opportunistic politics. As already noted, this last requirement is no easier to accomplish in Indian Country than it is in other settings, and it may be a good deal more important. One of the things that makes the Indian situation dramatically different from that of Chicago or Boston, or Moscow or Manila, is the greater relative importance of a single development project. Far more is at stake with a supermarket, a small assembly plant, or even a locksmith or beauty salon on a reservation than in a major metropolitan area. The potential impact on employment and income is greater, as is the potential impact on the reservation's reputation with investors. These high stakes mean that both the competition for control of resources and the social costs of the politicization of those resources are much greater as well. Chicago can afford a few politicized contracts and burned investors. Indian tribes cannot. In addition, the potential impact on social sovereignty may be greater for small tribes with few development options, which may risk becoming corporate-appendage economies dependent on a single outside investor for the majority of individual or tribal income.

These four models of tribes' potential economic systems are by no means mutually exclusive. Successful development policies may mix them in combination, or at least in some combination of the last three, although one or another is typically dominant. The right choices for tribes must be driven by the kinds of internal and external factors that we have discussed near the beginning of this chapter (see Table 2). Tribes have to find the economic system and accompanying institutions of self-government that match both their respective cultures and the resource and opportunity situations they face. Tribes differ a great deal in these dimensions, and one tribe's answer is certainly not guaranteed to work for another. Just because tribal ownership, for example, has worked relatively well for Mescalero does not mean it will work for Rosebud Sioux; just because Flathead has pursued development of the private sector does not mean the same will work for Crow.

Finally, it is clear that the crucial choices must be made by tribes themselves. The central role played by culture in either supporting or undermining tribal institutions leaves no alternative. The problem of getting a good fit among economic system, governing institutions, and cultural standards will not be solved in Washington, by professors or consultants, or even by other tribes. The problem will be solved by tribal leaders and members who understand the linkages among these things and can invent their own solutions.

2. DEVELOPMENT ACTIVITY

Many American Indian tribes face a barrage of ideas, proposals, offers, and enticements—some from within the tribe, many from outside it—aimed at establishing specific development or investment projects on the reservation. These projects range from chopstick factories to gambling casinos, from hazardous waste facilities to resort hotels. The reasons behind such suggestions and invitations vary from efforts by tribal members to bring jobs onto the reservation, to legitimate outside investor interest in the labor, tax, and regulatory advantages that many reservations can supply, to disreputable attempts to capitalize on tribal inexperience or desperation.

The challenge for both tribal decision-makers and individual tribal members is to separate the good from the bad opportunities, the solid prospects from the boondoggles, the likely successes from the probable failures. As we have stressed, tribal government has the necessary task of laying in place the environment in which wise and productive decisions can be made. It does this with its basic governmental (constitutional) form, its judicial institutions (see Andrea Skari's volume in this chapter), its regulatory institutions (see Paul Nissenbaum and Paul Shadle's chapter), and its economic policies (see preceding sections of this chapter, as well as Michael Cameron's chapter). But, given these institutions, tribes and individuals ultimately have to face very specific choices regarding the allocation of workers, resources, and capital: Should we invest in a carpet factory? Should we open a mine? Should we allow gaming? Should we encourage tourism or the commercial hunting of our wildlife?

Making choices of these kinds—and making them so that the resultant development activities are successful—requires basic technical and business skills: reading a balance sheet, understanding market conditions of supply and demand, interpreting risk and return trade-offs, and so on. In fact, numerous training efforts have been undertaken to increase management skills in Indian Country, and continued and enhanced efforts will be needed in the future.[31]

While basic management skills are certainly necessary, the success of tribal development activities depends also upon the *strategic* skills of decision-makers. Picking "winners" is crucially dependent on these skills. The heart of the strategic problem is the appropriate matching of particular development activities and projects to the governance capabilities, asset endowments, and cultural attributes of the tribe.

Table 5 presents some general patterns in this matching of activities to critical ingredients for success. The list of ingredients shown down the lefthand side of the table is not exhaustive; other factors may be important in various situations. Similarly, the list of development activities across the top of the table is hardly complete, and is intended simply to illustrate some of the opportunities many tribes face. The point of the table is to indicate which ingredients are especially important to which development activities. A check mark in the table indicates that this particular ingredient is especially important to the success of this particular activity. The table should not be interpreted to mean that unchecked ingredients are not supportive of success, but only that the checked ingredient is often found to be critical in Indian Country. Thus, for example, having a highly experienced and skilled workforce is a significant "plus" for any kind of development activity. Nevertheless, such a workforce is almost always especially needed in either large or small-scale manufacturing. These are sectors in which national and international competition increasingly penalizes low-skill workers and businesses. Except in instances in which a tribe has an especially hard-to-duplicate niche in the market, a tribe pursuing manufacturing activities cannot expect to insulate itself from the need for a skilled workforce. Certainly the experience on reservations such as Mississippi Choctaw and Passamaquoddy demonstrates that a skilled reservation workforce can compete successfully in the manufacturing sector.[32]

As we have emphasized, capable institutions of governance are necessary for any sustained, successful development. This is reiterated in the top rows of Table 5. In addition, success in certain development activities depends on the particular assets of the reservation and their economic value. For example, success in natural resource activities, such as agriculture and mining, obviously requires *both* endowments of harvestable or extractable resources *and* the market demand that makes those resources valuable. It makes no sense to undertake aquaculture in the desert or a new coal mine in a glutted energy market (although outside investors hoping to capture public loan and grant monies continue to propose precisely such projects to various tribes).

Activities such as large-scale manufacturing and natural resource development also commonly require access to large amounts of financial

TABLE 5
Critical Ingredients for Success
In Selected Development Activities

	Large-scale manufacturing	Small-scale manufacturing	Retail and service	Tourism	Natural Resource Extraction
Governance: Third-party dispute resolution	X	X	X	X	X
Governance: Separating politics from day-to-day biz management	X	X	X	X	X
Assets: High natural resource endowment				X	X
Assets: Skilled and experienced workforce	X	X			
Assets: Access to major financial capital	X				X
Assets: Near markets and/or low transportation costs	X	X			
Cultural: Receptivity to workers/bosses hierarchies	X				X
Cultural: Receptivity to interaction with non-members	X			X	
Cultural: Receptivity to commercialization				X	X
Cultural: Tribe as a whole is primary locus of identity/loyalty	X				X

capital. Money must be available to pay workers and buy materials during the construction and development phases of production in these sectors. Even in the case of agriculture, competition in the market for most crops compels large-scale operations and capital investment in order to achieve sustained success. This premium on access to capital is less pronounced in most retail, service, small-scale manufacturing, and tourism (except major resort) enterprises.

Being close to markets or low cost transportation facilities is particularly important in manufacturing. Proximity to the marketplace holds down the delivered prices of reservation-produced goods. In the case of natural resources, nearness to the marketplace can be important for success, but most natural resource use and extraction takes place in a rural setting, and nonreservation competitors face transportation problems similar to those of tribes.

"Success" in development activities does not mean solely jobs and income. The fact that American Indian tribes, like other societies, have goals of political and social sovereignty means that development success must also be assessed in political and cultural terms: Will this project bring large numbers of non-Indians onto the reservation who may challenge tribal sovereignty? Is this project going to introduce social or political strife among tribal members? Is factory work going to appeal to our young people? Would building that road up to the mine damage important religious sites? Will tribal members object to non-Indian hunters roaming the wilderness areas of the reservation?

Table 5 lists four cultural attributes—there may well be more—that frequently have implications for development choices. For example, because of their nature, large-scale manufacturing and resource development enterprises typically require (relatively) hierarchical, workers-and-bosses management structures. The larger the enterprise, the more likely it is that the necessities of specialization and coordination will require some people to tell other people what to do. Notwithstanding mass media stereotyping of American Indian societies as uniformly communal and nonhierarchical, the multitude of tribes that make up Indian Country differ a great deal from one another in this regard. Reservation societies that are not particularly receptive to workplace hierarchies are poor candidates for large-scale manufacturing and resource enterprises. Such societies are more likely, all else equal, to be able to successfully develop small-scale manufacturing, retail and service businesses, and tourism service activities.

Another cultural attribute affecting whether particular development activities are appropriate to a tribe is receptivity to interaction with nonmembers. Members of one tribe, for example, may be reluctant to expose their religious or social practices to tourists. Another tribe may see this as a welcome economic opportunity. Again, despite common stereotyping, neither of these tribes is more or less "Indian." They simply have different understandings of what is culturally appropriate for them. Such a difference has to be taken into account in decisions regarding the promotion of tourism. In a case where (many) tribal members are fundamentally unreceptive to interaction with tourists or to tourist demands for access to ceremonial activity, and at the same time tribal leaders or individuals aggressively undertake tourism development, the result is likely to be not only social strife but, eventually, a failed tourism enterprise.

Similar issues of interaction with nonmembers arise frequently in large-scale manufacturing undertakings. The large amounts of capital needed in such activities and the needs of high-skill labor often force tribes to turn to nonmembers for assistance. Joint ventures with large private corporations, for example, can provide access to capital, and high-skill labor (including senior management) can be imported from off the reservation. Such relationships, however, increase the affected tribe's interaction with nonmembers, and may place nonmembers in positions of power in certain reservation activities. Some tribes have been receptive to these sorts of relationships and have taken advantage of them to gain access to skills and capital resources not otherwise available to the tribe; other tribes have chosen not to. Where a tribe is unreceptive, going ahead with such interaction may lead to community discord, poor worker performance, and evaporating support for large-scale manufacturing on the reservation.

Perhaps no development activity provokes as much controversy today as the commercial development of natural and cultural resources. Receptivity to the commercialization of tribal resources is particularly necessary for development activities in the tourism and natural resource sectors. This is true not only in Indian Country but outside it as well. Changing the face of a mountain to build a ski resort, advertising to attract tourists, harvesting wildlife, strip-mining the reservation—these kinds of development activities are controversial because they force the society to confront trade-offs between economic development and cultural values. The White Mountain

Apaches, for example, receive substantial tribal income from commercial hunting of their wildlife. These hunts seem to fit comfortably with Apache concepts of proper resource use (which appear to attach high cultural value to particular places, relative to the things found in those places[33]). Yakima, on the other hand, has rejected the commercial hunting of big game on the reservation, in part because it does not fit with Yakima cultural standards of proper use of the habitat where their harvestable game is found or of the wildlife resource itself.

American Indian societies also differ markedly among themselves in the degree to which tribal members' primary source of identity and loyalty is the tribe as a whole, as opposed to subtribal organizations such as clans, bands, or other units, usually kinship based, within the tribe. Subtribal identity and loyalty appear to be most pronounced where the tribal unit has been made to include within a single political authority previously autonomous units such as villages (e.g., Hopi) or bands (e.g., the Oglala Sioux at Pine Ridge), or where historically separate and even hostile groups were forced to share a reservation (e. g., the Shoshone and Arapahoe at Wind River in Wyoming). On the other hand, some groups have proven adept at overcoming such divisions to create relatively united communities (e. g., the Confederated Tribes of the Warm Springs Reservation in Oregon, or the Confederated Salish and Kootenai Tribes of the Flathead Reservation).

Strong subtribal identities and loyalties can cause problems for some types of development activities. Large-scale manufacturing and major natural resource development (such as the operation of a sawmill or a mine), for example, often involve the concentration of a lot of a tribe's "eggs" in a single "basket." Given population size and economic conditions on most reservations, the chances are good that a major mine or factory will be the primary employer and income source—in some cases, virtually the only one outside tribal government—on the reservation. This highly concentrated form of development can encounter difficulty where members' loyalties and identities are dispersed among a number of subtribal units. First, tribal government may have difficulty mobilizing and sustaining support for development strategies in which power and responsibility are concentrated in the hands of the tribal government itself, as is usually the case with large-scale development activities. Second, in such situations these activities tend to become the focus of intratribal politics as subtribal units compete for control over enterprise activity and its benefits. Tribal dealings with the big mine or factory—whether Indian-owned and operated or not—on matters such as taxation, employment, land use, and production levels are likely to be especially unstable. Politicians lose the support necessary to negotiate from strength, the tribe fails to follow through on commitments, and investments deteriorate.

Thus, for example, the relatively poor track record of the Sioux in pursuing large-scale enterprises (particularly tribally owned enterprises), as compared to the Choctaws or the Apaches, may be due to the historic and enduring importance of subtribal allegiances in Sioux society (see the discussion in Section III.B.1 above). This does not mean that the Sioux cannot successfully pursue economic development. Rather, as suggested by Table 5, culturally appropriate development activities are more likely to lie, other things equal, in small-scale and localized manufacturing, retail and service businesses, and tourism.

Of course, knowing whether people identify primarily with the tribe or with a subtribal unit, or whether a society is or is not receptive to such attributes of development activity as workplace hierarchies, or commercialization of natural resources, or interaction with nonmembers, is not easy. Cultural characteristics are subtle, dynamic, and often in turmoil both within and across the members of a society. In some contexts, worker/boss relations may be perfectly acceptable to younger employees and unacceptable to older ones—or the reverse. In another context they may be seen as unworkable by the entire group. Commercialization of one portion of a reservation's forest may be noncontroversial, while logging activity in an adjacent area may be abhorrent to most of the population. Warm Springs vigorously pursues the development of a spa on one portion of the reservation, and turns down the development of a ski resort on another, without in any way being inconsistent: The tribe is simply pursuing what it sees as the appropriate uses of its various resources. Northern Cheyenne, on the other hand, finds itself deeply divided over the opportunity to mine its coal resources, with some tribal members urging the tribe to go forward and others viewing strip-mining as culturally unacceptable.[34]

None of this is to say that there is an inherent conflict between economic development and social sovereignty. Although the hard data is scarce, field experience suggests that strong assertions of sovereignty, supported by tribal government policies and institutions capable of backing up that sovereignty, have reinvigorated tribal identities on reservations such as Mississippi Choctaw, Mescalero Apache, White Mountain Apache, and Cochiti. It even appears that in some cases, tribally controlled development may be accompanied by such phenomena as a resurgence of indigenous language and reductions in reservation crime.

Resolving conflicts surrounding the cultural appropriateness of various economic activities is not a problem unique to Indian Country, nor is it a problem new to contemporary tribes, many of whom have had to manage such disputes ever since Europeans arrived in North America— and probably long before. We return to our central theme: effectively resolving conflicts over development activities today requires capable governmental and nongovernmental social institutions. If these institutions are not able to lay in place an environment in which conflicts can be resolved and productive investments in the future can be made, reservation economic development—of whatever kind—will be impeded. On the other hand, once those institutions are in place, then the choices tribes make over development activities will have a much greater chance of leading to sustainable—and culturally appropriate—development.

IV. IMPLICATIONS FOR POLICY

There are no quick solutions to the problem of economic underdevelopment in Indian Country. There also are no uncomplicated solutions. Successful and sustained economic development requires many ingredients—capital, skills, resources, stable institutions, and attractive market opportunities, to name a few. It also requires informed, thoughtful policymaking. Most of this chapter has been about the sorts of policy decisions that tribes face. But what about policy at the federal and state levels? What does the evidence indicate about how policy at those levels can help get reservation development underway?

We believe the available evidence clearly demonstrates that tribal sovereignty is a necessary prerequisite of reservation economic development. Each present instance of substantial and sustained economic development in Indian Country is accompanied by a transfer of primary decision-making control to tribal hands and away from federal and state authorities. Sovereignty brings accountability and allows "success" to be properly defined to include Indians' goals of political and social well-being along with economic well-being. Decades of control over reservation economic resources and affairs by federal and state authorities did not work to put reservation economies on their feet.

This conclusion does not imply that tribal-federal/state relations are or should be hostile or uncooperative. In fact, the federal government in particular has made a number of encouraging efforts to enhance tribal control over economic affairs. Public Law 638, which enables tribal contracting of otherwise federal services; the Indian Gaming Act, which codifies tribal authority over certain activities; and BIA efforts such as the "Self-Governance Project" are examples of steps in the right direction. The objective of federal and state policy should be to enhance tribal sovereignty over economic matters, with federal and state efforts aimed at support and technical assistance. In the role of consultant, federal and state governments need not always devolve back to the role of decision-maker.

The vast bulk of federal and state assistance to Indian tribes comes in the form of program-specific expenditures: health, education, infrastructure investment, loan and grant programs, direct general income assistance, and so forth. Capable tribal governments should be granted "Super 638" powers to elect to receive most of that assistance in the form of no-strings block grants, much in the way that the states now relate to the federal government. Criteria for eligibility should shift the burden of proof away from the tribe by presuming eligibility upon the tribe's request, unless it can be shown that the tribe is incapable of self-management of its block grant.

Sovereignty has many dimensions, from taxation and resource control to civil rights and child welfare.[35] Our research is confined to the economic sphere. Within that sphere, we believe the evidence on development success and failure supports the conclusion that tribal sovereignty over economic affairs should be founded upon a government-to-government relationship between Indian nations and the United States. This means tribal preeminence in taxation and business regulatory policy, as well as in land, water and resource use, and environmental policy. Split or shared jurisdiction, as under the Indian Gaming Act, does not go far enough.

One of the consequences of enhanced tribal sovereignty in the economic arena is likely to be greater variation in the economic conditions prevailing across reservations. There will be successes—and there will be failures. American Indian tribes are no more guaranteed than other developing countries that self-government will quickly and unfailingly produce dramatic improvements in economic, political, and social well-being.

The prospect of failure raises difficult policy and jurisdictional issues: Under the federal trust doctrine (under which Indian reservations are managed by the federal government in the role of trustee), does the federal government have the responsibility to bail out tribes that stumble as sovereigns? We believe that an appropriate long-range objective of federal policy should be to empower tribes with the information and decision-making apparatus by which they might knowingly and voluntarily elect to waive explicitly the federal trust responsibility upon the assertion of sovereignty powers (e.g., over the use of current trust funds, natural resource development, or environmental regulations). This would un-doubtedly expose tribes to risks. But sovereignty without such risks is a contradiction in terms.

V. CONCLUSION

Three things emerge as crucial pieces in the development puzzle. The first is sovereignty. Perhaps the greatest development asset Indian nations possess is sovereignty: the power to make decisions about their own futures. It is a tenuous power, dependent on the good will of Congress, the unpredictabilities of the courts, and, ultimately, the support of the public. But it is a key to economic development.

The second is institutions. Sovereignty alone is hardly sufficient for overcoming the immense problems tribes today face. Our research clearly indicates that, in the development arena, the single factor that most clearly differentiates "successful" tribes from "unsuccessful" ones is their ability to *effectively exercise* their sovereignty, to turn it from a legal condition or rhetorical claim into a practical tool for nation-building.

Institutions are key to that transition. But the transition is difficult. It requires, in many cases, institutional innovation. It requires the develop-ment of governing institutions that can pass two tests. The first is the test of *adequacy*: The institutions themselves have to be effective at solving the problems of managing sovereign societies. The second is the test of *appropriateness*: In order to be fully effective, tribal institutions not only have to be designed to work in the abstract; they have to fit the informal institutions—the culturally derived norms and preferred ways of doing things—of the tribal community.

The third factor is development strategy: choosing the economic policies and the specific development projects to pursue. Here again, adequacy and appropriateness matter. On the one hand, development strategies have to confront the realities of the external market and of the internal natural, human, and capital resource assets of the tribe. On the other hand, both overall economic policies and the selection of development projects have to pay attention to the culturally derived norms and preferences of the community.

Tribes that pay adequate attention to these issues can overcome, to some degree at least, significant disadvantages in other areas such as natural resources, workforce experience, or location. At the same time, tribes that fail to grapple effectively with these issues are less likely to be able to turn certain advantages, such as market access or significant resource endowments, into sustainable development.

The odds against successful economic development in Indian Country are high. On the basis of our research, however, we believe it is possible for Indian tribes to reload the dice, and significantly improve their chances in the development gamble.

NOTES

1. Brief portions of this chapter appeared in Stephen Cornell and Joseph P. Kalt, "Pathways from Poverty: Economic Development and Institution-Building on American Indian Reservations," *American Indian Culture and Research Journal* 14, no. 1 (1990): 89–125, and in idem, "Culture and Institutions as Public Goods: American Indian Economic Development as a Problem of Collective Action," in *Property Rights and Indian Economies*, ed. Terry Anderson (Lanham, MD: Rowman and Littlefield, 1992).

2. See, for example, the various cases discussed in Robert H. White, *Tribal Assets: The Rebirth of Native America* (New York: Henry Holt, 1990); some of those covered in Sam Stanley, ed., *American Indian Economic Development* (The Hague: Mouton, 1978); and those briefly described in Cornell and Kalt, "Pathways from Poverty."

3. C. Matthew Snipp, "Public Policy Impacts and American Indian Economic Development," in *Public Policy Impacts on American Indian Economic Development*, ed. C. Matthew Snipp, Development Series No. 4 (Albuquerque: Native American Studies, University of New Mexico), p. 16, and Table 2, p. 17.

4. See Stephen Cornell and Joseph P. Kalt, "Where's the Glue? Institutional Bases of American Indian Economic Development," Harvard Project on American Indian Economic Development, Project Report Series, John F. Kennedy School of Government, Harvard University, 1991; also Cornell and Kalt, "Pathways from Poverty."

5. Of course managing the forest itself is considerably more complex and typically requires more sophisticated skills. Some tribes have made themselves expert at this; see the chapter by Matthew Krepps in this volume.

6. For an excellent summary of the legal status of Indian sovereignty, see Joseph W. Singer, "Sovereignty and Property," *Northwestern University Law Review* 86, no. 1 (Fall 1991): 1–56.

7. See Stephen Cornell and Joseph P. Kalt, "The Redefinition of Property

Rights in American Indian Reservations: A Comparative Analysis of Native American Economic Development," Harvard Project on American Indian Economic Development, Project Report Series, John F. Kennedy School of Government, Harvard University, 1988; also Cornell and Kalt, "Where's the Glue?"

8. John W. Meyer and W. Richard Scott, "Centralization and the Legitimacy Problems of Local Government," in idem, *Organizational Environments: Ritual and Rationality* (Beverly Hills: Sage Publications, 1983), especially pp. 200–202.

9. See the discussion in Cornell and Kalt, "Where's the Glue?"

10. On the IRA constitutions, see Graham D. Taylor, *The New Deal and American Indian Tribalism: The Administration of the Indian Reorganization Act, 1934–45* (Lincoln: University of Nebraska Press, 1980), chapter 6; Kenneth R. Philp, *John Collier's Crusade for Indian Reform 1920–1954* (Tucson: University of Arizona Press, 1977), 161–167; and Vine Deloria, Jr., and Clifford Lytle, *The Nations Within: The Past and Present of American Indian Sovereignty* (New York: Pantheon, 1984), 173.

11. See Deloria and Lytle, *The Nations Within*, 172; Philp, *John Collier's Crusade*, 162, 166–67.

12. Deloria and Lytle, *The Nations Within*, 212.

13. There are exceptions, but the basic model is replicated, with minor variations, across a broad spectrum of tribes. See the discussion in Taylor, *New Deal and Tribalism*, 95–98.

14. On indigenous Apache government and leadership, see Harry W. Basehart, "Mescalero Apache Band Organization and Leadership," in *Apachean Culture History and Ethnology*, ed. Keith H. Basso and Morris E. Opler, Anthropological Papers of the University of Arizona, no. 21 (Tucson: University of Arizona Press, 1971), pp. 43–47; Keith H. Basso, *The Cibecue Apache* (New York: Holt, Rinehart and Winston, 1970), pp. 5–9; Morris E. Opler, "An Outline of Chiricahua Apache Social Organization," in *Social Anthropology of North American Tribes*, ed. Fred Eggan, enlarged edition (Chicago: University of

Chicago Press, 1955), especially pp. 233–35; and D. C. Cole, *The Chiricahua Apache, 1846–1876: From Warfare to Reservation* (Albuquerque: University of New Mexico Press, 1988), pp. 27–32. On the meaning of the Apache term for leader we are indebted to Mr. Edgar Perry of the White Mountain Apache Tribe, in conversation.

15. What remains unexplained in the Apache cases is the successful transition several Apache groups appear to have made from band or subtribal to tribal allegiance and identity. However, the pattern is not entirely consistent: the San Carlos Apaches appear to have had more difficulty making this transition than either the Mescalero or the White Mountain Apaches, perhaps in part because of a more heterogeneous mixing of Apache peoples at San Carlos when the reservation first was established. For some discussion see Stephen Cornell and Marta Gil-Swedberg, "Sociohistorical Factors in American Indian Economic Development: A Comparison of Three Apache Cases," Harvard Project on American Indian Economic Development, Project Report Series, John F. Kennedy School of Government, Harvard University, 1992.

16. Accounts of indigenous Sioux political organization vary in their details, but the overall scheme is fairly consistent. This brief summary draws on James R. Walker, *Lakota Society*, edited by Raymond J. DeMallie (Lincoln: University of Nebraska Press, 1982), pp. 25–39; Royal B. Hassrick, *The Sioux: Life and Customs of a Warrior Society* (Norman: University of Oklahoma Press, 1964), pp. 13–31; and William K. Powers, *Oglala Religion* (Lincoln: University of Nebraska Press, 1977), pp. 40–42.

17. Hassrick, *The Sioux*, 28.

18. See Raymond J. DeMallie, "Pine Ridge Economy: Cultural and Historical Perspectives," in *American Indian Economic Development*, ed. Sam Stanley (Chicago: Aldine, 1978), 239–40, 274.

19. See Douglass C. North, *Institutions, Institutional Change and Economic Performance* (Cambridge: Cambridge University Press, 1990), and, for systematic evidence from Indian Country, Cornell and Kalt, "Where's the Glue?"

20. From the tribal ordinance establishing the Rosebud ethics board, quoted by Rose Bordeaux, board member, interview, Rosebud Reservation, summer 1988.

21. See note 14 above.

22. See Robert H. Lowie, *The Crow Indians* (Lincoln: University of Nebraska Press, 1983), pp. 3–17; Fred W. Voget, *The Shoshoni-Crow Sun Dance* (Norman: University of Oklahoma Press, 1984), chapter 2; and Rodney Frey, *The World of the Crow Indians: As Driftwood Lodges* (Norman: University of Oklahoma Press, 1987), pp. 26–27.

23. This system, while significantly changed over the years, is clearly rooted in traditional forms of Cochiti governance. For a discussion of those forms, see Charles H. Lange, *Cochiti: A New Mexico Pueblo, Past and Present* (Albuquerque: University of New Mexico Press, 1990 [1959]), chapter 7.

24. For a more complete discussion of these findings, see Cornell and Kalt, "Where's the Glue?"

25. On separations of powers in Indian societies, see, for example, Edward H. Spicer, *Cycles of Conquest: The Impact of Spain, Mexico, and the United States on the Indians of the Southwest, 1533–1960* (Tucson: University of Arizona Press, 1962), pp. 374–84; Grenville Goodwin, compiler, *Western Apache Raiding and Warfare*, ed. Keith H. Basso (Tucson: University of Arizona Press, 1971), pp. 253–55; John H. Provinse, "The Underlying Sanctions of Plains Indian Culture," in *Social Anthropology of North American Tribes*, enlarged edition, ed. Fred Eggan (Chicago: University of Chicago Press, 1955), pp. 344–55; Stan Hoig, *The Peace Chiefs of the Cheyennes* (Norman: University of Oklahoma Press, 1980).

26. See the chapter by Krepps in this volume; also Cornell and Kalt, "The Redefinition of Property Rights"; and cf. White, *Tribal Assets*.

27. See, for example, the chapter by Krepps in this volume.

28. See Spicer, *Cycles of Conquest*, pp. 408–410, and the discussion in Cornell and Gil-Swedberg, "A Comparison of Three Apache Cases."

29. Richard T. Sherman, "A Study of Traditional and Informal Sector Micro-Enterprise Activity and its Impact on the Pine Ridge Indian Reservation Economy," Aspen Institute for Humanistic Studies, Washington, D.C., September 1988, p. 41, and Figures 3 and 4, p. 42, and Figure 7, p. 47.

30. In some tribes, in fact, it may be culturally more acceptable to have workers under the direction of nonmember management. See Ronald L. Trosper, "Multicriterion Decision-Making in a Tribal Context," *Policy Studies Journal* 16 (1988): 826–42.

31. For a review of past and existing Indian management training programs and their implications for future efforts, see Manley A. Begay, Jr., "Designing Native American Management and Leadership Training: Past Efforts and Future Options," Harvard Project on American Indian Economic Development, Project Report Series, John F. Kennedy School of Government, Harvard University, 1991.

32. See White, *Tribal Assets*.

33. See, for example, Keith H. Basso, "'Stalking with Stories': Names, Places, and Moral Narratives Among the Western Apache," in *On Nature: Nature, Landscape, and Natural History*, ed. Daniel Halpern (San Francisco: North Point Press, 1986), 95–116.

34. Rubie Sooktis and Anne Terry Straus, "A Rock and a Hard Place: Mineral Resources on the Northern Cheyenne Reservation," *Chicago Anthropology Exchange* 14, no. 1 and 2 (1981): 27–35; also Duane Champagne, *American Indian Societies: Strategies and Conditions of Political and Cultural Survival* (Cambridge: Cultural Survival, Inc., 1989), chapter 4.

35. For a discussion, see American Indian Lawyer Training Program, *Indian Tribes as Sovereign Governments* (Oakland, CA: AIRI Press, 1988).

2

A PROTOTYPICAL ECONOMIC DEVELOPMENT CORPORATION FOR AMERICAN INDIAN TRIBES[1]

Michael W. Cameron

One of the key problems all societies face as they organize for sustained economic development is how to protect enterprise management from political interference. Where tribes own their own businesses, one major challenge is to allow those businesses to be productive and profitable—which they tend not to be when they are run according to political criteria—while assuring that they continue to serve the long-term strategic interests of the tribal community.

One solution to this problem is to place tribal enterprises under the overall direction of a semi-independent economic development corporation. This mode of organization keeps long-term, strategic decision-making in the hands of elected tribal leadership. Day-to-day business decisions, however, are firmly in the hands of managers or boards of directors who are protected by the corporate structure from inappropriate political interference in nonstrategic, short-term business matters.

Michael Cameron's chapter provides a detailed outline of such a development corporation. Mr. Cameron's study was undertaken originally at the request of the Crow tribe of Montana, and was revised subsequently in response to a request from the Rosebud Sioux tribe. The present chapter takes into account further research and experience, and provides a generic outline that tribes can modify to suit their own needs.

As American Indian tribes continue their efforts to advance reservation standards of living, many are vigorously pursuing local economic development so as to provide employment and training for their citizens and revenue for tribal government programs. In doing so, a number of tribes have discovered that certain circumstances continue to get in the way of development planning and implementation. Some of these are circumstances over which tribes have little, if any, control; others appear to be rooted in tribal policy, organization, and practice.

This paper describes one organizational approach that can help to overcome certain of these obstacles to economic development: the semi-autonomous, tribal development corporation. The appropriateness of a development corporation for any particular tribe depends to a significant extent on the kinds of obstacles the tribe faces; many tribes, however, may find that a development corporation can help to solve a number of management problems while retaining ultimate control over development in tribal hands.

This paper is divided into three sections. Part I describes several common barriers to economic development on Indian reservations, and explains why an economic development corporation might be an appropriate way to deal with those barriers. Part II outlines in detail what such a corporation might look like: its structure, staffing, powers, responsibilities, and relationship to the tribal council. Part III offers some concluding comments. In addition, three appendices discuss implementation, outline the enterprise development process, and provide a glossary of terms.

PART I.
WHY ESTABLISH AN ECONOMIC DEVELOPMENT CORPORATION?

Three of the principal impediments to the development of tribal economies appear to be:

- **The potential for tribal political interference in enterprise operations.** The structure of many tribal governments allows elected officials access to the daily operations of tribally owned businesses. In addition, the short terms of elective office prescribed by most tribal constitutions politicize nearly all official decision making, including business decisions, as tribal leaders understandably act to preserve their elected positions. This frequently makes business planning difficult, leads to instability in business management, and places extraordinary burdens on tribal enterprises, discouraging growth and politicizing resources. Successful management of businesses requires some degree of insulation from the often short-term orientation and rapid changes of tribal politics.

- **An uncertain and risky business environment for potential nontribal investors.** The close association of tribal politics and tribal business, combined with the unique legal status of American Indian tribes, raises the risks to outside investors of conducting business with the tribe. Political instability, the possibility of opportunism on the part of tribal officials, and the difficulty of processing disputes or claims against the tribe discourage would-be investors, placing the tribe at a disadvantage in the competition for capital and expertise that could be devoted to enhancing tribal economies and community welfare.

- **A lack of sufficient indigenous managerial expertise.** The economic and political dependence that many tribes long had—and some still have—on the federal government discouraged the development of managerial expertise or entrepreneurialism among tribal members. Reservation retail sectors have been small or virtually nonexistent; the actions of tribal governments have been subject to federal approval; independent Indian decision making has been difficult. In many cases managerial decisions—in both business and public administration—have been made by the Bureau of Indian Affairs (BIA). Few tribal people have had the opportunity to own or operate business enterprises. For want of exposure, many tribal members lack the skills necessary for contemporary business management and economic success.

One of the striking differences between reservations and other local economies in the United States is that many Indian reservations lack a well-developed private sector. The primary, if not sole, source of capital is the tribal government, which typically is the channel for capital coming onto the reservation from the federal government or private sources. The power to invigorate the economy consequently rests almost entirely in the hands of the tribal government through its capacity to invest or to channel investments by others.

The expenditure of tribal funds on business development or any other program carries with it the responsibilities of prudent investment. It is the role of elected tribal officials to closely monitor the use of those funds. Such oversight by elected officials is both necessary and appropriate for government-run programs such as education and health services, which lack success indicators equivalent to a year-end profit statement. For these programs, citizens rely on the voting booth to express their preferences and their approval or disapproval of government performance in this role.

These systems of checks and controls that motivate tribal officials, while appropriate for certain public programs, are less suited to tribal or private enterprise. Businesses require a stable operating environment and stable management, while governments are subject to rapid turnover and quick changes in policy. This is only slightly less true at the federal and state level than it is at the tribal level, which is one reason why, through more than two hundred years of history, the United States has chosen to keep government and commerce relatively independent. As a matter of reality, for-profit enterprises, whether tribal or nontribal, become competitively disadvantaged when business decisions are made according to nonbusiness considerations.

To counter such tendencies, a tribal development corporation ensures (1) that public funds invested in business enterprises serve the interests of the tribe, and (2) that those enterprises have the necessary flexibility and freedom from political interference to be profitable and thereby attract needed outside capital, create and sustain jobs and revenue, and survive for the long term. **The corporation attempts to accomplish these two goals by assuring the tribe of a major role in the setting of long-term business goals and strategy, while preserving to enterprise managers freedom from interference in short-term, day-to-day business decisions.**

As noted above, however, another impediment to development is the lack of indigenous managerial expertise. This is attributable partly to the absence of American Indian commerce in recent tribal history. Successful operation of tribal enterprises may require an infusion of outside—i.e., nontribal and perhaps non-Indian—business expertise, until tribes can build up sufficient skills and experience among their own members. **A well-designed development corporation should facilitate access to such outside expertise without yielding too much influence to individuals from outside the reservation.**

Finally, the potential for tribal political interference in business operations, coupled with the special legal status of Native American tribes, poses added risks to would-be investors, putting the tribe at a disadvantage in its efforts to attract outside capital. **The development corporation should present outside investors with a stable and reasonably secure investment environment.**

Of course, an alternative to a semi-autonomous development corporation is to have each tribal enterprise report directly to the tribal council or to the tribal chair. In contrast to such an arrangement, which is common on many Indian reservations, a corporation offers a number of advantages:

- It frees the elected council and chair from the time-consuming and burdensome task of detailed monitoring of tribal businesses, allowing those officials to focus on long-term strategy and overall development goals;

- It places such monitoring in the hands of persons—the board of directors of the corporation—specifically chosen for their business skill and knowledge;

- It provides a crucial buffer—again, the board of directors—between enterprise managers and tribal politics;

- It allows the formulation of economic development and business policies that are less subject to changes caused by the cycle of electoral politics, bringing continuity and stability into business management for the tribe.

The following section describes a generic model of a semi-autonomous tribal development corporation, designed to achieve these objectives. It is presented here as a prototype. Obviously it can be altered to fit a particular tribe's situation or preferences. However, it is important to recognize the central purpose of the corporation, which is to facilitate economic development by overcoming the obstacles noted above. Changes in the prototype should be carefully considered so as to make certain that they do not undermine the system of checks and balances built into the design, making it impossible for the corporation to accomplish what it is intended to do.

It should be noted also that a development corporation is not sufficient in and of itself to ensure economic development. The effective functioning of the corporation itself depends in some cases on other aspects of tribal organization and leadership. But a well-designed development corporation can contribute significantly to successful reservation development.

PART II.
A PROTOTYPICAL TRIBAL ECONOMIC DEVELOPMENT CORPORATION

The concept of the development corporation is that of an organization wholly owned by the tribe but vested with sufficient autonomy to make effective and prudent business decisions. The task of the corporation is to manage and direct those tribally owned enterprises assigned to it by the tribe, and to explore, where appropriate, new opportunities for tribal enterprise development. The corporation also serves as the business arm of the tribe in cooperative ventures with outside investors or in arrangements for the establishment of nontribal enterprises on the reservation.

The creation of a development corporation presumably will follow whatever guidelines might be laid down in the constitution or charter of the tribe in question. If there are no such guidelines, the corporation could be created through an ordinance of the tribal government. The problem with creation by ordinance is that a subsequent government could dissolve the corporation simply by rescinding or altering the original ordinance. In other words, creation through the action of the tribal council leaves the corporation vulnerable to political events which might lead the same or a subsequent council to abandon the corporation.

Surely the council should have some say in how the corporation goes about the tribe's business; the task is to make certain that the corporation itself is protected from the short-term vagaries of tribal politics. The best way to do this is to establish the corporation through the tribe's constitution or charter, usually requiring the consent of a majority of tribal members, so that dissolving it likewise would require the approval not simply of the council but of a majority—perhaps a substantial majority—of the tribe.

The basic organizational chart of a generic tribal development corporation is shown in Figure 1. The corporation consists of a board of directors, a chief executive officer (CEO), tribal enterprise managers, and such additional staff as are necessary to maintain efficient operations. The size of the staff depends on the number and size of the enterprises the corporation has to manage, and on the other activities it may be asked to carry out by the tribe. Some enterprises may be large enough to internalize many of the management services of the corporation. Others will rely almost entirely on corporate staff. A tribe with few enterprises presumably will need little in the way of staff; a tribe with many enterprises to manage may need a larger staff to manage those enterprises effectively.

The following discussion describes the roles and responsibilities attached to each of these entities or positions, beginning with the tribal council, which, while not part of the corporation, typically oversees its activities.

THE TRIBAL COUNCIL

As the body ultimately responsible for tribal governance on most reservations, the tribal council also bears responsibility for overseeing the development corporation. It appoints the members of the corporation's board of directors, approves annual budgets and strategic plans, and puts together an overall economic development plan that specifies the role of the corporation in the tribe's future. The participation of the council in the affairs of the corporation is limited in its frequency but significant in its power. Its role is designed to achieve the delicate balance of giving the corporation sufficient autonomy to operate independently of politics while keeping the corporation accountable to the overall strategic interests of the tribe.

The tribal council is the organ of tribal government that interacts directly with the corporation. It makes those development decisions which are necessarily political, such as development priorities, overall spending levels, and the like.

The council serves two primary functions in the development process. First, it is the source of authority and direction from which the corporation

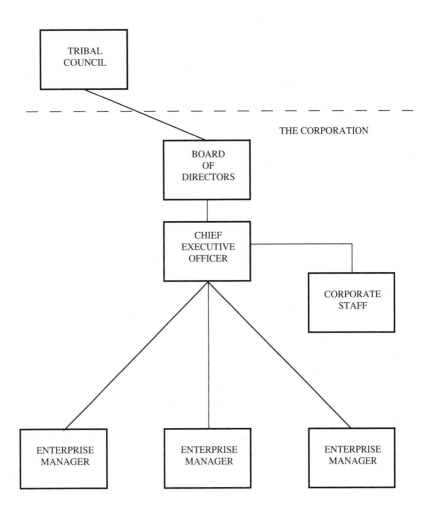

FIGURE 1. A prototypical economic development corporation

receives its mandate. By setting long-term priorities, formulating an overall development plan, appointing board members, and approving annual budgets, the council sets corporate strategy and assures a good fit with tribal objectives. In effect, it points the corporation in the right direction.

Second, the tribal council demonstrates to the outside world that the tribe is serious about economic development. The council empowers the corporation to make business commitments, and to place tribal assets at risk in the form of investments in tribal and nontribal enterprises. To demonstrate its commitment, the council may also have to grant limited waivers of immunity for development projects. Such tribal investments and waivers may be necessary to attract outside financing and talent capable of meeting tribal needs and objectives.

On the other hand, while corporate budgets and plans require annual tribal council approval, day-to-day business decisions are not accessible to the council. This inaccessibility of business decisions is essential if the corporation is to maintain the independence necessary for efficient business management and to attract outside investment.

In the prototypical development corporation, specific duties of the tribal council relative to the corporation are as follows:

A. SOURCE OF DIRECTION AND AUTHORITY

1. FORMULATE A LONG-TERM DEVELOPMENT PLAN

The development corporation is an integral part of the tribe's economic development strategy. Those who run the development corporation have to know what is expected of them. It is the task, typically, of the tribal council to set long-term development goals, to decide how the corporation can support those goals, and to communicate those decisions to the board of directors of the corporation.

Development goals have to bear the tribe's needs and interests in mind, as well as the accessibility and size of markets for tribally produced goods and services. In determining what the tribe's needs and interests are, the council may wish to seek tribal members' input through public meetings or by other means.

Among the issues a long-term development plan should consider are the following:

(a) The relative priority of:
- income
- job creation (quality & quantity)
- training (job, management, investment, etc.)
- provision of goods and services needed by the community
- tax revenue
- stimulation of ancillary businesses
- Indian ownership

(b) The availability of:
- skilled labor
- financial capital
- natural resources

(c) Acceptable levels of:
- capital costs
- tribal liability
- environmental pollution
- natural resource depletion
- presence of non-Indians or nontribal members on the reservation

(d) Acceptable/unacceptable forms of economic activity.

Through deliberate attention to issues such as these the council formulates general policy in the area of economic development, setting broad guidelines for the activity of the development corporation. The corporation's board of directors and chief executive officer can then decide how to operate within those guidelines.

2. APPOINT MEMBERS OF THE BOARD OF DIRECTORS

The tribal council appoints the members—let's say seven—of the board of directors of the corporation, selecting from a list of nominees provided by the tribal chair and the council itself.[2] The council selects directors based on objective qualifications. (See the section on the board of directors, below.)

The tribal council can remove a board member, but not easily. Removal of a board member requires a two-thirds vote of the tribal council, and must be for good cause. Good cause is limited to impropriety, malfeasance, gross incompetence, persistent absenteeism, or conflict of interest. Directors cannot be removed simply because they do not follow the wishes of the council.

Obviously, this is an area of difficulty. The council, which bears ultimate responsibility for tribal welfare, must have some control over the board. On the other hand, the whole objective of the corporation is to insulate tribal enterprise from politics. One can easily imagine a situation in which a board of directors that refused, for example, to alter its financial allocation policies to suit tribal council preference found its recalcitrant members charged with gross incompetence, and ultimately dismissed. The power to remove a member of the board is the most dangerous power the council has vis-à-vis the corporation.

The best protection against such interference is a strong, independent judiciary or personnel grievance procedure within the tribal government. Such truly independent mechanisms of dispute resolution are rare on Indian reservations, which is another reason why economic development often is difficult there. The design of an independent judiciary or some equivalent mechanism is beyond the scope of this paper, but it is important to note that there must be some check on the tribal council's ability to interpret just cause so as to serve its own, short-term political interest. In other words, should a member of the board of directors be dismissed by the council, the board member must have a route of appeal other than to the council. An independent tribal judiciary that can rule conclusively on the propriety of council personnel decisions would normally be the appropriate body to hear such an appeal.

3. APPROVE BUDGETS AND OPERATING PLANS

The annual Plan of Operation of the corporation is subject to review and consent by the tribal council. Each year the corporation's board of directors submits for council approval its Plan of Operation for the coming year, including projected budgets, appropriations, major acquisitions, enterprise strategies, and the like. In addition, the council may be asked by the board from time to time to approve or disapprove major changes in those plans as such changes become necessary. The council may also dictate that certain kinds of board decisions always require council approval. For example, the council may wish to retain the power of review over the expenditure of any tribal funds above a certain amount—e.g., $25,000— or over all decisions significantly affecting the use of reservation lands, and so forth. However, the sorts of business decisions that require council approval should be as few as possible.

The precise detail of the Plan of Operation, the format of the budget reports, and so on are determined by the tribal council and the board of directors. Appropriation or operating plans may be general or specific, depending on the nature of the enterprise, the perceived level of risk, and other considerations. The council's primary concern, however, should be that the Plan of Operation fit the long-term strategic interests and overall development objectives of the tribe. The level of detail should be only so much as required to meet this general criterion, leaving as much flexibility as possible in the hands of corporation and enterprise managers.

Finally, the review process should be limited to approval or disapproval. The tribal council should not be able to amend, and hence micromanage, corporation plans. If a plan and/or budget is disapproved, it should be returned to the board of directors, with explanation, for revision—similarly with occasional decisions regarding major expenditures, and the like. For example, the council may approve or disapprove a proposed corporate expenditure of $50,000 for center pivot irrigation, but it should not attempt to dictate what equipment is purchased, or from whom, or how the equipment is to be used. Allowing the council to amend budgets and plans directly removes business decisions from the hands of those best qualified to make them: the managers of the corporation and its enterprises.

B. GUARANTOR OF FINANCIAL COMMITMENTS

1. INVEST TRIBAL RESOURCES IN DEVELOPMENT PROJECTS

Because the corporation is a legal extension of the tribe, all assets of the corporation rightfully belong to the tribe. Consequently, all expenditure and contractual authority of the corporation must be delegated to it by the tribe, that is, in most cases, by the tribal council. Such authority should be granted annually through the Plan of Operation or other budget approval process. Thereafter, the corporation should have the authority to invest tribal resources in the manner indicated by the budget.

2. ALLOW LIMITATIONS TO SOVEREIGN IMMUNITY

Attracting nontribal private financing may require the tribe to share the investment risk through limited waivers of sovereign immunity. Under a limited waiver the tribe stands to lose its investment should an enterprise fail. Such a waiver can be made only by the tribe, that is, by the tribal council.

THE BOARD OF DIRECTORS

The board of directors serves as the steering committee for the corporation, and bears primary responsibility for corporate management. It has several tasks: to ensure that the operations of the corporation serve the long-term interests and objectives of the tribe, as specified by the tribal council; to serve as liaison between the tribal government and the corporation's chief executive officer; to insulate that officer and corporate decision-making from inappropriate interference on the part of the elected government; and to ensure that the operations of the corporation follow sound business practices.

The board also serves as a source of business advice for the tribe, and a source of reassurance to would-be investors. As a multimember body, ideally composed of individuals with business experience and acumen, and substantially protected from political pressures, the board is well set up to provide the tribe with objective judgments on business issues, and to reassure investors of the predictability of the reservation business environment.

A. NATURE OF THE BOARD

The number of members, their selection, representation, terms of office, and source of appointment, are all designed to give the board maximum stability and competence while keeping it accountable to tribal interests.

1. NUMBER OF MEMBERS

The board of directors has seven members. A minimum of five of these are members of the tribe, while up to two may be nonmembers. This division protects tribal interests from adverse outside influences while making it possible to give a significant managerial role to outsiders whose business expertise may exceed that available within the tribal population.

2. TERMS OF OFFICE

Members serve four-year terms, with staggered appointments made every odd year (nonelection years).[3]

3. APPOINTMENT

Board members are appointed by the tribal council. Appointment to the board is based primarily on business experience, acumen, and a commitment to the development goals of the tribe. Especially desirable areas of expertise include business management, economic development, marketing, finance, law, and accounting. No more than one-third of the members of the board (e.g., in a seven-member board, no more than two members) may at the same time serve as members of the tribal council.

4. REMOVAL

A member of the board may be removed by a two-thirds vote of the tribal council, but only on the grounds of gross incompetence, persistent absenteeism, conflict of interest, impropriety, or malfeasance. A board member can appeal dismissal to an independent judicial body.[4] A member of the board may resign at any time.

5. VACANCIES

Vacancies are filled by interim appointments made by the tribal council. Appointees serve the unfilled portion of the vacated term.

6. FREQUENCY OF MEETING

The board meets monthly on a fixed day (e.g., the second Tuesday of every month). Special meetings may be called by the board's chair when necessary. If requested by the chief executive officer of the corporation, the chair is responsible for calling a board meeting within two weeks of receiving the CEO's request.

7. MANNER OF ACTING

A simple majority of directors present at a meeting at which a quorum (five members) is present constitutes a decision by the board.

8. OFFICERS

Board members elect from among their number a chair, a vice chair, and such other officers (e.g., secretary, treasurer) as they see fit. The chair assumes responsibility for calling and running meetings of the board. The vice chair assumes the duties of the chair should that person be absent. The chair may not at the same time be a serving member of the tribal council.

9. COMPENSATION

Directors receive a modest per diem (e.g., $100) for each meeting they attend, plus reimbursement for the cost of travel to attend meetings. Directors are not salaried and should not serve for the purpose of financial gain.

B. POWERS AND RESPONSIBILITIES

The primary task of the board is to oversee the operations of the corporation. These operations should follow sound business practices and reflect the strategic interests and objectives of the tribe. The board's responsibility is to see that they do, and to keep the tribal council informed, via regular reports, of progress and problems against these objectives. Where tribal objectives may conflict with prudent business practice, it is up to the board to make clear to the council what the alternative courses of action and their likely consequences are, and to work with the council to resolve such conflicts.

It is the further responsibility of the board to make recommendations to the tribe regarding strategic decision-making about both current operations and future opportunities.

1. HIRING

The board selects and hires the chief executive officer of the corporation. Other hiring decisions are that officer's responsibility.

2. REPORTING

The board, in cooperation with the chief executive officer, provides the following reports to the tribal council: an annual Plan of Operation, including budgets; annual audit statements; an annual report describing progress against corporate goals in the past year; quarterly corporate balance sheets and profit and loss statements.

3. PLANNING

The board's task, in cooperation with the chief executive officer, is to establish a Plan of Operation for the corporation each year, and to monitor progress against that plan on at least a quarterly basis.

4. CORPORATE OPERATIONS

The board is responsible, along with the chief executive officer, for drafting and submitting to the tribal council the annual Plan of Operation of the corporation; it has the power of review and approval over all corporate expenditures over a sum to be determined by the board (e. g., $5,000), and below the level requiring tribal council approval (e. g., $25,000); and it has the power to overrule, should it so decide, decisions of the CEO. However, the CEO should be free to make the vast majority of business decisions without board review.

5. RULE AND POLICY MAKING

The board has the authority to create and implement a set of bylaws governing corporate operations, and to establish from time to time, in consultation with the CEO, policies necessary to effective operations. The bylaws and policies of the corporation must be consistent with those provisions, constitutional or otherwise, by which the corporation was created, with the constitution or charter of the tribe, and with the overall tribal objectives as determined by the tribal council or other appropriate tribal leadership. The board may propose to the tribe changes in those provisions and objectives, but such changes are appropriately up to the tribe, not to the board. On the other hand, the establishment of bylaws and business policies are appropriately the province of the board of directors of the corporation, not of the tribal council.

CHIEF EXECUTIVE OFFICER

The chief executive officer (CEO) is the single most important position in the corporation, and the focal point of responsibility and accountability. As overseer of day-to-day enterprise activities, the CEO to a significant degree determines the success or failure of tribal enterprises. He or she implements the annual operating plans approved by the board of directors and tribal council, and is authorized to make daily operational decisions, including spending decisions, consistent with those plans and with annual budgets. The CEO has to be both competent as a manager and able to understand and appreciate the needs and goals of the tribe. He or she has primary responsibility for hiring enterprise managers and other corporate staff; for delegating authority to members of the staff; for setting, in consultation with the board of directors, operational goals, policies, and procedures; and for organizing and overseeing those business systems found necessary for efficient corporate operations. Enterprise managers report to the CEO, who in turn reports to the Board of Directors.

A. NATURE OF THE POSITION

The CEO position is designed to give maximum latitude to the CEO so as to facilitate quick and efficient business decision-making, while at the same time assuring that corporate operations respect the broad guidelines set by the board of directors and the tribe.

1. APPOINTMENT

The CEO is appointed by the board of directors. The appropriate criteria for selection are business experience and acumen, the demonstrated skills necessary to assume the responsibilities and powers of the position, and a willingness to operate within the guidelines set by the board and, at a more general level, by the tribe. Tribal membership may be desirable, but should not necessarily be a criterion of appointment.

2. TERM

The CEO typically is hired to a multiyear (e.g., three-year) contract with a specified probationary period (e.g., six months).

3. REMOVAL

The CEO may be removed by decision of the board of directors whenever he or she is in violation of contract or has demonstrated incompetence in the position. The CEO may resign at any time.

4. COMPENSATION

The CEO should be paid a competitive salary commensurate with other persons of similar skill and experience.

B. POWERS AND RESPONSIBILITIES

1. MANAGEMENT

The following functions are those which must rest in the office of the CEO to ensure accountability and coordination.

    a. Day-to-day business management

        The CEO is the chief operating officer of the corporation, and as such has control over corporate business operations of all kinds. Day-to-day business decisions (e.g., hiring, contracting, payroll, pricing, schedules, and so forth) are the province of the CEO, unless otherwise delegated by the board of directors, and are not the province of the tribal council or other tribal officers.

    b. Hiring corporate staff

        The CEO is responsible for hiring such staff as are necessary to carry out the corporation's functions. All corporate staff report ultimately to the CEO.

    c. Operating policies and procedures

        It is the responsibility of the CEO to develop and implement operating policies and procedures for tribal enterprises, including personnel, financial management, contracting, purchasing, marketing, and other areas as needed.

    d. Annual Plan of Operation

        Each year the CEO submits to the board of directors a Plan of Operation for the corporation and its enterprises. This Plan includes the following items:

        • Operating budgets
        • Capital budgets
        • Production/sales targets
        • Staffing requirements (including training)
        • Expense/revenue projections

• Reinvestment and profit-sharing plans
The board of directors has the power of review and approval over this Plan.

e. Accounting for corporate funds
The CEO is responsible for keeping accurate, up-to-date
financial records and accounts of all corporate business,
and for hiring or contracting with necessary resources (e.g.,
a certified public accountant, etc.) to do so. Balance
statements should be available to the board on a monthly
basis.

f. Coordination with the Bureau of Indian Affairs
The CEO's responsibility is to keep the BIA advised of all
tribal business activities for which BIA notification is
required. The CEO serves as the conduit through which the
tribe makes its business developments known to the BIA.
He or she also monitors BIA compliance with any agreements between it and the tribe as they pertain to economic
development.

2. HIRING TRIBAL ENTERPRISE MANAGERS

The CEO selects and hires the managers of individual tribal enterprises.
(See the section on enterprise managers, below.)

3. DEVELOPMENT PLANNING

Depending on overall tribal goals and long-term development plans, the
corporation may be asked by the council to look for and explore new
business opportunities. As the person most immediately familiar with
business conditions on the reservation, with the tribe's business capabilities, and with tribal development goals and policies, the CEO is best
qualified to oversee such explorations and to initiate planning for new
business development. The CEO may hire such staff (e.g., an economic
development planner) as efficient planning for new business demands.

When pursuing new business development, the CEO is responsible for
developing a Business Plan that indicates how any new venture will
contribute to the achievement of tribal goals. The Business Plan should
include

a. identification of potential enterprises

- type of business (agriculture, manufacturing, etc.)
- type of ownership (tribal, joint)
- key production factors: capital, infrastructure, labor, and resource requirements
- facility location
- tribal benefits (fiscal and nonfiscal)
- relationship to long-term development goals

b. market analysis
  - key market determinants
  - market trends
  - competition
  - market projection

c. financial analysis
  - projected budget and profits (five years), income, and cash flow, plus balance sheet measures of performance (employment, internal rate of return)
  - structure of financing: equity, debt, bonds, loans, grants
  - break-even analysis

d. implementation plan and schedule.

All plans for new business development are reviewed by the board of directors and ultimately are subject to approval by the tribal council.

4. NONTRIBAL ENTERPRISE DEVELOPMENT

Although the CEO's primary concern is maintaining the health of tribally owned enterprises, he or she also serves as primary contact for nontribally owned enterprise development on the reservation, should such development be contemplated by the tribe. As the person most directly involved in business planning, operations, and development on the reservation, the CEO is in the best position to search out, screen, and evaluate proposals for nontribal enterprises. Part of the CEO's responsibility is to advise the tribe on such proposals. In the case of proposals deemed acceptable by the tribe, the CEO is responsible for arranging the terms under which the proposed project will be developed. This includes designing plans for technical assistance and financing arrangements intended to attract the project to the reservation. Of course, all such development plans are subject to the approval of the board of directors and, ultimately, the tribal council.

5. TECHNICAL ASSISTANCE, TRAINING, INFRASTRUCTURE

The CEO is in the best position to identify needs for improvement in reservation infrastructure, in manpower training, and in other areas relevant to the operation of tribal enterprises. Part of the CEO's job is to advise the tribe on such needs, and to coordinate corporate activities in this area with other tribal departments and services. The CEO also has the authority, within the constraints of sound business practice, to contract with vendors within or outside the tribe for training, technical assistance, or other consulting services necessary to the effective operations of the corporation and its enterprises.

6. TRIBAL MANAGEMENT TRAINING AND PLACEMENT

Where possible within the business resources and objectives of the corporation, the CEO may initiate special programs to prepare tribal members to fill managerial and nonmanagerial positions within the corporation and its enterprises. For example, he or she may assign tribal members as assistants or apprentices to enterprise managers or other corporate staff for the purpose of management training. Assuming that tribal members have or develop appropriate qualifications, the CEO attempts to place them in available positions in the corporation.

7. FINANCING

The CEO has the authority, in consultation with the board of directors, to solicit governmental and private financing or assistance, so long as it does not conflict with the Plan of Operation of the corporation or with the overall development goals of the tribe.

8. REPORT AND ADVISE

It is the task of the CEO to keep the board of directors advised of the state of corporate business operations, typically through attendance at the monthly meetings of the board. The CEO is responsible for bringing issues of concern to the attention of the board promptly, and for providing periodic assessments of corporate performance as it relates both to board-established policies and objectives and to the long-term economic development plan of the tribe. The CEO also may be called upon to report directly to the tribal council on occasion on corporate progress and problems, or to offer advice on business decisions.

9. HIRE A PLANNING STAFF

A number of these responsibilities clearly require the services of an economic development planner and possibly additional planning staff. The CEO may hire such staff as are necessary, within the available resources of the corporation. Ideally the planner will be familiar with the development goals of the tribe and with the nature of tribal government, competent at applying for development grants, experienced in the areas of particular development potential for the tribe, skilled at development planning, and able to arrange technical assistance contracts to attract desirable enterprises onto the reservation. While it may be desirable that the planner be a tribal member, this should not be a criterion of employment.

ENTERPRISE MANAGER

Each tribal enterprise has a manager, hired by the CEO of the development corporation. The enterprise manager is responsible for the day-to-day operation of the enterprise, and is authorized to make operating decisions in a manner consistent with the corporate Plan of Operation. Specific responsibilities of managers are determined by the CEO of the corporation, in consultation with the board of directors, and are likely to vary with the size and complexity of the enterprise in question. Typically they include all hiring of enterprise personnel, expenditures within those limits set by the CEO and the budget, and the organization and oversight of all enterprise operations and activities. The enterprise manager reports to the CEO.

The selection of managers, as of all other personnel, is based as much on objective qualifications as possible. Managerial ability and experience are the primary criteria. In addition, managers should be skilled at managing people and willing to operate the enterprise within the broad guidelines set by the corporation and the tribe.

PART III.
CONCLUSION

This outline of a prototypical development corporation is intended to serve two purposes. First, by presenting a detailed organizational design, it intends to raise a particular set of issues that need to be addressed by tribes as they pursue the development of tribally owned enterprises. Among these issues, the primary ones are

1. insulating business decisions from internal tribal politics;
2. developing the organizational capability to make informed, sound, and systematic business decisions;
3. building an institutional base within the tribe that will encourage would-be investors of money, time, or energy— whether tribal members or not—to invest; and
4. giving the tribe increased control over its own economic future.

Second, the intention here is to present a set of root ideas that can serve as starting points for the design of an institution appropriate to the tribe in question. While many of the details can be altered without jeopardizing the successful operation of the corporation, the following are considered vital to this model:

1. The role of the elected tribal government in business operations must be limited and clearly defined. Its primary role is strategic: creating a long-term vision and direction for economic development. The appointment of directors and the annual review of budgets and plans also should remain in the hands of the tribal council, as should approval of certain kinds of major business decisions. But interference beyond these functions should be kept to a minimum.
2. Members of the board of directors should have staggered terms that overlap those of elected tribal officials, and should be appointed during nonelection years.
3. Directors and the CEO should be well qualified for their

jobs. Demonstrated competence in business management should be required. Grounds for removal must be clear and strictly limited to objective evidence of poor performance.

One other caution should be noted here. As already pointed out, one of the most important conditions for the success of a tribal economic development corporation lies in other governmental institutions, and in particular in the presence of a strong and independent judicial mechanism within the tribe. It is a mistake to assume that the tribal council—any more than any other governing body, in Indian Country or elsewhere—can consistently rule fairly in disputes inwhich it is an interested party. Some sort of independent judicial mechanism that can help to resolve occasional conflicts over corporate operations and personnel will greatly increase the chances that the development corporation will successfully fulfill its intended purpose, and better serve the interests of the tribe.

Ultimately, of course, no matter how well designed, the development corporation will only succeed if tribal members and the tribal government want it to succeed. Strong leadership and an overall commitment to the purpose of the corporation are necessary for success. With that support, the development corporation can help tribes achieve their political, economic, and social goals.

APPENDIX I.
IMPLEMENTATION

The timing of the development corporation's evolution is difficult to predict. Considerable care should be given to the drafting of the charter of the corporation. The ultimate success of the corporation depends a great deal on achieving the delicate balance of power between the corporation and the tribal government. The constitutional measure or ordinance establishing the corporation should anticipate both future political turmoil and potentially misguided business decisions by the corporation. With the right balance of power these competing problems can be prevented from causing extreme harm to tribal economic development.

Once the corporation becomes a legally established entity, the tribe may consider hiring a temporary CEO for the purpose of initiating corporation activities.

The complete process of creating a long-term development plan, identifying promising enterprises, and arranging for their development may take more than a year or two, and it may take several years for tribal enterprises, once established, to return a profit to the tribe. Positive results are unlikely to materialize immediately.

Finally, the needs of the corporation, in terms of its budget and staff, will become clear as the tribal economy develops. At first the corporation may have only a CEO and a secretary. In time, however, as enterprises multiply and develop, the staff will grow and the CEO typically will delegate many of the office's responsibilities to enterprise managers and other staff. When and to what extent staff additions and delegations become necessary will probably become apparent in time.

APPENDIX II.
THE ENTERPRISE DEVELOPMENT PROCESS

It is difficult to imagine the dynamics of the development corporation based on the static definitions of responsibility given in the body of this paper. The following flow chart of the development cycle (Figure 2) describes the process of enterprise development itself.

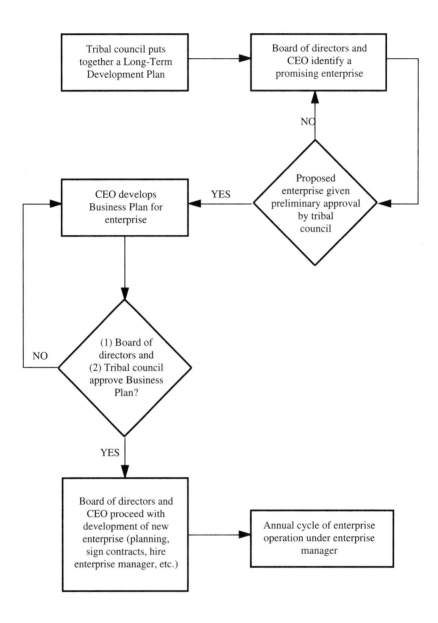

FIGURE 2. Enterprise development cycle

APPENDIX III.
GLOSSARY OF TERMS

Long-term development plan: A strategic plan for economic development put together by the tribal government, presumably in consultation with the members of the tribe. It summarizes long-term development goals and priorities, and outlines relevant tribal policies in regard to resource use, relations with non-Indians, jobs, appropriate development activities, etc.

Annual plan of operation: Prepared by the CEO in consultation with the board of directors. Outlines budgets, goals, staffing levels, production levels, anticipated profits, and major activities of the corporation for the coming year. Subject to tribal council approval.

Business plan: A plan for future enterprise development. Details the type of project, costs, resource use, anticipated impacts on unemployment, staffing, etc. Subject to board of directors and tribal council approval.

Tribal enterprise: A for-profit business owned by the tribe and operated by the development corporation.

Nontribal enterprise: A for-profit business which is owned not by the tribe itself but by an individual or other group (tribal or nontribal) and operated privately.

NOTES

1 . I would like to thank the Crow tribe of Montana and the Rosebud Sioux tribe for their assistance in the development of this paper.
2 . The number of directors and the process for developing a list of nominees should be determined by the tribal council.
3 . In starting up the corporation, three board members should be appointed to two-year terms and the other four to four-year terms so as to initiate the staggering of terms from the beginning. Thereafter, regular appointments are for four-year terms.
4 . Both the process for initiating removal of a director and the appeal process should be defined by the tribal council.

3

THE TRIBAL JUDICIARY: A PRIMER FOR POLICY DEVELOPMENT

Andrea Skari

One of the keys to self-government is a sovereign society's right to establish and enforce the laws by which it is organized and through which conflicts are resolved. Accordingly, tribal judicial systems are cornerstones of Indian self-rule and critical elements in successful economic development.

To be effective, such systems must be able to confront the real world problems of the reservation. These include matters of both on-reservation law enforcement and cross-boundary dispute resolution. The challenges are far-reaching, from constitutional interpretation and civil disputes to intergovernmental conflict and contract enforcement. To meet such challenges requires expertise, resources, and, ultimately, legitimacy and credibility in the eyes of the tribal community.

This chapter by Andrea Skari provides a review of judicial systems adopted by seven Indian tribes. There is no single judicial system that is right for all tribes, and the author presents an analysis of the pluses and minuses of alternative answers to such questions as the appropriate terms of office for judges and the role of the tribal attorney.

This study was written originally as a report to the Gila River, Hopi, Navajo, Pascua Yaqui, San Carlos Apache, Tohono O'Odham, and White Mountain Apache tribes.

I. INTRODUCTION

This study outlines choices tribes face when they are developing or revising their judicial systems. The range of options outlined on the following pages is by no means exhaustive. These options, however, should stimulate dialogue between tribal members and leaders involved in the process of change. Ultimately, a tribe must choose its own system, whether an amalgamation of the possibilities outlined below, a traditional system, or a combination of both.

If tribes want to act to the fullest extent as sovereigns, they have to take responsibility for the consequences of those actions. "Today Indian nations are realizing that the best way to prevent interference in their internal affairs is to take firm control of those governmental functions which are crucial to their continued survival."[1] Taking "firm control" may mean small changes in the governmental forms of the tribe, or it could mean massive revision. Whatever the decision, tribes should understand the importance of all their institutions and of the interconnections among those institutions.

No political decisions are made in a vacuum. Changes made to the judiciary will have an effect on the council and the other institutions of the tribe. Therefore, such changes must be considered carefully and thoughtfully. As Vine Deloria, Jr., and Clifford Lytle comment,

> Like most political communities, Indians have responded to reservation problems only after they have become apparent. The customary "band-aid" solution to political and legal problems inevitably takes precedence over planned action. This natural expediency has been true in the development of most tribal court systems from their inception. While awareness of a necessity for long-range planning is always discussed, it seldom receives any real attention.[2]

By learning from others and from their own experiences, tribes and their governments will be able to take firm control of their governmental functions as well as make long-range judicial plans to prevent further erosion of their sovereignty.

Mike Myers, a Seneca law consultant, describes sovereignty as follows:

> Ideally, sovereignty is the unrestricted right of groups of people to organize themselves in political, social and cultural patterns that

meet their needs. It is the right of a people to freely define ways in which to use land, resources and manpower for their common good. Above all, sovereignty is the right of people to exist without external exploitation or interference.[3]

Tribes still maintain sovereign powers, although they have been eroded by time and the United States government. These governmental powers, "with some exceptions, are not delegated powers granted by express acts of Congress, but are inherent powers of a limited sovereignty that have never been extinguished."[4] Among them are the power to establish a form of government and police power and to administer justice; the power to determine membership and to exclude persons from the reservation; the power to charter business organizations; and the power to tax.[5]

II. THE JUDICIARY

Ideally, the judicial branch of a tribal government administers justice for the tribe. The judiciary provides "for a tribal forum for redress of grievances and to settle disputes . . . . A judicial article [in the constitution] is included to provide a constitutional basis for establishing an independent court system to deal with the tribe's judicial responsibilities."[6]

However, judicial activity has taken many forms, depending on culture and circumstances. As noted by Samuel J. Brakel,

> Historically, law, order, and justice in Indian societies were dispensed in widely varying ways, matching the wide variety in cultures and life-styles among the tribes. Much was left to private means of enforcement—appropriate action in many conflict situations being the responsibility of the family or clan. If resort to more public means was had, it might be to political (tribal) councils, soldier or hunter societies, secular or religious leaders, generally respected and/or elder individuals, or combinations of these. But there were no "courts" and "judges" in the sense of the "independent" and "exclusively adjudicative" institutions and personnel that Anglo-American ideals have them to be.[7]

Tribes that are developing or revising their court systems face many choices: Which points of Anglo law and court composition should be adopted? What traditions, such as marriage and property rights, can be retained or reinstated by the tribe? Should the tribe accept jurisdiction over all possible areas, or accept only limited jurisdiction? Although the Bureau of Indian Affairs and state and federal governments have encouraged adoption of courts modeled after United States' systems,

> Federal law recognizes that Indian tribes may adopt whatever form of government best suits their own practical, cultural, or religious needs. Tribes are not required to adopt forms of government patterned after the forms of the United States government. Since Indian tribes are not limited by the United States Constitution, they are not subject to such principles as the separation of powers or the religious establishment clause.[8]

Regardless of the degree to which a tribe's judiciary is modeled after United States-style, traditional, or mixed systems, the judiciary of an effective sovereign power must consider taking on three primary roles: redress of grievances, dispute resolution, and judicial review of the acts of other parts of tribal government. Redress of grievances entails the capacity and authority to dispense justice (in such forms as fines, imprisonment and/or injunctions) when wrongs are committed against individuals or the tribe. Dispute resolution puts the judicial system in the position of being a forum in which individuals, organizations, and even governments can settle disagreements over such matters as contracts, land and resource use, property, and jurisdiction.

Judicial review by tribal courts is the power to determine the legitimacy (especially the constitutionality) of actions taken by the council and chair. In this role, the courts ideally aid governmental stability and ensure that the main precepts of the tribal government are upheld. They can ensure that revisions to codes and the constitution are made in a manner that is consistent with the form of government that the tribe has adopted. Judicial review can also be used to limit the actions of the council and chair to those actions that are consistent with the tribe's governmental principles. This power of discipline may ensure, along with other social and political pressures, that officials' actions serve the public's interests, rather than solely the self-interest of council members or the chair.

In order to effectively exercise any or all of its powers, a tribal judiciary is likely to need some degree of insulation from influence and control by other tribal officials, private parties, and the politics of the moment. The principles of judicial independence and separation of powers are important ingredients in United States-style court systems, where the legislative (council) and executive (chair) branches might otherwise compete for and concentrate power in ways that contradict the principles of sovereign governance in the people's interest. But independence and separation of powers have been common to effective indigenous judicial systems as well. Traditional institutions, such as warrior societies or councils of elders, have had their powers and legitimacy delineated and defined by tribal cultures. This gives them insulation from politics and special interests that might otherwise overwhelm tribal interests.

Judicial independence and separation of powers might be rooted first and foremost in basic constitutional and/or cultural precepts. Independence and the separation of powers also depend, however, on a host of other decisions and policies, ranging from how tribal courts are funded to how judges are selected. Important issues for a tribe to consider when designing a judicial system include: judicial selection, developing an appellate court, establishing other judicial institutions and offices, considering adoption of a council judiciary committee, funding, and relations with the police. These topics form the core of the analysis that follows. In each case, the strengths and weaknesses of various approaches are examined, along with the practices of a set of tribes surveyed in 1989 in order to illustrate options and experience.

III. JUDICIAL SELECTION

Selection of the judiciary is one of the most important actions a tribe can take. Observers and/or users of the courts include federal, state, and county officials, as well as those reservation and nonreservation persons who come before the courts in criminal or civil cases. To be effective, judges and court officials over the long run must be credible and capable. Therefore, judicial selection and requirements help determine the success or failure of the judicial system.

The following charts survey the selection criteria of seven tribal judiciaries.

CHART III.A
Judicial Selection

Tribe	Terms of Office	Elected, Appt'd	Review, Removal	Native Language Fluency	Experience	Training Update	Requirements in Const.
Pascua Yaqui	4 years (X)	apptd by council (X)	by council	no	no—chief judge yes—associate judge (X)	no	those checked (X)
Gila River	4 years	elected at-large	recall by community members	no	no	no	no *see note
Navajo	two-year probation, up to 70 years old	apptd by chairman, council confirms	designated, members of the three branches	yes	law-related experience	yes	no constitution
White Mt. Apache	4 years	apptd by council	general election, council	yes	no	no	no
San Carlos Apache	4 years	apptd by council	council	yes	no	no	no
Tohono O'Odham	6 years (X)	apptd by council (X)	council, recall (X)	no	no	yes—continue or begin training	those checked (X)

* As of 1989, the Gila River Indian community had a revised constitution pending approval by the secretary. The revisions put terms of office, election, and removal procedures within the constitution.

CHART III.B
Terms of Office

	Two Years	Four Years	Six Years	Life
Positive aspects	Terms of poor judges could be allowed to lapse without significant effort from the council	Judges could, if elected, cycle with other elected officials, so election money would be saved	Allows terms to cycle separately from elected officials—will aid in separation of powers	After a selection and review period, political pressures are removed, which aids in separation between council and court
Negative aspects	With a short time horizon, judges are more likely to be influenced by political pressures. With a high turnover rate, judicial training is much more expensive.	Judges are still under political pressures, if appointed with every new council. Judicial impartiality is required if fair decisions are to be made by the court.	If the judge is incompetent, greater effort is required to remove the judge. This power must be used infrequently and with great consideration.	If the judge proves incompetent after probation period, the life appointee must be impeached. This may undermine confidence in judicial impartiality.

CHART III.C
Mode of Selection

	Appointment	Election	Combination
Positive aspects	A judiciary committee or the regular council may be much more informed about judicial qualifications and requirements than the voting public. Judges may avoid some political pressure.	Control of the selection of judges will be in the hands of the tribal members, not the council, which may aid in separation of powers.	After the judge has been appointed and has served out the term successfully, popular approval could be sought. The tribe could acquire a competent judge through original selection, yet opinion could be expressed by, and power transferred to, the people.
Negative aspects	The council will have the final choice in judicial selection, and potentially large influence over decisions of the judiciary. This causes breaches of judicial impartiality.	Tribal members may not understand the skills and duties required of those in the judiciary. Selection then becomes political and may undermine attempts to upgrade selection and training requirements.	While a real possibility, logistically there would be much work required, first to correctly outline procedures, then to explain the system clearly to all parties involved.

CHART III.D
Review, Removal

	Review and Removal by Council	Recall	Combination
Positive aspects	The judiciary committee or the council will generally have greater knowledge of the judge than the public. Checks between the court and the council are preserved.	When the public has the right to recall judges, as well as other public officials, they gain more control over tribal decision-making.	Checks and balances between the council, the judiciary, and the public would exist. Ideally, a 2/3 vote would be required to remove any official from office.
Negative aspects	Checks and balances can be easily tilted toward a strong institution. If the council is allowed, it will influence judicial decisions. Threat of removal from office is a strong lever against the judiciary.	Possible public outrage and a move toward recall over a controversial, though correct, decision may encourage judges to make noncontroversial decisions.	Governments must ensure that removal of any public official is a difficult, though not impossible, procedure. Ease of removal will contribute to instability and frequent changes in leadership, already a major problem on many reservations.

CHART III.E
Native Language Requirement

	Yes	No	Combination
Positive aspects	The judge may be more culturally sensitive if she/he speaks the language of the tribe. In some cases, tribal members may speak only their tribal language, so cases before the court could be conducted in that language.	If no language or residency requirements exist, emphasis during selection can be placed on competency and experience. If the tribe wishes, language can be an influencing factor in selection.	If the tribe has more than one judicial position, a percentage could be fluent. This will ease the hiring restrictions and improve the selection pool while preserving cultural integrity.
Negative aspects	In many cases, judges with both experience and language fluency are difficult, if not impossible, to find. The tribe either hires a competent temporary judge and waives the language requirement, or hires a less competent judge.	On reservations where many speak only the native language, interpreters have to be hired, which increases court costs and lengthens trials and hearings. Those who speak no English may feel the judiciary is not effectively serving them.	Priorities between language fluency, competency, and experience are developed by either the judiciary committee, the council, or the judiciary itself.

CHART III.F
Experience Requirements

	Yes	No	Combination
Positive aspects	To preserve sovereignty, each tribe must ensure that a separate and respected judiciary exists for their members and those who deal with them. Experienced judges assist in that goal.	The tribe may have members who are inexperienced but with time will become excellent judges. The courts exist for the tribes and, ideally, should have judges from those tribes.	A combination of those with and without experience is possible until a sufficient hiring base develops on the reservation.
Negative aspects	Lack of funds may halt any attempts to hire those with experience. Courts are expensive to run properly, and those with experience expect higher wages.	Training is expensive and requires time. Many tribes cannot afford this time because of pressures they face to develop a strong court quickly.	Those with training would spend valuable time with inexperienced members, decreasing court efficiency and possibly creating case backlogs.

CHART III.G
Judicial Requirements Placed in Constitution

	Yes	No	Combination
Positive aspects	Requirements placed in a constitution are more difficult to change than those in a code. This allows for greater and more consistent separation of powers if the constitution is upheld.	Many pre-1970s constitutions do not mention the judiciary. Tribes thus are able to write their regulations into the tribal codes and can work more flexibly to perfect their systems.	Ideally, tribes use a combination of both constitutional and code regulations. Length of term, jurisdiction, and an outline of powers (preferably complete separation of powers) should be included.
Negative aspects	Tribes could write requirements into their constitutions that they are unable to follow. This compromises the legitimacy of the document every time guidelines are waived or ignored.	If codified but not constitutionalized, the powers of the judiciary can be easily appropriated by the council. Separation of powers is crucial to the maintenance of sovereignty.	Tribes may experience difficulty in deciding where to place each requirement, so several revisions may be necessary.

IV. APPELLATE COURT

The appellate process is critical in any judiciary. This process allows litigants to resort to a superior court to review the decision of an inferior (trial) court. The appellate court reviews and, if necessary, revises the action of the inferior court, and, unless the court is granted original jurisdiction or *de novo* review (where all evidence is presented again as before the trial court), rules only on points of law. This second hearing increases the chances that substantial fairness will be afforded the appellant by determining whether or not the trial court made proper application of case law or code to the facts of the case.

The following charts present a sampling of tribal appellate process and procedure.

CHART IV.A
Appellate Court

Tribe	Terms of Office	Selection	Standing Ad Hoc	Number of Judges	De Novo Review	Membership Requirements
Pascua Yaqui	2 years, staggered	council appoints	standing	3	no	no
Gila River	none	neighboring judges who are available	ad hoc	2	yes	no
Hopi	minimum 1 year	tribal chair appoints	standing	3	yes, if attorney requests	no
Navajo	2-year probation, up to 70 yrs. old	apptd by chair, council confirms	standing	3	no	yes
White Mt. Apache	chief—life, others by need	council	standing, ad hoc	3	yes	yes
San Carlos Apache	none	judges from other tribes	ad hoc	1	yes	no
Tohono O'Odham	6 years	candidate	ad hoc list submitted to jud. comm.	3 judge (pro tem)	no panel	no

CHART IV.B
Terms of Office

	None	Two Years	Four Years	Six Years	Life
Positive aspects	Appellate trials are easier to schedule if a variety of judges is available. Prompt appellate hearings should be a goal of the court.	Since many appellate judges are not full-time, replacement of those who yield their appointments is simplified.	Appointment of judges can cycle with elections of officials.	Aids in separation of powers, since terms do not correspond directly with those of elected officials.	After probationary period, threat of removal by council would be minimized. Goal of separation of powers is promoted.
Negative aspects	Continuity of decisions is at risk, and familiarity with tribal codes is not guaranteed.	As in trial courts, a short time horizon may prove detrimental to judicial impartiality. Judges are more prone to political pressure.	Judicial impartiality may be compromised if political pressures interfere with or influence judicial decision-making.	Part-time or volunteer judges may want shorter terms.	Removal of incompetent judges is difficult, and frequency should be minimized. Part-time judges will tend to desire shorter terms.

CHART IV.C
Appellate Court Selection

	Appointed by Council	Appointed by Judicial Comm.	Elected	Chosen from Trial Judges	Chosen from Neighboring Judges
Positive aspects	The council is familiar with the requirements for the post, and also chooses the trial judges. This promotes consistency in selection	A judiciary committee is more likely to have court experience and can make informed decisions about candidates.	The people choose and the influence of the council is lessened. This may assist in separation of powers	If the tribe's own judges are used for appeals, they are conveniently available, and scheduling is simplified. They are also familiar with tribal codes.	If an extensive candidate list is developed, schedule problems are minimized. If judges are used consistently, familiarity with the tribal code will develop.
Negative aspects	Separation of powers is jeopardized if the council exercises too much power. If appointees do not live on the reservation, scheduling of trials is a problem.	A judiciary committee is in position to influence the makeup and decisions of the court, and may lessen court independence.	The general populace may not understand the duties and requirements of the judgeship, so selection becomes politicized.	The trial judges may be too closely involved to allow a fair appellate hearing.	Familiarity with the judicial codes may not be sufficient. Trained candidates from neighboring tribes may not exist.

CHART IV.D
Standing, Ad Hoc Court

	Standing	Ad Hoc	Combination
Positive aspects	A standing appellate court promotes consistency in decision-making, simplifies scheduling of hearings, and assures that judges are familiar with tribal codes.	Ad hoc (for this special purpose) appellate courts are ideal for those tribes with few appellate trials. There is less expense than with a standing court, but if judges are trained well, decisions can be as consistent.	For those without the resources to maintain a standing appellate court, a combination is ideal. A standing list of candidates is approved, and judges are selected from that list. This minimizes scheduling problems by developing a pool of qualified candidates familiar with the tribal codes and constitution.
Negative aspects	Many tribes do not have the the funds or personnel to maintain a standing appellate court.	Scheduling of trials may become a severe problem, and those who are appealing deserve to have a timely hearing. Many courts with this system have huge case backlogs. Judges may not have sufficient knowledge of tribal codes or familiarity with tribal customs.	Developing a sufficient pool may take a considerable amount of time, particularly if the tribe is isolated. Backlogs can develop.

CHART IV.E
Number of Appellate Judges

	One	Two	Three	Four or More
Positive aspects	If only one judge is required to hear an appellate trial, scheduling problems are fewer.	Two judges can confer over the records of the lower court and decide if the law was properly interpreted and applied.	One of the three judges can serve as chief justice and handle the proceedings of the hearing. If the court has an odd number of judges, a majority opinion can be established.	Technically, the tribe could have as many judges hear a case as are available. However, the number should be kept to a manageable level. A greater number of opinions may standardize decisions.
Negative aspects	Because an appellate court's function is to review points of law cited in the lower court trial, the opinions of more than one judge are preferable. Fairness is then better served.	With only two judges, no majority opinion can be developed. This complicates the final decision process.	Funding of three judges is more expensive, and hearings are more difficult to schedule.	Funding, finding room for the hearings, and scheduling of hearings must be considered.

CHART IV.F
De Novo Review

	Yes	No
Positive aspects	De novo review, a hearing that contemplates an entire trial in the same manner in which the matter was originally heard, has the advantage that the plaintiff has a more exhaustive remedy. Both parties have ample opportunity to establish the facts of the case before each court.	Appellate hearings that only consider points of law (not the facts of the case), are shorter, less expensive, and easier to conduct, because witnesses do not have to appear. Judges can utilize their time to review how the points of law cited in the original case were used, and how those uses support or challenge current tribal laws.
Negative aspects	Because many courts are experiencing serious backlogs in trials and hearings, de novo review, by lengthening the hearing process, exacerbates the problem. Witnesses must be recalled and the facts reestablished. Courts currently have difficulties in convincing witnesses to attend hearings, so doubling the hearings would cause even higher attrition.	If the facts were poorly presented in the lower court trial, there is no chance to reconsider the relevant facts.

V. OTHER LEGAL INSTITUTIONS, OFFICES

Ideally, each tribe should provide for several types of legal counsel. In small tribes, a single attorney may serve in more than one capacity. This is workable unless a conflict of interest develops, or a case is brought by one of the branches of government against another branch.

Many tribes have a lawyer or trained person in the position of attorney general, general counsel, or tribal attorney. This person advises the council and the tribe on legal matters, negotiates contracts, and may represent the council and/or tribe in tribal court and before other legal bodies. A related position is that of solicitor. He or she advises the tribal courts, and can represent the court in suits or hearings against the council or chair.

A third position is the office of prosecutor. The prosecutor generally handles the criminal cases of the court. All criminal cases are "crimes against the state," that is, unlike petty theft or contract disputes, the sovereign state itself (in this case the tribe) is considered to be the entity that has been wronged. Therefore, unlike civil cases where the accuser is represented by his or her own attorney, the prosecutor represents the entity of the state in criminal cases.

A familiar institution in United States-style legal systems is the grand jury. The grand jury has the task of determining whether there is sufficient evidence that a crime has occurred, and that a particular party has committed that crime, to justify bringing charges against that party. Ideally, the grand jury provides an independent device for guaranteeing against false and frivolous law enforcement.

The legal staffing (as of 1989) of a selected group of tribes is shown in the following charts.

CHART V.A
Other Legal Institutions, Offices

Tribe	Attorney Gen., Gen. Counsel Tribal Attorney	Prosecutor	Solicitor	Grand Jury
Pascua Yaqui	general counsel	yes, part-time	no	no
Gila River	general counsel	yes—3	no	no
Hopi	general counsel	yes, chief and deputy prosecutors	no	no
Navajo	attorney general, staff, general counsel	yes	yes, plus staff	no
White Mt. Apache	general counsel	yes	no	no
San Carlos Apache	tribal attorney, lay advocates	yes	no	no
Tohono O'Odham	general counsel	yes	no	no

CHART V.B
Attorney General, General Counsel, Tribal Attorney

	Yes	No
Positive aspects	The duties of the attorney general include serving as the chief legal advisor to the tribal government, investigating and prosecuting offenses against tribal law, representing the tribe in court cases, and possibly supervising the prison system. Without this post, there is no one to represent the tribe in matters such as tax evasion or contract violations.	If the tribe is small and as an institution has limited dealings with off-reservation companies or persons, a general counsel or attorney general may not be necessary. Many tribes hire off-reservation firms to represent them in lawsuits. These firms may have greater resources and expertise. If there is only an occasional tribal lawsuit, money may be saved in the long run.
Negative aspects	The tribe may not be able to financially support an attorney general or general counsel. There also may not be a trained attorney available to fill the post. Since the tribal attorney may be prosecuting cases against those who have experienced attorneys, the importance of having a trained, experienced tribal representative cannot be minimized.	An in-house attorney general or general counsel would be able to devote his/her time to tribal matters, while a hired firm will not. A tribe would probably not hire an expensive firm for smaller, though still important, matters.

CHART V.C
Prosecutor

	Yes	No
Positive aspects	If the tribe has an attorney general, the prosecutor would serve under that person. He/she would take charge of a case and perform the function of trial lawyer for the people. In a large tribe, both offices may be required, particularly if the tribe has many dealings with off-reservation companies and individuals.	Each tribe must decide what the job entails. The tribe may need only one person serving as tribal attorney, and although terminology is not important, job description and duties are. If the tribe is small, they may not need a full-time attorney who represents the tribe in criminal prosecutions and civil suits.
Negative aspects	The tribe may not need both an attorney general and a prosecutor. Funding may be better used in other areas, or training may be supplemented for those currently serving. Off-reservation firms could possibly be utilized for less money.	Scheduling of hearings and prosecution of cases may be more efficient with on-reservation tribal representation.

CHART V.D
Solicitor

	Yes	No
Positive aspects	The duties of a solicitor include representing the judicial branch in its suits. Few tribes have this office, but if there are many dealings between the council and the courts, and if the judiciary is to be truly independent, an official serving in the solicitor's position may be necessary.	A tribe may find maintaining a solicitor's position to be expensive and unnecessary. In a suit called by the court against the council, the tribal attorney would probably represent the council, but a temporary advocate could represent the court. If the court has few problems with acts of the council, an ad hoc representative is preferable to a full-time and expensive solicitor.
Negative aspects	The position of solicitor may not be required full-time, or if the court never has major disagreements with the council, may not be required at all.	Arrangements should be made to provide for the possibility of a suit against the council or chair. However, the representative does not have to be full-time.

CHART V.E
Grand Jury

	Yes	No
Positive aspect	The duties of a grand jury include receiving complaints and accusations in criminal cases, hearing the evidence presented by the tribe's representative (generally the prosecutor or attorney general), and deciding if there is enough evidence so that a trial should be held. This added step serves the tribe, because lengthy and expensive trials can be avoided in cases where evidence is weak or absent.	The tribe may not have enough criminal cases to call for a grand jury. The selection and management of the jury may be more time- and resource-consuming than holding the actual trials without the intermediate decision of the grand jury.
Negative aspects	The grand jury would require building space, and the time of the prosecutor or attorney general. Because of the Major Crimes Act, those cases brought before grand juries generally are not tried in tribal court.	Time and money may be saved if the grand jury system exists. Individuals and businesses may feel more comfortable dealing with the tribe if it has a grand jury system.

VI. JUDICIARY COMMITTEE

A judiciary committee, or law-and-order committee, serves as an interface between the courts and the council and chair, and as a judicial oversight committee of the council. The functions of selected tribal judiciary committees are detailed in the following charts.

CHART VI.A
Judiciary Committee

Tribe	Judiciary Committee	Number Serving	Selection	Length of Term	Duties
Pascua Yaqui	no				
Gila River	no				
Hopi	law and order committee	7+	villages choose 1 rep. each	cycles with council	oversight of court, rangers, legislation
Navajo	yes	6	selected by chairman	4 years	oversight, advise removal, selection, legislation
White Mt. Apache	no, replaced by justice commissioner				
San Carlos Apache	yes	5	tribal chair	4 years, staggered	judicial complaints, funding legislation of ordinances
Tohono O'Odham	yes	5	council	standing	oversight, 4 years does not initiate, advises council

CHART VI.B
Judiciary Committee

	Yes	No
Positive aspects	A judiciary committee serves as an interface between the full council and the court. It oversees the operations of the courts. It should educate the council on matters of the court, fulfill budgetary duties, and recommend judicial appointments to the council and/or chair.	If the council and/or tribe is very small, a judiciary committee may be unnecessary and cumbersome.
Negative aspects	The judiciary committee may become too involved in court matters, and may exert political influence on the court.	Without a committee, the chief judge (or designate) must come before the entire council to discuss court administrative matters. This uses valuable council time. Some council members may not understand the functions and duties of the court, and educating them is also time-consuming.

CHART VI.C
Judiciary Committee Selection

	Chosen by Chair	Chosen by Full Council
Positive aspects	Appointment by the chairman is quick. He/She should understand the importance of this committee, as well as the importance of appointing those with judicial or police experience.	If the whole council appoints the judiciary committee, while the executive has veto power, the checks and balances between the executive, legislative, and judiciary are served. The council would retain some measure of control, aiding separation of powers.
Negative aspects	In tribes where the chair already wields a large amount of power, the council should have input into the selection of the judiciary committee. The chairman could conceivably "stack" the court if he/she chooses both the candidates and the judicial committee.	The full council may not understand the powers and duties of the judiciary committee. The committee should aid, not hinder, the court, and those with experience in court matters are more likely to assist in that.

VII. FUNDING THE JUDICIARY

Funding for the judiciary can be procured from several different sources. The most directly accessible funds are those provided under Public Law 638 (obtained by contracting under the Indian Self-Determination and Education Assistance Act of 1975, Public Law 93-638):

> Through grants and contracts, the Act encourages tribes to assume administrative responsibility for federally funded programs administered by employees of the Bureau of Indian Affairs and the United States Indian Health Service.[9]

When contracting, tribes agree to perform specific functions and to accept certain restrictions placed on them by the United States government.

Public Law 638 funds typically are inadequate to operate a sophisticated and competent judiciary. Tribes generally supplement their budgets by allocating other tribal funds and, occasionally, by lobbying and applying for extra funds or joint-venturing with the states.

The funding strategies of a number of tribes are shown in the following charts.

CHART VII.A
Funding the Judiciary

Tribe	638 Funds	Designate % of Total Budget	Extra Funds	% from Tribal Funds
Pascua Yaqui	yes	no	no	none
Gila River	yes	no	yes, through contracting	25%
Hopi	yes	no	no	none
Navajo	yes	no	no	60–80%
White Mt. Apache	yes	no	no	none, except for building maintenance
San Carlos Apache	yes	no	no	none
Tohono O'Odham	yes	no	yes—state/tribe joint ventures, lobbying	75–80%

CHART VII.B
Designate Percentage of Tribal Budget to Courts

	Yes	No
Positive aspects	If a set percentage of all government grants is designated to the courts, either in the code or the constitution, the council cannot use the budgeting process as political leverage against the court. The head of the court does not have to come before the council to lobby for funds.	If the government is not bound by budgetary restrictions, it can distribute monies to best benefit the tribe, which may include increasing—or decreasing—the budget for the judiciary.
Negative aspects	Tribal councils have their discretionary hands tied. They give up some authority in exchange for a more stable judicial budget.	With no directives, the council could conceivably cut funding to the courts, with political repercussions. The council may justify a pre-set minimum as "enough," refusing more funds even when needed.

CHART VII.C
Extra Funds

	Yes	No
Positive aspects	Current 638 funding levels are not sufficient to run a strong judicial system. By lobbying for and receiving extra funding, or joint-venturing with the state, the tribe has greater options—increasing salaries to attract experienced judges and personnel, funding building and library improvements, and increasing training funds and programs.	The lobbyist spends considerable time searching for, defining, and, if successful, establishing these programs. Monies generally are transferred to the tribe only when the receiving program has been clearly outlined and appears feasible. This process also takes time and resources. Grantors serve an oversight role, possibly compromising judicial independence.
Negative aspects	Lobbying for extra funding or creating joint-ventures with the state or counties is time-consuming, and the effort is not always profitable. Funding secured for the judiciary may limit funds available for other pressing uses.	Tribes may be able to save money by decreasing duplication of services with the state, and by amalgamating training programs. Tribes can use joint ventures and monies to target specific areas.

CHART VII.D
Percentage from Tribal Funds

	Yes	No
Positive aspects	638 funds are too small to run a competent, comprehensive judiciary. If the tribe can supplement those funds with general revenue, the chances of developing and maintaining a well-respected, well-run judiciary improve.	Tribes must choose the funding areas they want to emphasize. By increasing funding to the tribal courts, the council has chosen to decrease funding to other areas such as economic development or social services.
Negative aspects	With a greater reliance on funds from the council, there may be an increase in political pressure placed on the judiciary.	Economic development, particularly involving off-reservation companies and individuals, is correlated with the success and respectability of the tribal courts. Without the option of a fair hearing in tribal court, many investors will stay off the reservation no matter what other incentives the tribe uses.

VIII. POLICE

Police are agents of a judicial system. They provide a direct mechanism for law enforcement, and their presence serves as a deterrent to law-breaking. Many tribes traditionally have possessed agents with police power. Under present conditions, with highly mobile tribal members and extensive interaction with nonmembers, police powers are an important component of sovereignty. Given no tribal initiative, the BIA and other governments assume police authority.

Those tribes that have assumed 638 contracting for police services have done so for several reasons: expanding control of and increasing jurisdiction over tribal members; tightening control over training, hiring and firing of police; improving the efficiency of the police department; improving evidence-gathering and case management for and with the tribal court; and increasing tribal sovereignty. When a tribe assumes police functions, it accepts responsibility for many areas, including decisions on funding and training requirements, relations with the state (in terms of cross-deputization and jurisdictional issues), and, in some cases, the responsibilities of the special agency officers.

CHART VIIIA
Police

Tribe	638	Training	Cross-Deputization	Special Agency Officers
Pascua Yaqui	no			yes
Gila River	no			yes
Hopi	no, but has rangers for fishing, hunting violations	police academy	yes—depends on duties of police	yes
Navajo	yes	yes, runs own training academy, certified in 3 states —NM, UT, AZ	not necessary—police state certified	no—replaced by tribal crim. investigator, federally trained
White Mt. Apache	yes	trained after hired, either BIA or state, prefer state	no—place people depending on training	yes
San Carlos Apache	yes	trained after hired, either BIA or state, prefer state	no, not if BIA-trained	yes
Tohono O'Odham	yes	state-certified	not necessary	no—contracted if state-certified

CHART VIII.B
638 Police

	Yes	No
Positive aspects	When the tribe assumes police functions, it gains greater control over the actions of the tribe. Familiarity with custom and usage is increased, since new police officers are either from the tribe or typically spend a greater length of time with the tribal police force.	Small tribes with limited budgets may choose not to contract for police services. 638 funds are generally insufficient to operate a well-run police force. A major reason to "638" police is to increase expertise and training, and if the tribe does not have the monies to hire experienced and trained police or train them while they are on the force, one major goal is lost.
Negative aspects	Police from the tribe may be susceptible to political pressures.	Tribes are seeking greater control over reservation affairs. This is one step in that direction.

CHART VIII.C
Police Training

	State Academy	BIA Academy	Both
Positive aspects	If the officers are certified by the state academy, they are usually able to serve in the same capacities as the state officers, and cross-deputization is then not necessary. Time is saved in investigations, since state officers do not have to be called in many circumstances.	The tribe does not have to pay when they send officers to train at the BIA academy. The officers are trained not only in regular police duties but also receive cultural training, aiding in sensitization to the traditions of the tribes.	Police have the benefit of both the cultural training from the BIA academy and the arguably better police training at the state academy. Cross-deputization is not necessary.
Negative aspects	If officers are trained after they are hired, the tribe must pay the state for the training, but not for training at the BIA academy.	With the BIA academy's emphasis on culture, less emphasis may be placed on regular police functions.	Having the tribe pay for both programs would be expensive and time-consuming. Hiring those with the required experience may be difficult.

CHART VIII.D
Cross-Deputization

	Yes	No
Positive aspects	If the police are not state-certified, they are not able to perform some functions that those with state certification can fulfill. Officers who are faced with these situations (frequently those involving non-Indians committing crimes on reservation land) must call in state-certified or BIA special officers. Valuable time and evidence thus may be lost.	Tribes frequently face resistance from states, their police, and citizens who question the authority of the tribal police to carry out the functions otherwise relegated to the state police.
Negative aspects	Role and jurisdictional confusion between state and local governments may result.	Failing to have either state-certified or cross-trained police constitutes a lost opportunity to perform the functions of a sovereign power and demonstrates less capacity to govern.

NOTES

1 . Kirke Kickingbird, Lynn Kickingbird, Charles J. Chibitty, and Curtis Berkey, *Indian Sovereignty* (Washington, DC: Institute for the Development of Indian Law, 1977), p. 37.

2 . Vine Deloria, Jr., and Clifford M. Lytle, *American Indians, American Justice* (Austin: University of Texas Press, 1983), p. 138.

3 . Ibid., p. 2.

4 . American Indian Lawyer Training Program, *Indian Tribes as Sovereign Governments* (Oakland, CA: AIRI Press, 1988), p. 35.

5 . See ibid., p. 39.

6 . U. S. Department of the Interior, "Developing and Reviewing Tribal Constitutions and Amendments," 1987, pp. 3–11.

7 . Samuel J. Brakel, *American Indian Tribal Courts: The Costs of Separate Justice* (Chicago: American Bar Foundation, 1978), p. 9.

8 . American Indian Lawyer Training Program, *Indian Tribes as Sovereign Governments,* p. 36.

9 . Ibid., p.15.

4

BUILDING A SYSTEM FOR LAND-USE PLANNING: A CASE STUDY FOR THE PUYALLUP TRIBE

Paul Nissenbaum and Paul Shadle

The legal status of Indian reservation lands creates both special problems and unique opportunities. On many reservations, interspersed ownership by Indians, non-Indians, tribes, states, and the federal government can produce jurisdictional disputes and complicate development efforts. At the same time, opportunities for development can be enhanced by sound tribal land-use policies.

Faced with jurisdictional complexity and a continuing stream of proposals for the use of reservation lands, many tribes find themselves needing to devise and implement comprehensive land-use policies and procedures. This chapter by Paul Nissenbaum and Paul Shadle presents a model system for processing land-use proposals. Designed at the request of the Puyallup tribe in Washington, the model seeks to allow tribes to weed out unacceptable proposals while expediting approval of options that promote tribal goals. The resulting system is one example of how a tribe can arm itself with capable institutions of self-government.

INTRODUCTION

The Puyallup tribe of Indians is a 1,500-member tribe with an 18,000-acre reservation located in the Tacoma, Washington, area. Several features of the Puyallup setting and history, including scattered control of land, hostility from neighboring populations, and traditional dependence on fishing, present them with a unique set of land-use management challenges. The tribe's current land-use management process is characterized by two central deficiencies: a lack of long-range planning, and the absence of a coherent land-use evaluation system. Both deficiencies must be addressed if the tribe is to reestablish control of its historic land holdings and realize the potential created by a 1988 land-claims settlement.

This study focuses on the second problem, the absence of a coherent land-use evaluation system. Land-use projects are often approved by tribal government on an ad hoc basis, with decisions dependent primarily on individuals and politics. The Puyallup community plays only a minimal role in this process. This report seeks to provide the Puyallup with a comprehensive system for evaluating land-use proposals, a system based on objective criteria and an inclusive, regularized process. Such a governing system, while flexible, would be objective and predictable. It would enhance the credibility of land-use decision-making both inside and outside the tribe. The specific reforms proposed here attempt to strike a balance between the complexity necessary to address the critical land-use management problems facing the tribe and the simplicity required to make such a system feasible to implement.

The report is divided into five sections. Section I begins by briefly reviewing the history of the Puyallup and their current economic conditions. It then describes the context within which the tribe operates—its assets and liabilities, including its economic environment, political setting, cash and land, legal powers, and tribal organization. Section II lays out the unique planning conditions facing the tribe, the deficiencies in the current land-management system, and potential reforms. Section III gives an overview of our proposal for a land-use evaluation system, and describes our research and design methods. The proposal itself is detailed in Sections IV and V. Section IV outlines the analytic model—the four baseline criteria and six variable criteria for development. Section V describes how these criteria should be implemented through a comprehensive permitting process.

I. BACKGROUND

HISTORY AND CURRENT CONDITIONS[1]

The Puyallup Reservation covers 18,000 acres at the mouth of the Puyallup River on Commencement Bay in Puget Sound. The portion of the reservation which the tribe actually owns outright is approximately 900 acres, smaller than that of any other tribe in Washington. They have had their territory and customs systematically eroded by non-Indian settlers during the last two hundred years.

The first agreement between the Puyallup and settlers was the Treaty of Medicine Creek in 1854, which created a 1,280-acre reservation on Puget Sound; but the tribe actually received only a small inland tract of land. In 1855–56, the Puyallup and a number of other tribes waged war against the settlers in order to obtain the land they had been promised. An 1857 settlement granted the tribe 23,000 acres of land on Commencement Bay (where the city of Tacoma is located today), but the official survey was lost and copies were destroyed in a fire. During the next fifty years, through the efforts of the federal government, railways, land companies, and lumber interests, marine access was severed, reservation acreage was reduced, and tribal land was sold to the public. By 1910, little more than thirty-five acres of the reservation remained. The United States Bureau of Indian Affairs (BIA) helped further erode the tribe's cultural identity through policies of assimilation.

After a number of decades of inactivity and decline in tribal population, the Puyallup began to demand that their rights be observed. In 1965, six Puyallup were arrested for asserting their right to fish—without licenses—for salmon. In 1970, a large group of Puyallup and their supporters built a fishing encampment on the banks of the Puyallup River, which the state of Washington immediately dismantled by force. In response to this and other tribal-state battles over fishing rights, the federal government sued the state on behalf of the Indians. A 1974 court decision granted twenty Washington tribes, including the Puyallup, the right to catch up to 50 percent of the salmon and steelhead in their traditional fishing grounds in and around Puget Sound.

Since the mid-1970s, the Puyallup also have sought, through a series of direct confrontations, lawsuits, and negotiations, to restore their legal control and use of reservation land—control which had been guaranteed by treaties signed in the nineteenth century. In 1976, a group of tribal members successfully occupied a former Indian hospital on the reservation, and evicted the state (which had been somewhat weakened by its 1974 lawsuit defeat). The hospital building and its grounds now comprise the Puyallup tribal headquarters in northeastern Tacoma. In 1981, the tribe won a court claim to twelve acres of riverbed owned by the Port of Tacoma. The filing of a 1984 suit asserting tribal ownership of 160 acres in the Tacoma tidal flats convinced a group of non-Indian interests, including local, state, and federal governments as well as affected businesses (such as the Union Pacific Railroad and Burlington Northern Inc.), to form a bargaining committee and begin negotiating with the Puyallup. After four years of meetings and a series of confrontations, an agreement was finally reached in 1988. This "Land-Claims Settlement" granted the tribe land, cash, and social support programs worth $162 million. The terms of the settlement were final; the Puyallup agreed to file no more claims for land or damages.

The number of registered Puyallup tribal members rose from a low of 300 in the early 1970s to 1,500 by 1990. Most of the Puyallup live near the reservation in Pierce and Thurston counties, an area that includes the city of Tacoma. Their traditional livelihood has been fishing, but they are now substantially integrated into an urban economy and thus have a variety of new occupations. They are part of a larger Native American community in the Puget Sound area that suffers from serious social and economic problems. Fewer than 2 percent of the 5,000 Native Americans in the Puyallup service area earn more than $7,000 each year. In Pierce County, 66 percent of Native Americans are unemployed. Ninety-five percent of local Native Americans have, or are affected by someone who has, a substance-abuse problem. An Indian living in Tacoma is forty-eight times more likely than other city residents to die in a fire. Like other economically disadvantaged urban populations, the Puyallup are in desperate need of social services, educational improvement, housing, and a means of promoting employment and economic development.

PUYALLUP ASSETS AND LIABILITIES: THE CONTEXT

In order to assess the Puyallups' current land-use management process and propose workable solutions, it is important to understand the context—

both internal and external—in which land-use management takes place. The external context can be broken into two parts: the economic environment and the political setting. While the tribe has so far been isolated from the economic fortunes of the region, today's Washington economy has the potential to be an asset for the tribe. Any effective land-use management system must also work with a number of external political forces that have historically been at odds with the tribe.

More importantly for this analysis, the Puyallup must recognize their internal strengths and weaknesses in three relevant categories, which are cash and land assets, legal powers, and organizational structure. Land-use planning, like other tribal functions, must include careful management of an improved cash and land resource base. An understanding of the tribe's legal powers on reservation land—particularly as they relate to land use—is also crucial. Finally, any land-use management system will have to operate within a complex tribal organization; it is useful to recognize how this organization is set up.

THE ECONOMIC ENVIRONMENT

The Seattle-Tacoma regional economy is anchored by Boeing Aerospace and is supplemented by the lumber industry, various services, and a booming foreign trade sector. In the second half of the 1980s, employment grew at an annual rate of 5.3 percent, more than double the average gain in the nation's top 100 metropolitan markets. The strong economy brought with it a significant population increase. Between 1986 and 1989, the population of Seattle grew at an annual rate of 2.2 percent, twice as fast as the top 100 other metro-areas. Total income growth in the region was also impressive, increasing by more than 7 percent during the same period.[2] While the city of Tacoma has grown at a somewhat slower pace than Seattle, it remains a strong market.[3]

Despite the national economic recession, the region is poised for continued growth through the 1990s. In Tacoma, a thriving port facility, with attendant transportation and maritime operations, promises to continue spurring growth. A January 1991 study claimed that the "Port is now on the verge of a significant increase in maritime traffic," including the potential for a doubling in container traffic.[4] Moreover, Boeing is planning an expansion project in Tacoma, and as Seattle becomes more crowded and costly, further growth spill-over into the Tacoma area is likely. Overall, the city should be able to withstand recession, with 1.3 percent annual employment growth and 6.4 percent income growth expected over the 1990s.[5] The tribe's assets and determination put it in a position to take advantage of the Tacoma economy and capture some of this growth.

THE POLITICAL SETTING

In order to be a successful sovereign entity, the tribe must develop and reinforce working relationships with a variety of political entities. Many of these entities were signatories to the 1988 settlement. They include the United States of America, the state of Washington, local governments within Pierce County, and several private entities. These parties know that this agreement "cannot reverse or erase all of the injustices and problems that have occurred," but they hope that it can "encourage a cooperative relationship which will reduce the danger of continued injustice and continuing conflicts in the future."[6] Officials in the tribal government have expressed an interest in building on the foundation laid by the agreement, and further enhancing relationships with what some term the "settlement partners." At the very least, the tribe knows it will have to maintain working relationships with these and other political forces.

Using powers granted by the 1988 settlement, the tribe's Land Use Division currently consults with local governments (Pierce County, the cities of Tacoma and Fife, and others) regarding any land-use decision contemplated by those governments within reservation boundaries. In the interest of building further cooperation, and thus tribal credibility, the Puyallup are ready to consult with their neighbors on their own development proposals.

Tribal development frequently has an impact on neighboring governments and private parties; it often involves a change in current zoning, and with new land acquisition it takes land off local tax rolls. While being sensitive to these impacts, the tribe can also build political alliances with outside interests—real estate groups, housing advocates, etc.—who may be supportive of particular projects and help move them forward. Puyallup land-use decisions should not be dictated by external political forces, but the tribe would be wise to make an effort to inform affected communities and residents, and in some cases build political alliances, when considering substantial land-use projects.

CASH AND LAND ASSETS

Aside from human capital, which is arguably any society's most important asset, the Puyallup tribe's primary resources are its cash and land. A critical tribal goal is the proper management and expansion of these two assets, and any land-use system will have to work toward this goal. It is important, therefore, to review the inventory of current cash and land holdings.

Prior to the 1988 settlement, the Puyallup tribe operated on little income and owned relatively few acres of land. Revenue came from tax and license fees on tribal businesses, fisheries and other activities, and from Bureau of Indian Affairs grants. The tribe's primary land holding was its headquarters campus, which contains the tribal government, school, health clinic, and burial grounds, and is the site of a planned bingo hall. There were also scattered private tribal businesses and residences throughout the area.

The 1988 settlement substantially boosted the tribe's cash and land assets. The agreement conveyed $162 million worth of resources, including:

-   A $22-million trust fund
-   $24 million in direct payments to tribal members
-   $10 million for fisheries
-   $10 million for economic development and land purchases
-   $2 million to assist tribal members in developing businesses
-   $2.2 million for social services
-   207 acres of land, in four parcels, adjacent to the port of Tacoma
-   57 acres of land owned by the Union Pacific Railway
-   27 acres of land in the town of Fife.

The tribe's revenue stream is now significantly enhanced by income from the settlement endowments. The Puyallup also hope to leverage financial resources and property conveyed in the settlement to generate additional revenue by investing in economic development activities. In early 1991, for example, the tribe began construction of a bingo hall and marina, both of which have the potential to generate positive cash flow. The Puyallup land holdings also increased, but at nine hundred acres still represent only a small fraction of the 18,000-acre reservation. Nevertheless, in light of the economic prospects for the region, the new land assets, particularly the port properties, hold the greatest economic development potential. The challenge for the tribe will be to maximize the potential of these new assets while ensuring that other critical social and economic needs are met.

LEGAL POWERS

Legal powers over those portions of reservation land which are held by the tribe are an important asset. United States law gives Indian tribes the choice of placing property they hold in "trust" or designating it "fee" land. Although trust land is legally owned by the federal government, trust status carries with it several advantages for tribes. First, trust land and any tribal income generated on it are exempt from federal, state, and local taxation. This tax-exempt status may be a determining factor in the degree of profitability of a development project. Second, Indian tribes retain substantial civil regulatory power, exempt from many state laws, on trust land. Tribes have the authority, for example, to allow certain gambling activities such as high-stakes bingo.[7] A third advantage is a tribe's power to rezone trust-land parcels to meet its own development needs. For example, a tribe can add value to land simply by purchasing a residential parcel at a low price and then rezoning it for commercial use. As discussed above, however, a tribe that is interested in maintaining peaceful relations with its neighboring residents and governmental authorities must act reasonably in this regard.

There are several disadvantages to trust status. First, a tribe must obtain approval from the Bureau of Indian Affairs to put land into trust. By the same token, a tribe cannot sell or exchange trust land without federal permission. In addition, it is difficult to obtain a mortgage against trust land. Because of the legal powers and independence granted by this special status, lending institutions are understandably wary of making mortgage loans secured by trust-land property unless a strict "willingness to be sued" clause is included in the contract. However, alternative mechanisms such as long-term leases may allow a tribe to raise the necessary capital for development.

Fee land, in contrast, is legally owned by a tribe or individual tribal members. The owner, therefore, must pay state and federal taxes on it, although courts have ruled in a number of cases that even fee land is exempt from taxes.[8] On balance, however, the advantages of trust status outweigh those of fee status, and most Indian tribes seek to place land in trust whenever possible.

TRIBAL ORGANIZATION

Political power is vested in the Puyallup tribe through a constitution that was written by the Bureau of Indian Affairs in 1938. The constitution creates a parliamentary system and designates the Puyallup tribal council as the central governing body of the tribe. The members of the tribal council are elected to three-year terms but are subject to special "recall" elections. The council's responsibilities include writing laws, controlling taxation and "per-capita" payments, setting tribal enrollment standards, appointing members to various tribal boards, establishing tribal policy priorities, and selecting a tribal chairperson.

Operating at the behest of the tribal council is an extensive tribal government. In fact, the number of tribal staff has grown from just seven in 1974 to three hundred currently.[9] The government includes more than thirty divisions, boards, and other administrative agencies that collectively are responsible for running the day-to-day activities of the tribe. They range from accounting and legal to the Chief Leschi School and the tribal court.

The extent to which each tribal agency is involved in land-use matters varies, but all of these divisions have some land-related requirements or responsibilities. At the very least, each needs its own office space. Some tribal entities, like the Bingo Committee, have plans that involve land-consumptive activities. Others, such as Environmental Protection, actually have regulatory responsibilities over land-related matters. One tribal entity that directly affects land-use management on the reservation is Puyallup International Incorporated (P.I.I.). P.I.I. was established by the tribal council as a subsidiary of the tribe and is responsible for planning economic development activities on the 1988 settlement properties.[10] Finally, at the center of the land management process, not surprisingly, is the Land Use Division itself. The division's current responsibilities include review of tribal and neighboring jurisdictions' specific land-use plans. Clearly, the Land Use Division should be at the core of any evaluation system.

II. PUYALLUP LAND-USE MANAGEMENT

Several features of the Puyallups' setting and history—including scattered control of land, hostility from neighboring populations, and traditional dependence on fishing—present them with a unique set of land-use management challenges. The tribe's Legal Division has suggested that the tribe simply adopt the "land use standards of overlapping jurisdictions" as regulations for all land within the reservation.[11] Because of the unique nature of their legal jurisdiction over the reservation, however, the Puyallup cannot implement standard zoning. Most of the ostensibly sovereign reservation area is not actually governed by the tribe. Instead of owning a large plot of land defined by contiguous boundaries, as would a municipality, the Puyallup control widely scattered sites in and around Tacoma. As long as large portions of the reservation are owned by non-Indians and governed in practice by a variety of municipalities and two counties, the tribe will not be able to assign standard residential, commercial, and industrial zone designations on the reservation in any legally meaningful way.

The Puyallup are also one of a small number of Indian tribes that possess real estate in the middle of a large, densely populated city. As mentioned above in the discussion of the local political setting, the tribe therefore must consult with other governments and citizens who do not live under its laws when pursuing development projects. When the Land Use Division makes a decision, it must consider the impact not only on the Puyallup, but also on non-Indian neighbors who have tremendous investments in communities that are well-established on reservation land. These people are only beginning to confront the newly and justly reinstated power of the Puyallup and are resistant to tribal efforts to assert authority in land-use matters. In the town of Fife, which is located entirely within the Puyallup Reservation, residents have been extremely hostile toward Indians and to the notion that they live on Indian land.

In addition to possessing scattered land and being located in a city, the Puyallup Indians have been dependent historically on fishing. During the last century, they have witnessed the destruction of their salmon spawning grounds by logging, industrial, and shipping activity. As a result, they place a particularly high value on protecting the natural environment and pursuing active measures to improve its health.[12] Tribal staff members therefore must scrutinize carefully all land-consuming development proposals to assess their impact on fisheries and the general health of the Puyallup River, Commencement Bay, and Puget Sound.

This combination of limited control over land, an urban setting, and special priorities creates a unique set of conditions for the tribe. These conditions will help shape the forms of land-use regulation that are feasible and the types of projects that will be approved.

CURRENT LAND-USE MANAGEMENT DEFICIENCIES

The land-use functions of the tribal government are in their infancy. As the Land Use Division stated in 1990, "the absence of a land base prior to the Settlement precluded the development of a government infrastructure typical of a landed people."[13] Consequently, the current Puyallup land-use management process is characterized by several shortcomings, including a lack of long-range planning and an ad-hoc means of project evaluation. The process is also noteworthy for its lack of assigned planning authority and the absence of community input.

The Puyallup tribe only recently began to reestablish its eroded land base, and therefore has not yet developed a coherent, long-range planning strategy for the reservation. It has not systematically assessed its land-related policy needs and priorities. For example, no specific housing or open-space needs analyses have been conducted, and thus no long-term plans weighing the relative merits of each have been developed. Consequently, it has been impossible to develop any type of comprehensive land-use plan for the reservation, even though such a plan is required by the 1988 settlement and necessary for long-term tribal success.

The tribe also lacks a mechanism for evaluating current land-use projects. Decisions often are made on an ad hoc basis, and projects often resist regulation, taking on lives of their own. Detailed evaluation takes place in some cases, but many projects pass through only a fractious political process. The resulting inconsistent and unpredictable management of land prevents the tribe from considering all of the issues related to developments.

There are numerous examples of the ad hoc nature of the current process. The Puyallup are currently building a bingo hall, adjacent to their headquarters, which is likely to be successful and may provide substantial financial rewards for tribal members. However, the committee that planned this facility considered only one location. A useful study might have analyzed the potential markets for bingo halls on various tribally owned land parcels and compared the value of alternative uses of the site chosen. In another case, cemetery workers, understandably worried that land adjacent to a sacred site was going to be used for a new building, bulldozed the area for "expansion" without consulting the Land Use Division. A large piece of rural land also was purchased recently, before staff members learned that it had no access to utility connections. Each of these examples can be attributed to the lack of a land-use evaluation system.

The problems associated with a deficient land-use management process are compounded by inadequately defined planning roles within the tribal government. Staff members generally assume responsibilities and discuss decisions informally among themselves. Observations and interviews with staff members suggest that planning and evaluation authority is not clearly assigned. For example, the Environmental Division might take the lead on evaluating a recreational use of land near the Puyallup River, and the Land Use Division might initiate consideration of a commercial project. Neither division has been officially assigned the authority to regulate these types of uses, but they must take action to fill voids in an undeveloped process.

Finally, tribal members are justifiably concerned that the present land-use management process provides no adequate mechanism for community input. Members currently have three outlets for participation: the tribal council, which holds regular public meetings; tribal committees, which are representative groups appointed by the council to manage specific issues or projects; and tribal activists, who operate informally to organize support for, or opposition to, tribal policies, and often promote recall petitions against tribal council members. These outlets have not given tribal members an adequate role in land-use decision-making. At a February 1991 community meeting, members expressed concern about the cost of a proposed marina to be built on tribal land in the port of Tacoma and were angry because the project had been initiated, designed, and approved without a community hearing. Construction of the new bingo hall also began with little systematic consideration of community feelings about its effect on other uses of the headquarters campus, such as the annual sale of fireworks. These cases seem to be typical of the current land-use assessment process.

As a result of these problems, land-based economic development is curtailed and valuable tribal government resources are wasted. The tribal council is forced to become involved in the details of every land-use decision, whether it involves a project as trivial as a private home alteration or as important as the construction of a new business. These responsibilities divert the council from pursuing its primary task—establishing broad policy objectives in all areas critical to the well-being of the Puyallup tribe.

We should point out that these problems are recognized by tribal leaders. This study has its origins in their desire for tribal betterment.

POTENTIAL REFORMS

The tribe must address several challenges if it is to properly manage its land resources in the future. First, the tribe needs to adopt a long-range planning strategy. Second, the tribe should implement a coherent system for evaluating pending land-use projects. Underlying both of these are, among other issues, the desire to provide the community with a meaningful role in the process, and the need to allow the tribal council to focus on a broad policy agenda rather than on day-to-day problems.

LONG-RANGE PLANNING

While the analysis below does not attempt to remedy the first problem, it is important to note several critical steps in the area of comprehensive long-range planning. The Puyallup should begin by conducting a thorough assessment of land-related needs as well as land inventory. If the tribe is unable to predict its long-term needs, it should at least develop a system for identifying them in the future. The Land Use Division has initiated the needs-assessment process by compiling a list of land-consumptive needs that are being actively pursued now.

Once the tribe has assessed its land-use needs, it can then begin to weigh competing land interests and prioritize those needs. The tribal council, relieved of specific land-use evaluation duties, will be able to focus more on the task of prioritizing land-use needs. Ultimately, the Puyallup will be able to use those land-use priorities to establish a comprehensive tribal land-use policy. These efforts are necessary to enable the tribe both to meet internal and external expectations set in the 1988 settlement and to reap the potential benefits of its newly acquired assets. Strong and consistent political leadership will be necessary if these goals are to be pursued successfully.

III. A LAND-USE EVALUATION SYSTEM: DEVELOPING THE PROPOSAL

The second fundamental land-use inadequacy cited in Section II—the lack of a system for evaluating pending proposals—is the focus of this analysis. In order to avoid making land-use decisions on an ad hoc basis, the tribe needs a comprehensive land-use evaluation system. Such a system would enhance objectivity and predictability in decision-making. A land-use evaluation system also would survive over the long-term without relying solely on the dedication of the particular people involved at any given time. Finally, such a system would enhance the tribe's credibility in the larger community and, more importantly, promote self-esteem within the tribe itself. Institutionalized systems like this support tribal sovereignty and are crucial to the long-term success of self-determination.[14]

The proposed land-use evaluation system, which is detailed in Sections IV and V, consists of two parts: an analytic model and an implementation process. The analytic model establishes a set of criteria by which to judge land-use projects. In the absence of a traditional zoning system, which we believe is impractical for the Puyallup, these development criteria will provide a consistent basis for assessing proposals. The second component of the system, the implementation process, lays out a decision-making apparatus for the tribe. It is essentially a comprehensive permitting process which seeks to coordinate the various decision-making institutions, apply the model criteria, and provide a role for the community. Although this system is not a substitute for long-range planning, it is a useful tool that can be implemented quickly. The establishment of land-use priorities and a planning policy would make it even more effective.

A well-implemented, coherent evaluation system should enable the tribe to use staff and other government resources more efficiently. Staff members will be able to avoid wasting time inventing new ways to evaluate each land-use proposal. More importantly, busy tribal council members will only need to become involved in the most critical projects. Consequently, they will save valuable hours and thus be able to spend their time addressing broader policy issues.

DESIGN AND RESEARCH

Before providing the details of the land-use evaluation system, it is important to explain how we developed the proposal. Our initial hope was that we could find a documented example of such a system for a comparable Indian tribe. Unfortunately, we were unable to uncover such a model. We were forced, therefore, to turn to other, less directly applicable land-use systems. We found useful concepts in several alternative approaches to traditional zoning which are used by a number of municipalities. Although none of these approaches is directly transferable to the Puyallup situation, we were able to draw elements from each into our proposal. These systems, known variously as "flexible zoning," "floating zoning," and "contract zoning," all differ from traditional "Euclidean" zoning in that they do not map out an entire jurisdiction into different "use" districts (i. e., residential, industrial, commercial, etc.). Instead, they allow the municipality to set standards and goals with which to guide market-driven development initiatives.

The most relevant of these alternative zoning schemes for our purposes is "flexible zoning." This type of regulation evaluates development proposals based on the compatibility of their individual characteristics with municipal policy priorities, rather than on whether they conform to predesignated uses for their particular locations. The city of Fort Collins, Colorado, for example, has adopted a "Land Development Guidance System," which clearly defines a set of flexible criteria for land use. *Absolute* criteria, which apply to all developments, cover "neighborhood compatibility, conformance with adopted plans, minimum requirements for engineering and public services, and compliance with standards for protecting resources, the environment, and site design."[15] *Variable* criteria assign "performance points" to proposals based on the type of use and community preferences. They are designed to guide projects toward the achievement of long-term development goals for the city.[16] Similar systems have been used successfully in Breckenridge, Colorado, and Hampden County, Kentucky. Until it has articulated policy priorities, the Puyallup tribe cannot adopt a plan that assigns specific weights to different criteria. However, the unique characteristics of the tribe's planning setting described in Section II suggest that it would benefit from using components of such a flexible regulatory tool.

Another means of regulation which provides inspiration is the notion of "floating zoning," which has been attempted in places such as Lower Gwynedd Township and New Hope, Pennsylvania.[17] Because all potential uses of land cannot be controlled or predicted, this method allows the marketplace to guide use determination within set standards for safety and compatibility. When certain land uses begin to dominate a particular area, the city then designates the area for those prevailing uses. Comprehensive long-term goals are not abandoned, but are achieved through market-driven investment. Over time, a set of zones is thereby established. Endowed with scattered land holdings and undetermined needs, the Puyallup will have difficulty making rational "Euclidean" zoning assignments. The concept of floating zoning justifies allowing current investment preferences rather than arbitrary decisions to determine use designations.

Another useful model is the concept of "contract zoning" which has been utilized by a number of cities and municipalities to regulate large developments. This method requires large-scale developers to meet with municipal officials to establish design specifications, payments or concessions, and other project components that must be provided before approval is granted.[18] For example, the city of Boston uses a system whereby commercial development proposals must be submitted to the city for design approval and investors must pay linkage fees to cover new public costs imposed by the project. Specific plans are created and conditions are agreed to through elaborate negotiations that take place before zoning and construction permits are granted. A similar process would allow the Puyallup tribe both to have input in the design specifications of projects and to reap a portion of the return on investments.

The most important underpinnings of our proposed land-use evaluation system are found not in any existing zoning scheme, but rather in the unique characteristics of the Puyallup tribe described in Section II. The system is based on the expressed interests and concerns of tribal members and staff as well as observations of the reservation and its setting. It reflects an attempt to incorporate needs into a coherent and workable system. We have deliberately omitted some issues which the tribe itself has yet to resolve and which we, as outsiders, are not in a position to address. In a number of instances, we have proposed various alternatives for the tribe to consider. The system's guidelines and procedures, although clearly established in our recommendations, are flexible and enable the tribe to set its own priorities.

Most of the data for the proposal were drawn from interviews and meetings with tribal members and governmental staff personnel. We also gathered information from various local publications, staff materials, and memos. The tribal constitution and a number of ordinances clearly outline the roles of various tribal divisions, and the 1988 settlement documents articulate the tribe's new rights and responsibilities. Finally, the Land Use Division provided a significant amount of research material and direction.

IV. ANALYTIC MODEL: CRITERIA FOR EVALUATING LAND-USE PROJECTS

Any systematic approach to land-use development appraisal must be based on a clear set of criteria. These criteria should serve essentially as a checklist by which all development proposals are judged. They should be based on both traditional measures of project worthiness and viability, and objectives unique to the Puyallup tribe.

We propose two types of criteria: baseline criteria and variable criteria. The baseline criteria are fundamental standards for development which can be clearly defined and measured, and they should be applied uniformly to all development projects regardless of land-use type or current tribal policy priorities. The proposed baseline standards fall into the following four categories:

- Building and safety
- Environmental
- Fisheries habitat
- Other land use.

The variable criteria are a set of more subjective standards that cannot easily be measured. They should be applied in varying degrees depending on the type of land-use project and tribal policy priorities at the time of project consideration. The proposed variable standards fall into the following six categories:

- Cultural enrichment
- Economic development

- Financial benefit
- Human service provision
- Natural resource preservation
- Sovereign identity promotion.

BASELINE CRITERIA

All land-use projects should be evaluated on the basis of a set of baseline criteria. Each of these standards should be defined by one or more specific threshold tests—thresholds which are measured quantitatively whenever possible (e.g., maximum emissions of a given pollutant, minimum level of building material quality, exact impact on size of spawning areas, etc.). These standards should be applied uniformly to any tribally regulated development project regardless of its location, size, or type of use (although certain standards obviously will be more relevant to particular locations, sizes, or uses).

Specific threshold levels may be revised to strengthen or weaken the regulations as new building and environmental technology becomes available, or as tribal priorities shift over time. If the tribe wishes to take advantage of its regulatory powers and encourage or discourage certain types of economic development, for example, it may decide to loosen or tighten requirements or allow trade-offs in any of these baseline categories. In order to maintain a credible and predictable system, however, the standards must be applied in a nondiscriminatory fashion and thus should not be revised for any *particular* project.

The establishment of baseline criteria is not a new concept. Municipalities, for example, whether they regulate land use through traditional zoning or not, include in their regulations minimum standards that apply to any development project. Moreover, the Puyallup tribe is already employing some minimum standards. For example, development proposals must include environmental impact statements that are subject to review by the tribe's Environmental Division. However, existing criteria need to be further refined—and new ones must be added—to ensure the development of a comprehensive land-use evaluation system. Indeed, the tribe's Legal Division, in a January 1991 memo, has confirmed a consensus among staff members that the current standards should be enhanced and solidified. In the short term, the tribe should consider filling gaps with standards borrowed from other jurisdictions (e. g., Pierce County, state of Washington, other tribes, etc.). In the future, however, the tribe probably will want to revise such standards to meet its particular policy goals.

The baseline criteria categories—building and safety, environmental, fisheries habitat, and other land use—represent commonly accepted areas of regulation, with an emphasis on specific Puyallup concerns. While a detailed checklist of requirements for each category should be established by each of the relevant tribal government divisions, this analysis can articulate the broad criteria definitions and some of the issues they should cover.

BUILDING AND SAFETY

Building and safety codes are employed by virtually all jurisdictions that have the authority to exercise police powers in order to protect the "public health, safety, and welfare."[19] The Puyallup tribe should be no exception. These codes cover issues such as quality of construction materials, proper lighting and design specifications, as well as engineering, electrical, and plumbing standards. In the short term, as the Land Use and Legal divisions have suggested, the tribe should adopt the "Uniform Building Code" or another relevant standardized building and safety scheme.[20] If the tribe chooses to strengthen or relax particular standards in the future for cultural or economic reasons, it should codify these changes in the regulations and apply them uniformly to all development.

ENVIRONMENTAL

Environmental impact criteria have been widely adopted at all levels of government as a means of reviewing development projects. For the Puyallup, environmental standards are particularly critical, given their historical connection with water and land. In fact, the tribe already has water quality standards in place. It needs to adopt additional environmental standards in order to control air quality, hazardous waste, and sources of erosion and run-off. In some cases, the tribe may simply want to employ United States Environmental Protection Agency or Washington State standards. In others, it may want to adopt more stringent standards to reflect its environmentally-dependent past and its future priorities.

Fisheries Habitat

One environmental area to which the Puyallup have always paid particular attention is the fisheries habitat. The tribe's roots are in fishing, and much of its recent history has been dominated by a struggle to reassert traditional fishing rights. In fact, the Puyallup government includes a separate Fisheries Division, responsible for protecting and expanding fish habitat. This division is several times larger than the Environmental Division. The Fisheries Division employs standards that are consistent with those agreed to by all signatories of the 1988 settlement. Technical Document #4 of the settlement requires that projects result in no net degradation of the fisheries habitat, and it sets standards for mitigation of negative impacts on fisheries.[21] Mitigation standards should be applied as a variable criterion ("natural resource preservation"). The baseline "no net degradation" criterion, however, should be applied across the board, although it will likely be relevant only for shoreline and other water-impact projects.

Other Land Use

A final group of miscellaneous standards should apply to all assessed projects. For example, there should be standards in place that ensure the existence or provision of necessary infrastructure such as sewers, utility lines, and roads of sufficient capacity to permit the land-use development in question. Other regulations might guide heights, setbacks, and floor-to-area ratios (FAR). In addition, the Land Use Division may require that all new residential units include off-street parking or that retail signage fall within specified size and design parameters. While these codes may evolve over time to suit tribal needs, they are not intended to be a random list of flexible standards. As baseline criteria, they should only include guidelines which can be codified and applied to all development.

Variable Criteria

While all development proposals should meet baseline codes, many should also be evaluated on the basis of a set of variable criteria. Projects that receive this additional scrutiny should be those which have a high impact on the tribal and local communities, such as commercial buildings, housing developments, cultural facilities, or parks. The precise cutoff for determining which proposals fall into this category, however, must be established by the tribe itself. This issue will be discussed further in the implementation section (V).

The variable criteria—cultural enhancement, economic development, financial benefit, human service provision, natural resource preservation, and the promotion of sovereignty—are a more subjective set of standards which should be weighed differently depending on the type of proposed land use and on tribal policy priorities at the time of project consideration.

Most proposals will fall into four broad categories of land use:[22]

- Cultural projects
- Human service projects
- Income-generating projects
- Land preservation.

The category into which a project fits will partially determine the degree of emphasis placed on each variable criterion. An income-generating proposal, such as a commercial project, will be evaluated more intensively against the financial benefit and economic development criteria than a cultural project, such as a museum, which will be required to meet high cultural enrichment standards. The remaining criteria would be applied to both projects, but will be given less emphasis than the primary standards.

The degree to which the variable standards are applied will also be partially dependent on the tribal policy priorities at the time of project consideration. If, for example, the Puyallup decide that job creation is the most important tribal objective over the next several years, then all proposals should be examined more closely against economic development standards. If the tribe is seeking to actively promote its sovereign identity, then the relationship of projects to the surrounding community should be carefully assessed.

The tests that are used to measure performance under the variable criteria categories are necessarily more qualitative than those used to determine baseline acceptability. Quantitative thresholds simply do not apply for some of the criteria, such as cultural enrichment and sovereign-identity promotion. These require a more subjective weighing of pros and cons to determine whether a project is acceptable or not. At some point in the future, the tribe may want to place quantitative weights on each of the tests (i. e., create a point system) to make project analysis easier and less subject to the judgment of particular staff—a solution used in the flexible zoning schemes of Fort Collins and Breckenridge, Colorado. Whether or not there is a point system in place, however, judgments will have to be made about the weights assigned to different standards for different project types. These decisions should be made based on tribal priorities when the evaluation system is established.

Like the baseline criteria, the six proposed variable criteria categories represent a combination of typical development criteria and specific Puyallup concerns, with an emphasis on the latter. They reflect what seem to be the current policy priorities for the tribe. Details within each category will have to be determined by the tribe. This analysis will articulate the broad criteria definitions and some of the issues that specific standards must cover.

CULTURAL ENHANCEMENT

Since the arrival of settlers in the Northwest, the Puyallup tribe has been subjected to the dilution and disintegration of unique cultural characteristics and identity. These characteristics include both a communal, supportive style of living and distinct forms of worship and artistic expression. Tribal members and leaders have expressed a desire to redevelop and preserve cultural identity as a means of strengthening the Puyallup community and asserting its presence in Tacoma.[23]

The cultural enhancement criterion should be used to measure the extent to which proposed land-use projects promise to contribute to this effort. For some proposals, most obviously cultural projects, this criterion will be the primary measure of acceptability, while for others it will have only peripheral importance. A proposal for a tribal museum, for example, would be judged primarily on the comprehensiveness and expertise with which it presents Puyallup culture. A fast food restaurant would have other priorities, but might be credited for using Puyallup cultural symbols in the design of its building and dining area. The cultural criterion may also be the most suitable means by which to review architectural and design aspects of projects.

ECONOMIC DEVELOPMENT

Another critical objective of the Puyallup is to reap economic benefits from assets gained through the 1988 agreement and from the growing economy of northwest Washington. The tribe has substantial economic development needs which have yet to be clearly identified and translated into policy goals. Long-term goals may include steps that increase economic well-being, such as job creation, tribal business ownership, small-business development, education, and community improvement. Some of these criteria may be subject to quantitative measurement.

The economic development criterion should be used to assess the extent to which projects promote these economic development objectives. The tribal community currently suffers from an unemployment rate of more than 60 percent, so any project that creates jobs is particularly valuable. A business or other income-producing project, such as the proposed Outer Hyllabos Marina, should be required to add commercial activity and employment opportunities to the community. All P.I.I. projects should be required to create economic development benefits. A review of a school proposal would include consideration of the long-term economic benefits of student training. If housing is proposed, the tribe would assess its potential impact on the economic condition of the surrounding Indian neighborhood. Given the tribe's urgent economic development needs, this criterion will probably be applied at some level to almost every proposal.

FINANCIAL BENEFIT

The Puyallup tribe seeks to build its financial resources, both to eliminate want among members and to support its various programs. Given the growing local economy, many land-use projects have the potential to provide income for the tribe.

The financial benefit criterion often can be accurately quantified and should be used to assess the amount of income that a development may generate or consume. Standard gauges may be used, such as rate of return on total assets and equity, cash-on-cash return, annual cash earned, and future value. P.I.I. initiatives, such as the Outer Hyllabos Marina and the proposed long-term lease of land to a waste disposal company for composting, should be judged in large part by this criterion. Proposals for tribally owned businesses, such as bingo halls or restaurants, also should be carefully assessed for their income-producing potential, though they may seek to meet other needs. Even reviews of private-business developments owned by tribal members should include consideration of the income they may produce through tax revenue. Some projects, such as most human service facilities and internal cultural activities, will actually cost money and should be judged against the financial benefits criterion only to determine the level of subsidy they will require.

HUMAN SERVICE PROVISION

In addition to managing internal affairs and representing the interests of the 1,500 tribal members with other governments, the Puyallup government provides a range of human services to almost 5,000 registered Indians in Washington State. A school (K through 12), an outpatient medical clinic, a dental care facility, a children's services center, a teen parenting program, a resident detoxification dormitory, a housing agency, and a job training program are all located at the headquarters site. The tribe also runs a police force and a court system. These programs are supported both by resources from the Bureau of Indian Affairs and by funds generated within the tribe.

The human service provision criterion should be used to assess the degree to which a land-use development will support these extensive programs. Projects may be judged according to their potential to generate either direct services or dedicated financial contributions. An investment designed specifically to provide a human service, such as a new school or elder-care center, would be assessed primarily by its performance under this criterion, and would be expected to meet a high standard. Commercial developments, such as the bingo hall or a restaurant, might produce revenues that could be dedicated to expanding human services and therefore would be given some credit for this contribution, though they would be judged primarily by other criteria.

NATURAL RESOURCE PRESERVATION

As noted previously, the Puyallup tribe attaches especially high value to natural resources, particularly to fisheries. Baseline requirements give fisheries special protection, but these are simply minimum maintenance standards. The 1988 settlement asserts further that an explicit goal is "to *increase* the current level of salmon and steelhead production released directly into the Puyallup River and Commencement Bay Basins and to *enhance* the fisheries resource [emphasis added]."[24] The agreement specifically calls for efforts to "increase the production of naturally spawning or artificially propagated stocks, or to improve the habitat of such stocks."[25] In interviews, tribal members repeatedly mentioned the importance of both enhancing fisheries and improving the general health of other natural resources on reservation land.

The natural resource preservation criterion should be used to assess the extent to which development projects will enhance the health of natural resources in general and fisheries in particular. The proposed Outer Hyllabos Marina, for example, would be given credit if it were designed to improve water quality in the Hyllabos Creek or if it dedicated a portion of its revenues to fisheries enhancement efforts. A plan for land acquisition and the creation of a tribal park would be judged primarily by this criterion. It would perform well if it protected open lands, and would be even more likely to gain approval if it also prevented alternative uses of these lands that might otherwise produce run-off or threaten fisheries. A project that threatens natural resources, such as the proposed composting plant, would be penalized under this criterion.

SOVEREIGN IDENTITY PROMOTION

The tribe has an overriding interest in asserting itself as a sovereign entity. In order to successfully do so, it must both exercise its authority on the reservation and maintain constructive relationships with local communities. Because the reservation is largely urbanized, tribal land-use decisions will have impacts on many non-Indians. Development projects will be noticed by outside groups and may lead to the cultivation of either support or opposition. The active hostility of local outside groups will hinder long-term tribal efforts to pursue its objectives. Consultation with and support from these groups may actually enhance tribal credibility and increase the tribes's ability to function as a sovereign government.

The sovereign identity promotion criterion should be used to assess the extent to which development proposals address their social context as well as how much they contribute to tribal prestige and self-esteem. This performance standard is particularly difficult to measure. A review of plans for the development of a smoke shop or liquor store in Tacoma should place some emphasis on whether or not residents near the site have been consulted and given a chance to contribute their concerns to the planning. The effects of the new bingo hall on local traffic patterns should also be assessed. A proposed new clinic at the headquarters could be judged on the degree to which it enhances the tribe's authority and prestige. Likewise, a marina or other significant new project should be given credit if it boosts the tribe's image, both internal and external. This criterion should be construed as a means of increasing tribal options, not limiting tribal power.

V. IMPLEMENTATION: A COMPREHENSIVE PERMITTING PROCESS

The analytic model (Section IV) alone is useless without some means of putting the baseline and variable criteria into practice—that is, a way of implementing the model. Any implementation scheme must apply the development criteria in a manner that addresses the shortcomings of the current land-use "process," particularly the scarcity of community input, uncoordinated decision-making, and the politicized nature of many current reviews. In order to accomplish these objectives, we are proposing a comprehensive permitting process. This process is composed of the following five phases (see the flowchart in Figure 1 for an overview of the process):

- Phase 1: Baseline Code Review
- Phase 2: Staff Analysis
- Phase 3: Community Evaluation
- Phase 4: Planning Commission Decision
- Phase 5: Tribal Council Oversight.

Any proposed land-use project, from minor building renovations to major commercial construction, would go through Phase 1. Small projects such as home alterations or other minor construction (hereafter referred to as "low-impact projects"), would pass only through Phase 1 before proceeding to Phase 5 for the required tribal council oversight. Projects of significant size or impact such as commercial developments or other major construction (hereafter referred to as "high-impact projects"), would proceed to Phases 2 through 5.

If amendments or additional requirements (like those often required by municipalities for the issuance of a certificate of occupancy) are added to a permit by the Planning Commission or the tribal council after a proposal has passed through the entire process, these changes would be sent back to Phase 1 to be reviewed as low-impact projects. This process should prevent delays in permitting that might occur through the excessive imposition of conditions.

The analytic model described in Section IV and the comprehensive permitting process detailed in this section together make up an overall land-use evaluation system.

PHASE 1: BASELINE CODE REVIEW

Every land-use proposal should begin the permitting process by going through a review that checks its compliance with the established baseline criteria. This initial phase is essentially a filtering step which ensures that all projects meet the minimum threshold tests outlined in the analytic model. It also guarantees that components added to proposals later in the permitting process are applied fairly and meet tribal standards. Projects which are obviously unacceptable are thereby eliminated early in the process, and developers are encouraged not to pursue frivolous ventures. These basic requirements will discourage wasteful ad hoc activity and conserve the tribe's scarce resources. The tribe currently conducts cursory regulation of development proposals; Phase 1 will improve that process by implementing the baseline criteria in a coordinated fashion (see Figure 2).

PARTICIPANTS

Project evaluation in Phase 1 would be carried out by staff members in the Environmental, Fisheries, and Land Use divisions. Environmental impact may be assessed using devices already agreed to by staff members, an "environmental checklist" and, for larger projects, an environmental impact statement (EIS) which should include all baseline environmental criteria.[26] The Fisheries Division should ensure that projects pose no threat of "net degradation to the fisheries habitat" and meet all other fisheries-related thresholds.[27] Compliance with building, safety, and other baseline land-use standards would be checked by the Land Use Division.

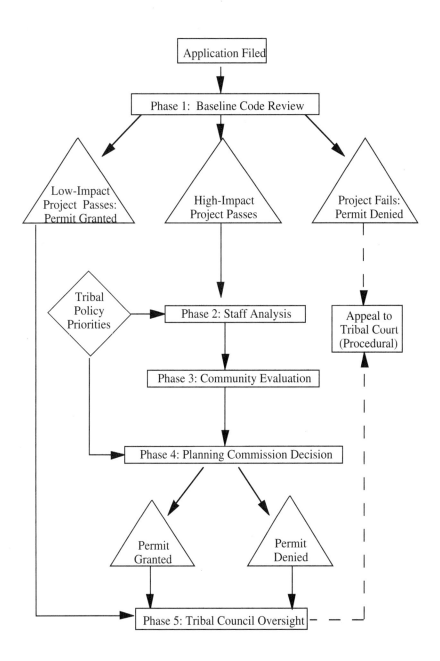

FIGURE 1. Comprehensive Permitting Process Overview

PROCESS

The mechanics of the review process should be straightforward. Staff members should develop an application form, which all permit applicants would submit along with general plans and maps specifying the location and impacts of development. The application would go to the Land Use Division, which would distribute copies to the Environmental, Fisheries, and Land Use divisions for simultaneous review. Phase 1 decisions must be made in a timely fashion, in most cases within thirty days, because time lost diminishes the value of a development.

Most low-impact projects, such as private home renovations and "ex post" conditions added to permitted proposals, would be comprehensively reviewed and either approved or rejected in Phase 1. Low-impact projects that are permitted at this stage would pass directly to Phase 5 for tribal council oversight. In order to avoid embroiling staff members in disputes, applicants should be allowed to file appeals based on procedural grounds with the tribal court. If permits are denied on substantive grounds, applicants would be able to make recommended changes and file new applications. A high-impact project that passes successfully through Phase 1 would proceed to Phases 2 through 5 as originally submitted or with required modifications.

ADDITIONAL ISSUES

The tribe must resolve a number of issues before implementing the Phase 1 process. In areas where staff members do not have expertise, such as surveying and inspections, the tribe may have to contract with outside consultants or governments to gauge the performance of development proposals.[28] In addition, comprehensive environmental impact statements, which may be required in some cases, may be impossible to complete within thirty days. To ensure adequate review, the time frame for completion may need to be flexible. Another issue that needs to be resolved is how exactly to distinguish low-impact projects, which need only go through Phase 1, from high-impact projects, which must proceed to Phases 2 through 5. Finally, the staff should have a procedure in place for reviewing the Phase 1 baseline codes regularly to reflect new technology or evolving priorities. The application form, therefore, also would need to be revised from time to time.

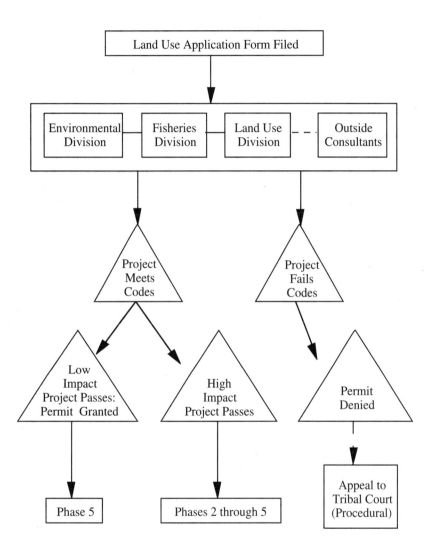

FIGURE 2. Phase 1: Baseling Code Review

PHASE 2: STAFF ANALYSIS

Any land-use application designated "high-impact" that passes Phase 1 would then move on to Phases 2 through 5. Phase 2 begins the process of implementing the variable criteria outlined in the analytic model. In this phase, the staff would analyze the strengths and weaknesses of the proposal against the six variable criteria in as objective a manner as possible. In contrast to Phase 1, no two proposals would undergo the same set of tests in an identical fashion. The weights assigned to the six variable criteria would be dictated by the type of land use (income generating, cultural, human service, or land preservation) and the tribal priorities at the time of the analysis. This procedure represents an effort to direct the ensuing evaluation process in a productive and consistent manner—to frame the debate. It provides the flexibility in assessment required by the Puyallup tribe's unique characteristics and needs, while applying a consistent set of standards to ensure that the remaining phases of the permitting process are as fair and predictable as possible.

PARTICIPANTS

Phase 2 review would be coordinated by the *staff* members who serve on the Planning Commission (the composition and mandate of the Planning Commission are described in detail in Phase 4 below). Commission staff would analyze project compliance with criteria in their respective areas of expertise. Performance under remaining standards would be evaluated by noncommission staff members, who would provide detailed written and/ or oral reports to the commission. In areas such as economic development and financial benefit assessment, where the tribe may lack in-house expertise, outside consultants should be hired to judge development proposals.

PROCESS (SEE FIGURE 3)

An application that passes Phase 1, and is required to go through Phases 2 through 5, would be sent to the Planning Commission staff, with or without modifications attached. The project would then be categorized by land-use type (income-generating, cultural, human service, or land preservation) which, along with any explicit tribal policy priorities, should determine the relative weighting assigned to the variable criteria. Staff members would then gather any necessary additional data, such as the job-creation potential, cash flow estimates, or neighborhood impact information. Any data collection and analysis that cannot be performed in-house should be contracted out at this point. Any information relating to the application should be placed in a file along with the Phase 1 results.

After all the data are collected, the staff should proceed by analyzing the pros and cons of the project under each criterion in order of importance. The results of this pro/con analysis should be reported in writing, with a separate page or pages for each variable criterion. This staff report should be completed within thirty days, unless outside consultants are required.

ADDITIONAL ISSUES

The primary unresolved question in Phase 2 is one that affects a number of aspects of the land-use process: What are the tribe's policy priorities? For example, the tribe may determine that job-creation and training are the top priorities for the next two years. This decision would affect the weighting given to the economic development criterion relative to the other criteria. Another issue that needs to be addressed is the appropriateness of the four land-use categories we have defined. While these reflect what tribal officials have suggested are the most salient categories, there may be other ways of dividing proposals in order to prioritize criteria. In addition, the flexible thirty-day time limit is merely a suggestion; experience may dictate a longer or shorter period. Finally, we have not specified the exact form of the Phase 2 staff report—only that it be in written form with separate pages for each criterion. The tribe will probably want to standardize this report as much as possible to enhance the consistency and clarity of this process.

PHASE 3: COMMUNITY EVALUATION

Each high-impact project should also go through a community review phase, including a community hearing and gathering of tribal comments (see Figure 4). In the past, as we have indicated, the tribal community at large often has been excluded from the land-use review process. This has been a source of internal conflict and has prevented the inclusion of valuable tribal feedback regarding development projects. Phase 3 repre-

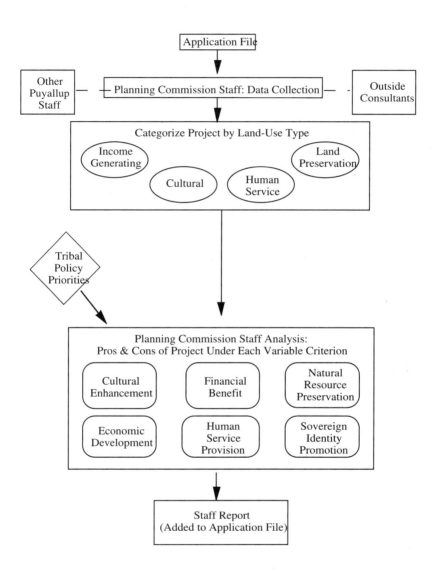

FIGURE 3. Phase 2: Staff Analysis

sents an effort both to inform the community about important projects before bulldozers arrive, and to provide members with regularly scheduled opportunities for participation. In this way, all members of the Puyallup community will be partners in the evaluation process.

PARTICIPANTS

The community review process would be coordinated by the Planning Commission. Written comments, which are likely to be submitted by concerned staff, members of key tribal committees, and the general tribal membership, should be gathered by staff members serving on the commission. Public hearings on development proposals should be open to the entire Puyallup community and should be conducted by the chairperson of the Planning Commission with assistance from staff. Typically, no outside, nontribal persons would be allowed to make comments during this phase; staff members should have assessed the external impacts of projects during Phase 2.

PROCESS (SEE FIGURE 4)

After an application has passed through Phases 1 and 2, it would be forwarded with staff comments to the Planning Commission. In order to promote broad participation, the commission should hold public hearings on development proposals. These hearings should be held on a quarterly basis, on a specified evening of the week after normal working hours, at the tribal community center. Hearing times, along with the agenda of projects to be discussed, should be announced through direct mailings to tribal members and notices in the *Puyallup Tribal News* to ensure that all concerned parties are informed of their opportunity to provide input. Written public tribal comments should be accepted for ninety days following an application's completion of Phase 1, and those comments received to date should be summarized at the public hearing. If the public hearing is held before the end of the ninety-day comment period, written comments should be accepted and added to the application file until this period has elapsed. Projects should be considered at the earliest quarterly community hearing following their completion of Phase 2.

In order to ensure procedural consistency and fairness, hearings should proceed according to a standard agenda. The Planning Commission

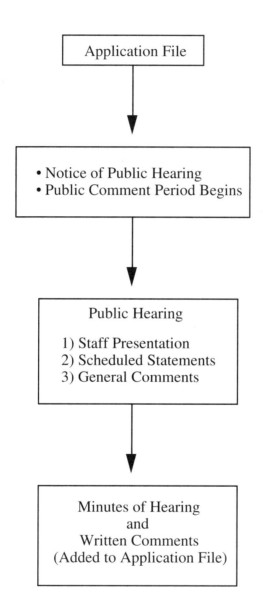

FIGURE 4. Phase 3: Community Evaluation

chairperson or a designated staff member should begin with an introduction and a description of the projects under consideration, followed by a summary of project results from Phases 1 and 2. Applicants or project sponsors should then be permitted to give a brief presentation or "pitch." The bulk of time should be reserved for a limited number of previously scheduled, prepared public statements and unscheduled general audience questions and comments. General comments should be unstructured in order to allow the airing of all reactions to proposed developments. Detailed minutes of the hearing should be taken by a Planning Commission staff member and added to the application file.

ADDITIONAL ISSUES

In order to promote thorough representation and broad participation as well as timely review of applications in Phase 3, a number of design issues must be resolved. For example, proposals that are submitted on the day of or after a hearing may be damaged or threatened by having to sit for three months before being reviewed by the public. In such cases, the Planning Commission may wish to schedule special hearings. The tribal members or leadership may believe that quarterly hearings are insufficient to meet the demand for community input, in which case it will be wise to hold them on a monthly basis. The ninety-day written comment period might also be lengthened in order to ensure inclusiveness. Finally, tribal officials often lament the lack of member participation in government and have actually provided small stipends to members who have attended certain public meetings in the past. The tribal council must carefully consider the social and financial costs of such a mechanism and decide whether or not to make payments in this case.

PHASE 4: PLANNING COMMISSION DECISION

Following the community review process, applications should be formally reviewed by the Planning Commission (see Figure 5). The purpose of this fourth phase is to synthesize all the information that has been gathered during Phases 2 and 3, and to make a decision on the application in light of the tribe's policy priorities. Because the commission review would be framed by the staff criteria analysis, it represents another application of the variable criteria. The Planning Commission should essentially serve in this phase as a buffer and conduit between the staff and community at large (Phases 2 and 3) as well as the applicant, and the tribal council (Phase 5).

The tribal constitution grants the tribal council the power to delegate its regulatory authority over land to a commission.[29] By exercising this power through the creation of a decision-making Planning Commission, the council would depoliticize the difficult task of conducting land-use application reviews. The commission, which would be subject to tribal council oversight in Phase 5, could make informed judgments about projects without the immediate threat of electoral action. With a diverse membership, it would be both representative of the spectrum of tribal interests and responsive to the council.

PARTICIPANTS

As of early 1991, the notion of establishing a Planning Commission had gained wide acceptance within tribal government. The Land Use Office originally proposed the idea in the *Interim Land Use Plan*, and the Legal Division reiterated it in a January 1991 memo.[30] Under these proposals, the commission would be composed of one representative each from the tribe's Environmental, Fisheries, and perhaps, Legal divisions, one member of P.I.I., one tribal council member, and two Puyallup members-at-large. While the tribe must make the final decision on commission composition, we propose several changes in this makeup based on our research. Government staff members should be part of the commission, but they should be made ineligible to vote in order to preserve the objectivity of their analysis in previous phases. P.I.I. should not be represented on the commission, because in many cases *its own* proposals will be under consideration. Finally, in order to separate the role of the tribal council in this process, and to avoid the difficult decision of selecting a councilor to serve, the tribal council should not have a representative on the commission. Instead, the number of Puyallup members who serve should be expanded (perhaps to five), and they should be the voting members of the commission. The tribal council should appoint these members at large in a manner that represents a cross-section of the community.

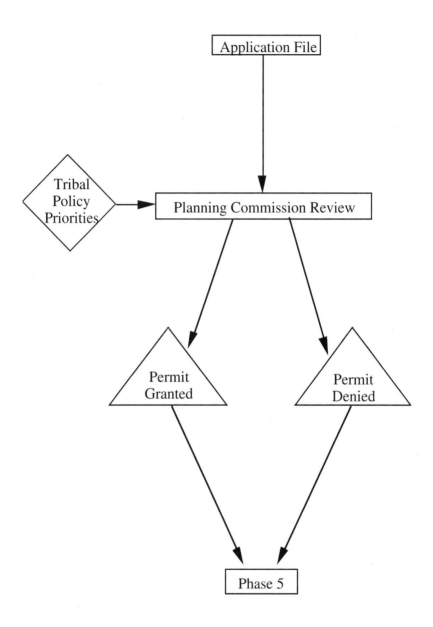

FIGURE 5. Phase 4: Planning Commission Decision

PROCESS (SEE FIGURE 5)

As soon as the public comment period outlined in Phase 3 has elapsed, the Planning Commission would schedule a meeting to deliberate and make a final decision on the application. The meeting should open with a staff briefing. The staff members of the commission should report the Phase 1 conclusions, present their Phase 2 analysis, and summarize the public comments and minutes of the public hearing from Phase 3. The commission should then deliberate, synthesizing the information presented and injecting comments of their own. Finally, the commission should vote to grant the permit, grant the permit with conditions, or deny the permit. The commission's decision should then be forwarded to the tribal council for final oversight (Phase 5).

ADDITIONAL ISSUES

The most important issue to be resolved in Phase 4 is the makeup of the commission. We have suggested an alternative to the recent Land Use and Legal division proposals based on our interviews and research. The details of the membership will have to be determined by the tribe. In addition, the tribe must decide whether to pay voting members for their participation, or whether to make service voluntary. Finally, once again, the question of a time frame must be resolved. Phase 4 may take as little as one day, or it may require several sessions, but the tribe should set some time limit for completion—perhaps two weeks—starting after an application completes Phase 3.

PHASE 5: TRIBAL COUNCIL OVERSIGHT

Planning Commission decisions regarding high-impact applications, and low-impact proposals approved in Phase 1, should be sent directly to the tribal council for final oversight (see Figure 6). While the comprehensive permitting process represents an effort to depoliticize land-use decisions, it is clear from our interviews that the tribal council needs to retain a degree of authority over crucial matters related to development. Indeed, such a process would be incomplete without some political control. Moreover, the power of the tribal council to review decisions made by a "subordinate committee" is clearly granted in the constitution, and it is consistent with tribal tradition.[31]

The assumption of these recommendations, however, is that the tribal council will have an opportunity for oversight in Phase 5, but will in most cases simply affirm Planning Commission and Phase 1 decisions. Observations and interviews suggest that the council may benefit by limiting its influence over the land-use permitting process.[32] The council is responsible for a broad range of policy-making and faces a chronic shortage of time. Even the smallest land-use issues can become mired in disputes that are difficult to resolve and likely to congest the council's schedule. By distancing itself from and routinizing permitting decisions, the council will be able to reserve time to address more pressing policy issues.

PARTICIPANTS

The five-member tribal council is the key participant in Phase 5. During the consideration of particularly important development applications, members of the tribal council may wish to sit in on Phase 4 deliberations, and even the Phase 3 hearing, so that they are prepared to conduct informed oversight. In order to provide strength and continuity in the process, the Planning Commission staff should provide any information and assistance requested by the council during this phase.

PROCESS (SEE FIGURE 6)

When an application has passed through the other required phases, the tribal council should add it to the agenda of one of its regularly scheduled meetings. The Planning Commission staff should be invited to this meeting to summarize the proceedings up until that point. The council may then want to debate the issue briefly. Virtually all decisions made by staff members in Phase 1 regarding low-impact land uses should be quickly affirmed by voice consensus. Most Phase 4 Planning Commission decisions on high-impact applications should also be accepted. It is to be expected that controversial projects will have been detected early in the evaluation process. In the few instances when the council decides to overturn an earlier decision, it should be required to vote unanimously— 5 to 0—to do so. As in other phases, a timeframe for completion should be established.

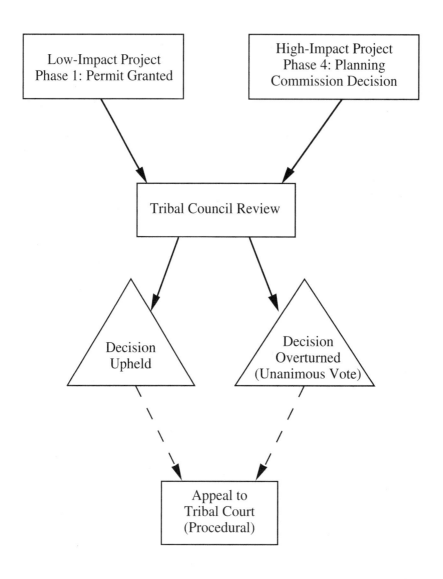

FIGURE 6. Phase 5: Tribal Council Oversight

ADDITIONAL ISSUES

While the proposed process appears to provide a good balance for the tribal council between involvement with, and insulation from, the contentious land-use permitting process, some members may believe that it grants them too much or too little authority. This issue must be resolved by the council itself, but two other alternatives may be feasible. If the council wants to distance itself further from permitting decisions, it could forego all reviews of Phase 1 and Phase 4 proceedings and allow earlier decisions to stand in *all* cases. If it wishes to assert more authority, it could give the Planning Commission the responsibility to make strong, detailed recommendations and reserve for itself the power to make final permitting decisions.

APPEALS PROCESS

If applicants or opponents of a proposed land-use development disagree with a final permitting decision, they should be granted the opportunity to file an appeal. As discussed by staff members and recommended by the tribe's Legal Division, an appeal based on whether required procedures have been followed should be taken to the tribal court.[33] Substantive issues should be addressed in the course of the five review phases; but applicants denied permits who believe either that their proposals meet baseline and variable tribal criteria, or can be satisfactorily revised, should have the option of reapplying.

CONCLUDING THOUGHTS

While the comprehensive system recommended here could bring immediate benefit to the tribe, a number of issues should be addressed in order to enhance its long-term effectiveness. First, the evaluation system—both criteria and process—should be presented to the tribal community as a whole if it is to be adopted and effectively implemented. Second, the tribal leadership should begin to remedy the other critical land-use management gap by developing a set of land-use policy priorities. Finally, the long-term effectiveness of any project evaluation process would be improved by additional stability in the overall political and electoral system.

In spite of the remaining unresolved planning and political issues, this recommended evaluation model could be useful immediately. The combination of a well-defined analytic model and a process for implementing it would allow the Puyallup tribe to manage and enhance its substantial resources in a rational and consistent manner. Furthermore, such a land-use management system—by advocating flexibility of standards and inclusiveness of tribal views—will itself help define future tribal priorities. Therefore, it will not only guide today's decision-makers, but will provide long-term direction as well. Finally, the framework for this system may be transferable to other tribes in Indian Country. If the Puyallup are able to make such a system work, it could become a model for other tribes and provide benefits to native peoples throughout the country.

NOTES

1. Data for this section are drawn from "The Puyallups: Tribe at a Crossroads," *Tacoma News Tribune*, October 21–26, 1990.
2. Glenn MacDonnell, *Washington: Chilling Out* (Boston: Data Research Incorporated-McGraw Hill, 1990), p. 163.
3. Ibid., p. 154. Total nonfarm employment expanded at about 3.5 percent annually during the 1980s, according to DRI.
4. Vickerman, Zachary, and Miller, Blair, *Waterway 2010 Plan: Executive Summary* (Oakland, CA: VZM Engineering and Architecture, 1991), p.1.
5. MacDonnell, *Washington: Chilling Out*, p. 154.
6. Puyallup Tribe of Indians, *Agreement between the Puyallup Tribe, Local Governments in Pierce County, the State of Washington, the United States of America, and Certain Property Owners* (August 27, 1988), pp. 2–3.
7. While states that allow bingo generally limit awards to $100–$250, high-stakes bingo on Indian reservations produces winnings in the $1,000s, with megajackpots sometimes reaching $250,000–$1,000,000. See Eduardo E. Cordeiro, "The Economics of Bingo," in this volume.
8. Margo S. Miller, *Tribal Responses to Federal Land Consolidation Policy*, Project Report Series, Harvard Project on American Indian Economic Development, John F. Kennedy School of Government, Harvard University, 1988, p. 40.
9. Interview with Rolleen Hargrove, Puyallup Tribal Council member, March 1, 1991.
10. P.I.I. is governed by a seven-member board, four members of which are non-Indians and the remaining three of which are Puyallup. The chief objective of P.I.I. is to maximize the financial return of its development projects to the tribe. As the chairman of P.I.I.'s board wrote, "The separation of business and politics is recognized as being vital to the success of economic development within Indian Country." From Puyallup International Incorporated, *Annual Report, 1990* (Tacoma, WA: P.I.I., 1991), p. 1.
11. John Bell, "Draft Memo to the Puyallup Tribal Council Concerning Tribal Permitting Procedures," Puyallup Legal Division, January 18, 1991, p. 5.

12. The importance of fisheries is clearly stated in both the tribal constitution and the 1988 settlement documents. During interviews held in early 1991, staff and tribal members reiterated the central role that fisheries play in Puyallup economic and cultural life.

13. Elizabeth Tail, *Interim Land Use Plan for the Puyallup Tribe* (Tacoma, WA: Puyallup Land Use Division, Puyallup Tribe of Indians, 1990), p. 3.

14. See Stephen Cornell and Joseph P. Kalt, "Reloading the Dice," in this volume.

15. Douglas R. Porter, *Flexible Zoning: How It Works* (Washington, WA: The Urban Land Institute, 1988), pp. 161–63.

16. Ibid., p. 163.

17. Charles M. Haar and Michael A. Wolf, *Land-Use Planning: A Casebook on the Use, Misuse, and Re-Use of Urban Land* (Boston: Little, Brown and Company, 1989), p. 216 and p. 279.

18. Ibid., pp. 283–89.

19. Ibid., pp. 141–43.

20. Bell, "Draft Memo," p. 5.

21. Puyallup tribe, *Agreement*, Technical Document #4, pp. 1, 34, and 42.

22. Interview with Elizabeth Tail, Land Use Division, Puyallup tribe, March 3, 1991.

23. Maiselle Bridges, tribal elder, in *Tacoma News Tribune*, October 21, 1990, p. A8.

24. Puyallup tribe, *Agreement*, Technical Document #4, p.1.

25. Ibid., p. 42.

26. Bell, "Draft Memo," p. 7.

27. Ibid., p. 8.

28. Ibid., p. 8. This option has already been tentatively approved by staff members.

29. Puyallup tribe, *Constitution*, June 1, 1970, Article VI, Section 1, Subsections C and D.

30. Elizabeth Tail, *Interim Land Use Plan*, p. 16, and Bell, "Draft Memo," pp. 5–6.

31. Puyallup tribe, *Constitution*, Article VI, Section 1, Subsection R.

32. Interviews with tribal council members, March 1, 1991.

33. Bell, "Draft Memo," p. 6.

5

CAN TRIBES MANAGE THEIR OWN RESOURCES? THE 638 PROGRAM AND AMERICAN INDIAN FORESTRY

Matthew B. Krepps

Public Law 638 (the Indian Self-Determination and Education Assistance Act of 1975) provides a mechanism by which tribes can assume management control over an array of reservation governmental services, including such functions as police, schools, and natural resource management. "638 contracting" typically operates by allocating to tribal management monies that would otherwise fund the activities of the Bureau of Indian Affairs (BIA). There is no guarantee, however, that tribal management will be superior to BIA management. Indeed, claims abound as to whether or not 638 contracting works well for tribes.

Matthew Krepps' chapter reports the results of a systematic, statistical study of over seventy tribes which have undertaken some degree of 638 control of forestry operations on their reservations. The results are striking. After accounting for differences across tribes in the quality and quantity of harvestable timber, the author finds that, as tribal control increases relative to BIA control, worker productivity rises, costs decline, and income improves. Even the price received for reservation logs increases. While no individual tribe is assured success, these findings indicate that tribal institutions and control can be keys to a productive reservation timber industry.

The directors of such [joint-stock] companies, however, being the managers rather of other people's money than of their own, it cannot well be expected, that they should watch over it with the same anxious vigilance with which the partners in a private copartnery frequently watch over their own... Negligence and profusion, therefore, must always prevail, more or less, in the management of the affairs of such a company.

Adam Smith, The Wealth of Nations, *1776[1]*

American Indian tribes have long been treated as wards of the federal government. This relationship was first codified by Chief Justice John Marshall in 1832, and until recently Indian tribes have lived under this legally mandated system of dependence.[2] Under the auspices of the federal trust responsibility, the United States federal government has historically conducted various enterprises, including the maintenance and marketing of Indian timber resources, on behalf of Indian tribes through the Bureau of Indian Affairs (BIA). Perhaps the trust responsibility was intended as a sort of quid pro quo for disenfranchising the Indians of untold millions of acres of land during the pursuit of America's "manifest destiny." Whatever the reason for this federal interest in Indian affairs, the federal government in effect has been serving as the executor of a will, while the decedent is alive and well.

Although this relationship between tribes and the federal government has persisted for more than 150 years, it has not always been endured willingly by the tribes. In response to repeated claims throughout Indian Country that tribal economic and political interests were not being properly served by BIA agents, Congress passed the 1975 Indian Self-Determination and Education Assistance Act (hereafter PL 638). PL 638 allows tribes to contract with the federal government to conduct various operations formerly conducted on their behalf. BIA funds are typically earmarked for specific programs or individual projects. By participating in the 638 program, a tribe takes over one or more of these aspects itself and receives the concomitant funding to dispense as it sees fit in the task. Restricting our focus to tribal forestry, a tribe could contract with the BIA to undertake a specific project such as inventory or to manage a particular program such as special forest development. The funding for these activities is the same funding that formerly paid the salaries of BIA workers performing the same tasks.

The implementation of PL 638 is feasible because it shifts the onus of accountability for tribal forestry onto the tribes themselves without necessitating any increase in federal appropriations. If federal derogations of the trust responsibility are now detected or even suspected, a tribe can demand and receive control of its portion of BIA forestry appropriations. Although PL 638 threatens to reduce the purview of the federal government by facilitating the transfer of control of certain enterprises from the United States government to the tribes, it is nonetheless very attractive to the politicians who control the BIA's purse strings. The political palatability of PL 638 derives from the fact that past proofs of BIA shortcomings invariably cost the federal government a significant amount of money to redress. In fact, the two most recent investigations of inadequacies in the BIA's fulfillment of the federal trust responsibility vis-à-vis Indian forestry (1977 and 1984) resulted in funding increases of 57 percent and 19 percent, respectively. By contrast, funding levels remained roughly constant in real terms for the years 1977–88 in which no investigations were conducted.[3]

WHY WRITE ABOUT INDIAN FORESTRY?

Since the passage of PL 638 in 1975, tribal participation in the 638 forestry program has been extensive and well-documented. Of the seventy-five tribes analyzed in this paper, forty-nine participated to some degree in the management of their forest resources through the 638 program during the years 1984, 1987, and 1989. Tribal involvement in forestry operations ranged from a completely hands-off approach with full BIA management to total tribal control of day-to-day operations.

However, despite this growth of tribal participation, there have yet to be any studies comparing the success of participating versus nonparticipating tribes. The lack of serious scholarly attention to the 638 forestry program is especially disturbing since some BIA officials have opposed expansion of tribal forestry participation on the grounds of economic efficiency. The often repeated argument that tribes lack the necessary human capital to successfully manage their own resources is again being heard in public debate. This institutional opposition to 638 is not surprising since over 4,000 BIA forestry workers have already been replaced by tribal forestry workers who have demanded and received an increased voice in how their timber is managed.[4] Given this opposition to increased tribal participation in forestry operations and decision making (as well as to 638 contracting in other sectors of tribal economies), it seems imperative to ascertain the success of the 638 forestry program thus far. In view of current levels of federal indebtedness, the increased sensitivity of Congress to issues of economic expediency, and the growing assertions of economic and political sovereignty by American Indian tribes, tribal involvement in the management of Indian natural resources seems likely to grow. Under such conditions, a systematic examination of tribal versus BIA performance could prove especially timely.

ANALYTICAL METHOD AND PREVIEW OF CONCLUSIONS

This study is an attempt to estimate the relative contributions of BIA and tribally employed workers to the productivity of Indian forests. Rather than simply report anecdotal evidence from a handful of reservations, this study subjects data from a nationwide sample of seventy-five tribes with significant timber resources to the rigors of statistical analysis. The primary question to be answered is: What effects does increased Indian forestry participation have on two components—quantity of timber harvested and price obtained—of the revenues received in forestry operations?

The central conclusion of this study is that tribal control of forestry under PL 638 results in significantly better timber management. A detailed statistical analysis of forestry operations reveals that tribal control dramatically improves productivity. Output rises dramatically under 638 contracting—by as much as 40 percent for the typical tribe able to move to complete tribal control—with no increase in the number of workers. Tribal control also results in better marketing and in sharply higher prices received by tribes for their resources. Shifting to total tribal control under PL 638 would allow the typical tribe to receive prices as much as 6 percent higher than under BIA management.

The analysis also indicates that the tribes with the most business experience are currently the most successful forest managers. Economists refer to this increased efficiency over time as a learning curve: unit costs of production decline as cumulative output rises because people get better with practice. The functional implication of the value of forestry experience is that if tribal foresters can gradually assume increasing levels of responsibility over time, while working alongside (and monitoring) experienced BIA foresters, their descent down the learning curve will certainly entail less economic hardship than would an abrupt withdrawal of the government presence.

ANALYSIS OF QUANTITY HARVESTED

In order to determine whether tribal participation leads to better forest management, a benchmark is needed to measure performance. Fortunately, the minimum optimal harvest rate for every forest is determined by Mother Nature. The quantity of timber harvested in one year at this rate is referred to as the biological annual allowable cut (AAC). To understand the concept of a forest's AAC, one must first understand the components of the harvest decision calculus.[5] The decision to harvest any given stand of trees is a function of the growth rate of the trees, current and expected timber prices, and the market rate of interest and/or the rate of time preference of the forest's owner (explained below). Standing timber represents an asset for which the expected annual return is equal to the annual increment to the forest's biomass multiplied by the expected change in the price of timber. The annual cost of holding this asset is the foregone interest that could have been earned by harvesting the trees and investing the proceeds. Therefore, a tribe concerned with the long-run maximization of timber income should harvest trees as long as the discount rate exceeds the expected value of the annual percentage increment to the value of the forest from its additional growth. In other words, if a stand of timber can generate more value as money deposited in the bank (earning at the discount rate) than it can earn by growing into a bigger harvest later, the stand of timber should be harvested now.[6]

At the beginning of every fiscal year, BIA foresters calculate the biological annual allowable cut for each Indian forest. This figure—the AAC—is the quantity of timber whose expected growth rate is economically negative. That is, the forest either has stopped growing altogether or is actually deteriorating. This timber represents foregone opportunities to invest the cash that could be realized from harvesting. It also serves only to delay replanting and the realization of subsequent harvest receipts.

Therefore, the AAC represents the minimum amount of timber a market value-maximizing tribe would offer for sale each year, and thus provides a benchmark by which to gauge the success of PL 638. If, all things being equal, tribes involved in 638 harvest a greater share of their AAC than tribes who participate on a lesser scale or not at all, then it follows that tribal involvement increases productivity. Unfortunately, all things are not equal. Tribes obviously differ in many regards other than the degree of 638 participation. These differences, if unaccounted for, could lead to spurious conclusions regarding the impact of tribal involvement on forest productivity. Economists therefore employ a technique known as multiple regression to simulate an all-things-being-equal situation.

Ideally, the sample of seventy-five forested Indian tribes would differ only in the degree of 638 participation, thereby facilitating a straightforward measurement of the impact of changes in tribal involvement on productivity. Although this is not the case, multiple regression obviates the need to have the sort of classical control group commonly employed in psychological and biological experiments, i. e., one that differs from the experimental group only with respect to the parameter being analyzed. In this study, the relationship of interest is the one between tribal involvement and forest productivity. Multiple regression essentially allows us to enter into a computer variables corresponding to any intertribal differences that might influence a tribe's harvest level, and then to calculate the correlation of each variable to the quantity harvested as if only that variable were changing. In this way, multiple regression creates the classical control group of psychological and biological experimentation.

The annual harvest level of a forest (measured in million board feet) is a function of four primary factors: the amount of timber available for sale, the maintenance efforts of low-skilled workers, the marketing efforts of high-skilled workers, and the internal rate of time preference (explained below) of the forest's owner.[7] The AAC (also measured in million board feet) is included in the productivity statistical analysis in order to control for size differences among tribal forests. The inclusion of AAC permits the measurement of how well a tribe performs given what it has to work with. Having controlled for intertribal scale effects, the foremost purpose of this multiple regression production analysis is to determine whether the productivity of forestry workers differs depending on whether they are employed by the BIA or the tribe, and if so, to quantify the differences.

The productivity of low-skilled labor is measured as the average contribution of each low-skilled worker to the value maintenance of the total growing stock of a tribe's forest. The productivity of high-skilled labor is measured as the average contribution of each high-skilled worker to the successful transformation of mature timber into harvest receipts. The computer-generated "coefficients" of these labor variables measure how much the addition of a BIA or tribal worker adds to forest output. They allow us to ascertain whether tribal workers are more or less productive than their BIA counterparts. If the answer is more, then PL 638 can be judged a success with respect to productivity, and the argument that tribes lack the sophistication to manage their own resources can be safely dismissed.

With inputs of labor and available timber controlled, we expect that intertribal differences in the rate of time preference will affect the quantities harvested by each tribe. The rate of time preference is a measure of the relative value placed by a tribe on present and future income. The market interest rate is commonly used to measure the rate of time preference because a dollar this year and a dollar plus interest next year are of equal value to those who invest wisely. However, two primary factors could cause a forested tribe's rate of time preference to diverge significantly from the market interest rate. These factors are the reservation unemployment rate and the percentage of timber harvested in a given year that was owned by individual tribal allottees rather than the tribal collectivity. Higher unemployment might bias the resource extraction decision toward current harvests because economic hardship tends to promote present-orientedness.[8] Higher allottee timber ownership might serve as an impetus to current harvests if individuals' rates of time preference do not include the full consideration of descendants that may characterize tribal decision makers.

The variables defined above—the AAC, the number of BIA and tribal workers of each skill class, and the rates of unemployment and allottee ownership—are the primary determinants of a tribe's annual harvest level. However, in order to fully understand the impact of 638 on forest productivity, it is necessary to account for differences in motivation and experience between BIA and tribal workers. First, we employ a variable representing the number of high-skilled tribal workers divided by the total number of BIA agents employed in each forestry operation. As mentioned above, 638 participation has already resulted in the replacement of over 4,000 BIA agents with tribal members.[9] An awareness on the part of BIA agents of this apparent cost of underperformance should induce all such agents to exert more effort when working alongside tribal foresters who might be monitoring their activities. This monitoring effect is important to quantify, otherwise the regression results will underestimate the degree to which tribally employed workers outperform BIA workers or will overestimate the degree to which BIA workers outperform tribal workers. Second, a variable representing the average quantity of timber per tribal member is included as a measure of the importance of timber to the individual and to the tribe. An individual tribal member's stake in a well-managed forest is a function of the quantity of timber per tribal member because the receipts from timber harvests redound to members in the form of tribally provided public goods (such as school systems) and/or per capita income. A further consideration is the solicitude that individual members have for their tribe. Notwithstanding personal gain, the strong cultural unity that is characteristic of many Indian tribes should enable them to counteract the free-rider problem, i. e., the tendency for individuals to desire something and expect others to perform the work of securing it for everyone. An additional factor that might induce tribal members to outperform BIA agents is the Administrative Deduction, a program which stipulates that 10 percent of a tribe's timber receipts be reinvested in the tribal forest. This 10 percent is often used to employ more tribal members as forest workers. Thus, when the harvest level falls and timber receipts decrease, tribal members are the first ones to lose their jobs.

Finally, we expect 638 participation to be most successful where the tribe possesses general business experience and/or specific experience in forest management. Therefore, variables are included to control for differences in these parameters. The rate of employment in tribally owned businesses serves as a proxy for a tribe's ability to mobilize and achieve sustainable economic activity. The inclusion of forestry experience is predicated on the assumption that Indian foresters face a learning curve.

It is hoped that the variables defined above account for all important determinants of the quantity of timber harvested by a tribe.[10] If significant influences on productivity are omitted, they are most likely specific to particular time periods and/or regions. Therefore, additional variables are employed to account for the geographic location of each forest and the time of harvest.[11]

RESULTS OF PRODUCTION ANALYSIS

The aforementioned variables were entered into a computerized regression program which generated an "effect coefficient" and a significance level for each one. The sign and magnitude of each effect coefficient reveal the direction and magnitude of the corresponding variable's influence on quantity harvested. The significance level represents the level of certainty with which we can reject the hypothesis that the variable in question bears no relationship to the quantity of timber harvested by a tribe. The significance level is essentially a measure of the confidence with which the computer-generated effect coefficients can be accepted.

The multiple regression analysis was performed on a sample of seventy-five forested Indian tribes throughout the United States in each of three years: 1984, 1987, and 1989. This time period corresponds to very detailed labor input data available in periodic BIA internal program evaluations. Whether or not a tribe is included in the data set depended on the following criteria: a positive AAC and some level of forestry employment, BIA and/or tribal. Tribes with no AAC were eliminated from the sample because it would be specious to infer anything about the productivity of labor inputs when the optimal harvest level is likely to be zero. Further, there is no point in attempting to assess the motivational implications of a tighter tribal-BIA nexus when there is nobody to motivate.

Table 1 reports the results of the statistical production analysis. The quantity harvested is less than the AAC for the typical tribe, indicating that tribal timber is typically harvested at less than the minimally optimal rate. The coefficients for both skill classes of labor indicate that tribal members working under PL 638 are significantly more productive than BIA workers given the amount of timber each has to work with. The addition of a typical high-skilled tribal 638 worker adds 24,000 board feet of harvest; adding one more high-skilled worker under BIA control may actually reduce a tribe's harvest (the effect coefficient is negative). Meanwhile, the typical additional PL 638 low-skilled worker that is added to the workforce is 75 percent more productive than an additional BIA-controlled worker. This differential labor productivity provides a compelling rebuttal of the argument that tribes cannot manage their own resources.

The positive influence of allottee ownership on quantity harvested suggests that tribal cultural unity is sufficiently strong to overcome the free-

TABLE 1.
Determinants of Tribal Timber Sale Quantities

EXPLANATORY FACTOR	EFFECT ON HARVEST (EFFECT CO-EFFICIENT)	PROBABILITY THAT EFFECT IS SIGNIFICANTLY DIFFERENT FROM 0
AAC	445,000 bf/yr per million allowable cut set by BIA	99.9%
BIA High-Skilled Labor	-14,000 bf/worker/yr given the quantity of timber available to sell	99.9%
Tribal High-Skilled Labor	24,000 bf/worker/yr given the quantity of timber available to sell	99.9%
BIA Low-Skilled Labor	40 bf/worker/yr given the total growing stock available to tend	99.9%
Tribal Low-Skilled Labor	70 bf/worker/yr given the total growing stock available to tend	99.9%
Percent Allottee Ownership	1.34 million bf/yr given the AAC and degree of tribal involvement	99.9%
Per Capita Tribal Timber Holdings	6.59 million bf/yr for each million bf increase in per capita timber holdings	99.9%
Past Tribal Business Experience	306,000 bf/yr for each 10% increase in employment in tribally-owned businesses	99.9%

Note: The model was estimated by generalized least squares jointly with the price equation presented in Table 2. Predicted effects of explanatory factors are for marginal increments to the means.

rider problem which would otherwise undermine a tribe's incentive to harvest the optimal quantity of timber. The unemployment rate appears to be positively correlated with the quantity harvested, but the variable was not reported for reasons outlined below.[12] The insignificance of the variable representing the monitoring capacity of Indian foresters reveals that the superior productivity of tribal labor derives from these workers' own efforts and not from any energizing effects on BIA personnel.

Additional factors that influence worker productivity are the importance of timber to tribes and their members and tribal business and forestry experience. Tribes for whom timber comprises only a small fraction of total income have relatively little incentive to harvest the optimal quantity, while tribes with little business or forestry experience may be incapable of harvesting the optimal quantity of timber. The positive influence of per capita tribal timber holdings on the harvest level demonstrates that tribal foresters do exert more effort when they can appropriate more of the benefits of their own productivity. Although a tribe's forestry experience appears unrelated to the quantity harvested, the significantly positive influence of employment in tribally owned businesses provides strong evidence that the productivity of Indian workers increases with the amount of general business experience possessed by tribes involved in 638 contracting. This finding constitutes a powerful argument in favor of pursuing economic development through tribally run businesses because it implies that there are positive spill-over effects of attaining business acumen. As tribes run enterprises, they will gain experience that will further increase their competitive advantage over the BIA.

The most important conclusion to be drawn from the preceding analysis is that replacing BIA agents with tribal members can significantly increase forest productivity. Figure 1 illustrates the potential for increasing productivity through 638 participation. Tribal members currently comprise an average of 20 percent of high-skilled labor and 40 percent of low-skilled labor inputs applied to a tribe's forest (represented on the graph by "0"), the remainder being BIA employees. The average tribe currently harvests approximately 12.5 million board feet of timber annually. Given the productivity difference that exists between similarly skilled tribal and BIA workers, Figure 1 illustrates the harvest levels that could be achieved with different proportions of BIA and tribal labor. It should be noted that these values are derived from extrapolation and are based on the assump-

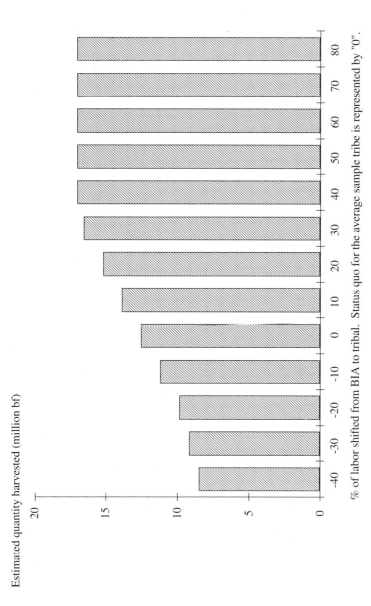

Estimated quantity harvested (million bf)

% of labor shifted from BIA to tribal. Status quo for the average sample tribe is represented by "0".

FIGURE 1. Shifting to Tribal Labor Can Double Output.

tion that the productivity gap is constant across the entire range of tribal involvement levels.[13]

As can be seen from Figure 1, shifting 10 percent of the forestry workforce from BIA to tribal control results in an increase in productivity of approximately 1.3 million board feet of timber for the average tribe in our sample of 75 forested tribes. This amounts to almost an 11 percent increase in output. Given that tribes currently receive an average of $45,570 per million board feet of timber, this means that shifting 10 percent of the workforce of the typical tribe from BIA to tribal control would bring in an additional $60,000 in revenue per year (even if increased tribal control does not allow the tribe to improve the prices it receives—see below). Assuming, for the sake of argument, that this relationship holds over the full range from the status quo to 100 percent tribal control (with quantity capped at the AAC level), 638 contracting could add as much as 40 percent to productivity and $200,000 to annual revenues for the typical forested tribe. Over all 75 tribes in this sample, this would mean additional annual revenues of roughly $15,000,000.

The analysis below indicates that increased tribal involvement leads to increased prices obtained for Indian timber. Therefore, the foregoing estimates of gains from tribal control are understated. Through greater 638 participation, tribes can realize higher prices as well as improved productivity.

ANALYSIS OF PRICE OBTAINED

In the preceding production analysis, the annual allowable cut served as a natural yardstick by which to gauge the performance of forestry workers. The AAC represented the minimum optimal harvest level for each forest and the labor productivity coefficients measured the contribution of each type of labor to the attainment of this optimum. A different yardstick is employed to assess labor performance with respect to timber marketing, namely the prices received for similar timber from contiguous national forests.

For each of the seventy-five Indian forests in our sample, there exists a nearby national forest administered by the United States Forest Service (USFS). Forest Service foresters, like their BIA counterparts, cannot keep any profits generated by the forests they manage. Therefore, with respect to motivation, national forests are organizationally analogous to Indian forests with no tribal involvement. These national forests hold constant the degree of owner involvement (at zero) and provide a base price yardstick against which shifting to tribal marketing under PL 638 may be evaluated on a tribe-by-tribe basis. Timber quality differences and divergent contract structuring methods preclude the making of qualitative judgments about the relative marketing performance of the BIA and USFS. Nonetheless, these differences are uniform throughout the United States so the nearby USFS base prices still permit intertribal comparisons of marketing success.

Using USFS timber prices as a base for comparison also effectively controls for the many region-specific and time-specific factors that can influence timber prices and are impossible to explicitly account for in any statistical analysis. If, for example, timber prices are depressed in a particular year in a particular region because of an economic recession in the region, this recession would be expected to affect both Indian and USFS forestry operations. Measuring Indian timber prices relative to USFS prices allows us to compare forestry performance across tribes even if there is (for example) a regional recession that impacts tribes differently. In fact, since we will be comparing concurrent prices from neighboring forests it is not even necessary to know what the region-specific and time-specific factors might be; they are effectively held constant by applying USFS revenue per species figures to the species bundle sold by the nearest Indian tribe.[14] Deviations from USFS prices serve as a proxy for relative management and marketing success.

The three primary determinants of a tribe's position relative to the base price index established by the USFS are: (1) Who markets the tribe's timber? (2) What are their incentives to obtain a high price? (3) How experienced are they?

The marketing of Indian timber is the province of high-skilled workers. The efforts of low-skilled workers are confined to maintenance of the forest's growing stock value. Timber sale administration consists of deciding what timber to sell and what market to target when advertising the sale to prospective buyers. Timber revenues are positively correlated with the efforts of high-skilled foresters because the market is fissured such that more effort on the part of the seller raises the prospects of finding buyers willing to pay top dollar. For example, in a well-documented case the BIA refused to support a move by the Quinault tribe in Washington to export timber. BIA agents were selling the tribe's timber for as little as $16 per thousand board feet while export prices for the same logs exceeded $1,000 per thousand board feet. When the Quinault Indians brought suit against the federal government for failing to fulfill its trust responsibility, the BIA responded by saying that seeking out more lucrative timber markets was not among the mandates of the trust responsibility to Indian tribes.[15] It is clear from this example that the efforts exerted by timber sale administrators can have a significant impact on stumpage prices obtained.

Due to the nature of Indian timber sale contract structures, harvest enforcement also plays a vital role in obtaining the highest possible stumpage prices. Harvest enforcement is important because Indian timber sale contracts frequently extend up to two years in duration, with the provision that the buyer will pay a per-species price that is only imperfectly indexed to prevailing timber prices at the time of harvest. Indian timber contracts adjust bid prices to fully reflect after-the-bid market price increases, and to reflect 50 percent of after-the-bid market price declines.[16] Because price declines are not fully absorbed by the seller, market downturns can eliminate the incentive to harvest.[17] When market prices fall, it becomes the task of high-skilled timber sale administrators to enforce contract provisions requiring that a certain quantity of timber be harvested by a predetermined date. Thus, in most situations, and especially in a declining market, the sale monitoring efforts of high-skilled workers can have a significant impact on stumpage prices received.

As in the quantity analysis, workers are separated in a statistical analysis into tribal and BIA so that the computer-generated coefficients on such labor measure the relative contributions of the two groups to the sale prices attained for Indian timber relative to nearby USFS timber. Three additional variables are included to capture possible motivational differences that distinguish tribal and BIA timber sale administrators. First, the quantity of timber per tribal employee is again employed to account for the importance of timber receipts to individual tribal members through tribally provided public goods and to the tribe as a whole as reflected in the individual's solicitude for fellow tribal members. Second, the reservation unemployment rate is again employed as an indicator of the importance to a tribe of current income (relative to delayed income from later harvests). The previous section suggested that high tribal unemployment might bias the resource extraction decision toward current harvests. If tribes experiencing high unemployment exhibit internal rates of time preference that exceed the market interest rate, tribes may harvest timber prematurely in a biological sense. Stumpage prices are an increasing function of log diameter; therefore, this propensity for tribes with high reservation unemployment to cut immature timber would depress stumpage prices.

The third factor that influences the motivation of Indian foresters to obtain high stumpage prices is the percentage of timber sold to the tribe and its members. This factor is included because tribes can set whatever price they like for timber that they sell to themselves, irrespective of market prices. In fact, Indian tribes often conduct referenda in order to secure tribal approval of artificially low timber prices on sales to tribally owned entities such as downstream milling operations.[18] This maneuver bolsters the apparent profits of tribal sawmills and safeguards employment therein. The proportion of timber sold to tribal entities should therefore have a negative influence on stumpage prices. Finally, the percentage of tribal employment accounted for by tribally owned businesses is again employed to control for the learning curve effects of prior tribal business experience.

RESULTS OF PRICE ANALYSIS

These variables were collected for the same sample of tribes analyzed in the section dealing with quantity harvested. Fifteen of the tribal observations were discarded from the price analysis because the only national forest within a reasonable distance did not sell the same types of timber as its Indian neighbor. In a few instances, national forest data existed only for classes of timber rather than individual species, e. g., cedar instead of western red cedar and Port-Orford cedar. In such cases, the aggregate national forest price was applied to all Indian timber species within that category. The region-specific and time-specific variables employed in the previous section are utilized in order to ensure that the USFS base price index does not miss any unidentified influences that are unique to Indian timber sales.

Table 2 reports the results of the multiple regression price analysis. The USFS base price is a good predictor of Indian timber prices and therefore serves as an effective control for unidentified aspects of the timber market

TABLE 2.
Determinants of Tribal Stumpage Prices

EXPLANATORY FACTOR	TIMBER PRICE INCREASE DUE TO A 10% INCREASE IN THE EXPLANATORY FACTOR (EFFECT COEFFICIENT)	PROBABILITY THAT EFFECT IS SIGNIFICANTLY DIFFERENT FROM 0
USFS Timber Price	5.2%	99.9%
BIA High-Skilled Labor	1.4%	85.4%
Tribal High-Skilled Labor	5.9%	96.2%
% of Timber Sold to Tribal Entities	-3.8%	99.1%
Tribal Unemployment	9.8%	99.9%
Per Capita Tribal Timber Holdings	1.7%	83.9%
Past Tribal Business Experience	17.2%	98.0%

Note: The predicted price increases associated with labor inputs are per additional worker. The model was estimated using generalized least squares jointly with the quantity equation presented in Table 1. Predicted effects of explanatory factors are for marginal increments to the means.

that might affect tribal stumpage prices. The effect coefficients of the workforce measures indicate that tribal control does a much better job of marketing timber. This result holds in spite of the fact that tribes often negotiate to sell timber to tribal entities at below market prices, as evidenced by the negative influence of sales to tribal entities on stumpage prices. The analysis indicates that adding an additional tribal 638 high-skilled worker adds 5.9 percent to the typical tribe's timber price, whereas the additional BIA-controlled high-skilled worker adds only 1.4 percent to price.

Both per capita tribal timber holdings and employment in tribally owned businesses are positively correlated with stumpage prices, thus attesting to the fact that both financial incentives and prior marketing experience are prerequisites to successful timber sale administration.

The one variable that behaves contrary to our predictions is tribal unemployment, which exhibits a significant positive effect on timber prices. As explained above, the tribal unemployment rate should be negatively correlated with stumpage prices if economic hardship promotes the harvest of premature timber. However, the positive coefficient is likely a result of the fact that the AAC was exceeded in only 24 percent of the tribal observations. What this statistic tells us is that even though high rates of internal time preference may have led tribes with high unemployment to cut more timber, this incentive probably brought them closer to the optimal harvest, rather than inducing them to exceed it. Another possibility is that tribal foresters who work on high-unemployment reservations place a higher value on their jobs than foresters who can easily find another job, and this fear of unemployment induces greater effort. The importance of 638 job creation to the sample tribes (whose average unemployment rate was 54 percent) is evidenced by the fact that most 638 contracting involves special forest development, the area which generates the most jobs per dollar of funding.[19]

The finding that high-skilled tribally controlled foresters do a better job of marketing tribal timber than BIA agents provides hard evidence to support anecdotal instances of BIA malfeasance like the Quinault case outlined earlier. In order to illustrate just how much tribally controlled foresters under PL 638 outperform BIA foresters vis-à-vis timber sale administration, Figure 2 transforms the effect coefficients from both the quantity and price analyses into dollars.

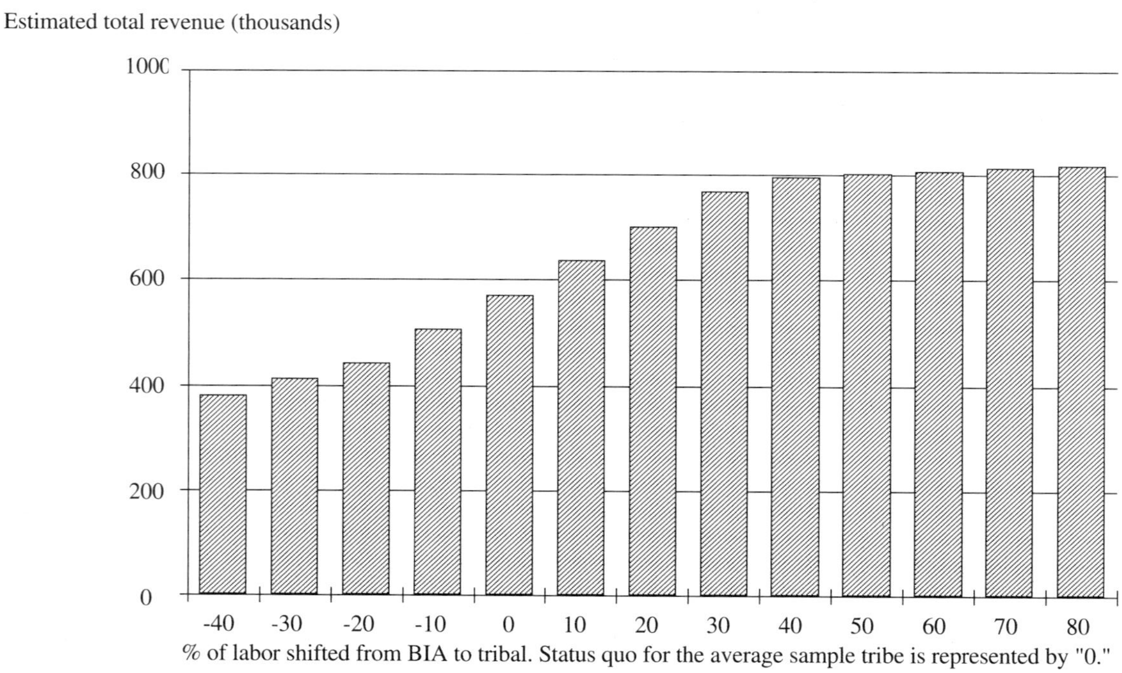
Estimated total revenue (thousands)
1000
800
600
400
200
0
-40
-30
-20
-10
0
10
20
30
40
50
60
70
80
% of labor shifted from BIA to tribal. Status quo for the average sample tribe is represented by "0."

FIGURE 2. Shifting Labor from All BIA to All Tribal Can Increase Total Revenue 115%

The statistical analysis contained in this paper provides strong evidence that tribal involvement leads to larger harvests and higher prices obtained. Therefore, Figure 2 represents the potential revenue increases realizable through 638 participation. The graph illustrates that shifting 10 percent of the typical tribe's workforce from BIA to tribal control potentially results in an increase in total forestry revenue of over $65,000 per year. Over all 75 tribes in the sample, this amounts to almost $5,000,000 per year. Moving from the current situation to 100 percent tribal control on all 75 sample reservations could conceivably mean an additional $18,750,000 per year in tribal timber revenues. The potential revenue difference between having 75 forests run entirely by the BIA and 75 tribally managed forestry operations could be as high as $33,000,000, or $440,000 per tribe. This much additional revenue could obviously help ameliorate some of the economic and social problems confronting Indian tribes today. However, demonstrating that tribes can manage their own resources is perhaps the most valuable benefit that accrues through 638 participation.

WHAT IS THE NEXT STEP?

The tribes who are best prepared to manage their own forests and who have the most to gain have not yet taken control from the BIA.[20] At the end of 1989, only eight tribes had complete control over the management of their forest resources. It behooves leaders throughout Indian Country to take a long, hard look at how the BIA manages their tribes' timber. Certainly, in some instances the BIA does a very good job; however, the quality of BIA management cannot be inferred from the size of the check sent to the tribe at the end of the year. In the absence of tribal involvement, the effects of poor BIA performance cannot be distinguished from the effects of uncontrollable market shocks. Therefore, to ensure that its timber is harvested in a timely fashion and sold at fair market value, every tribe needs to be involved to *some degree at least* in the management of its forest resources. This is not to say that 638 participation is a riskless opportunity to further tribal economic interests. On the contrary, the results of this paper indicate that some tribes are more suited to forest management than others: for example, those with prior business experience, and those for whom timber comprises an important part of tribal income. What is suggested is that all tribes, regardless of wealth or experience, enjoy a decided motivational advantage over BIA foresters who are paid flat salaries, regardless of how well they manage Indian forests.

With the termination effort still fresh in the minds of today's tribal leaders, the suggestion to push for tribal control of Indian forests will naturally be met with skepticism. Many tribes rely heavily on the fulfillment of the trust responsibility to provide needed services. But if the federal trust responsibility has come to signify undercutting Indian forests and selling tribal timber for a fraction of its value, then greater tribal involvement is the only recourse.

NOTES

1. This quote appears at the beginning of Michael Jensen and William Meckling's seminal work on the principal-agent problem, "Theory of the Firm: Managerial Behavior, Agency Costs and Ownership Structure," *Journal of Financial Economics* 3 (1976). A version of the principal-agent model is developed in this paper and receives more rigorous econometric treatment in a companion paper from which much of the analysis contained herein is drawn. See Matthew B. Krepps and Richard E. Caves, "Bureaucrats and Indians: Principal-Agent Relations and Efficient Management of Tribal Forest Resources," Department of Economics, Harvard University, September 1991.

2. United States Supreme Court, *Worcester v. Georgia,* 31 U. S. (6 Pet.) 515 (1832); *Cherokee Nation v. Georgia,* 30 U. S. (5 Pet.) 1 (1831).

3. United States Senate, Select Committee on Indian Affairs, Special Committee on Investigations, *The Federal Government's Relationship With American Indians: Natural Resources on Indian Lands,* Part 11, 101st Cong., 1st sess. (1989), p. 258.

4. Telephone interview with Derek Parks, BIA Office of 638 Administration, Washington, D.C., November 11, 1990.

5. For a lucid explanation of the factors affecting the resource extraction decision, see Forest L. Reinhardt, "Forest Products Firms and Their Timber Suppliers: Essays in Economic Organization and Behavior," Ph.D. dissertation, Harvard University, 1990, and David H. Jackson, "The Microeconomics of the Timber Industry" (1980).

6. In fact, this formulation is too simple, but it can be made more general once we recognize that the value of unharvested timber may also include aesthetic, cultural, religious, and/or recreational values that could compel a tribe to rationally forego harvesting.

7. Primary data sources for this analysis are U. S. Department of the Interior, Bureau of Indian Affairs, Department of Forestry, *Forestry Program Funding and Position Analysis* (Washington, DC: Government Printing Office, 1985, 1988, 1990); U. S. Bureau of the Census, 1980 Census of Population, vol. 2, *Subject Report: American Indians, Eskimos, and Aleuts on Identified Reservations and in the Historic Areas of Oklahoma (Excluding Urban Areas)* (Washington, DC:

Government Printing Office, 1986); and U. S. Department of the Interior, Bureau of Indian Affairs, Area Annual Reports, Branch of Forestry. For a detailed discussion of data sources, see Krepps and Caves, "Bureaucrats and Indians," op. cit.

8. For a discussion of the link between economic hardship and one's internal rate of time preference, see Emily C. Lawrance, "Poverty and the Rate of Time Preference: Evidence from Panel Data," *Journal of Political Economy* 99 (1991), p. 54. This link is also a basic tenet of Franco Modigliani's life-cycle consumption theory.

9. Derek Parks (see note 4 above).

10. The adjusted R-squared for the production function regression is .903, indicating that the variables included in the model account for all but 10 percent of the variance in tribal harvest levels.

11. Although not reported, the dummy variables did contribute to the explanatory power of the model. The region-specific dummy variables represent tribal forests located in the northwest Plains, north-central, East Coast, and Southwest regions of the United States; the Pacific Northwest is the omitted region. The time-specific dummy variables indicate tribal timber sold during 1984 and 1987; 1989 is the omitted year. The inclusion of year-specific variables is also necessary, because observations for a single tribe in different years would otherwise confer upon the model an undeservedly high degree of explanatory power. For a full discussion of the variables, see Krepps and Caves, "Bureaucrats and Indians," op. cit.

12. The correlation matrix of the data set indicates that the tribal unemployment rate is negatively correlated with tribal business experience and 638 participation. The unemployment rate was dropped from the model because it infected the model with multicollinearity and did not successfully control for time preference.

13. This assumption is supported by the random distribution of residuals from the multiple regression estimation.

14. In order to control for unidentified influences that affect only Indian timber sales, the region and time variables from the production analysis are again employed.

15. United States Senate, *The Federal Government's Relationship with American Indians,* op. cit., p. 258.

16. Interview with Kenneth Lathrop, BIA forester, Portland, January 3, 1991.

17. For a discussion of contract enforcement and the incentive to harvest, see Randal R. Rucker and Keith B. Leffler, "To Harvest or Not to Harvest? An Analysis of Cutting Behavior on Federal Timber Sale Contracts," *Review of Economics & Statistics* 70 (1988), p. 207.
18. Telephone interview with Larry Schmidt, BIA timber marketing expert, Phoenix, October 9, 1990.
19. Personal interview with Clifford Reed, manager, Branch of Natural Resources and Planning, Bureau of Indian Affairs, Portland, January 5, 1991.
20. See Krepps and Caves, "Bureaucrats and Indians," op. cit.

6

THE ECONOMICS OF BINGO: FACTORS INFLUENCING THE SUCCESS OF BINGO OPERATIONS ON AMERICAN INDIAN RESERVATIONS[1]

Eduardo E. Cordeiro

The fastest-growing industry in Indian Country in the last decade has been gaming. Large-scale gaming operations began to appear on Indian reservations in the late 1970s. In the 1980s, gaming skyrocketed, and while precise figures are elusive, by the early 1990s some estimates placed aggregate reservation gaming revenues in the billion-dollar range.

High-stakes bingo is a centerpiece of many tribal gaming operations. In this chapter, in order to learn what factors are most closely associated with successful bingo operations, Eduardo Cordeiro analyzes some of the only systematic data on gaming revenues available: bingo revenue figures from a 1987 Bureau of Indian Affairs survey. His key finding—that the most important factors are the size of the regional market and the extent of nearby competition—not only fits with what economists would expect, but almost certainly applies to other gaming activities as well.

INTRODUCTION

In recent years a significant number of American Indian tribes have taken up bingo and other forms of gaming as an economic development strategy. In 1987, the Bureau of Indian Affairs (BIA) estimated that the Indian bingo industry included 113 tribes, with total estimated gross revenues of approximately $225 million.[2] By 1991, according to the Indian Gaming Commission, more than 130 tribes were involved in some form of gaming in the United States, including 150 separate gaming operations,[3] while the *Los Angeles Times* reported that gross revenues were expected to reach $1 billion.[4]

Over the last decade or so, as gaming has spread and as non-Indians have flocked to reservations to play, some of these operations have had dramatic effects on Indian economies. By 1986, the Seminole Indians of Florida—who started using bingo to generate revenue in 1979—were running four separate bingo operations which grossed an estimated $45 million in one year alone.[5] As a result of the Seminoles' success with bingo, their reliance on federal funds dropped dramatically. The percentage of the tribal budget received from the federal government fell from 60 percent in 1977 to 20 percent in 1984.[6] In Minnesota, by 1984 the Shakopee Sioux were averaging 25,000 players per month and were able to pay off a $1 million debt on their bingo facility in only nine months of operation.[7] The Tulalip tribe of Washington State grossed $15 million in a single bingo operation in 1986, just a year and a half after its start-up.[8] In August of 1991, the Oneida tribe in Wisconsin claimed annual net earnings of $15 million from gambling operations.[9] The Lac du Flambeau band of Lake Superior Chippewa Indians in Wisconsin today uses revenues from the band's casino gambling operations to fund a substantial share of the tribe's programs and services.[10] Creek Indians in Oklahoma "use bingo proceeds to support a hospital, scholarships and a ranch,"[11] while the Sycuan band of Mission Indians near San Diego, California, uses gaming proceeds to fund housing, a fire department, health insurance, modest per capita payments for tribal members, and a tribal trust fund. The tribe is now investing in other businesses that will be less vulnerable to changes in the regulatory environment or competition from other gaming operations.[12]

While casino gambling is growing and other forms of gaming are increasing, the single most common gaming activity on Indian reservations is bingo. This is not bingo as it is widely known in the rest of the United States: games for very low stakes run by churches and other nonprofit organizations. As some of the above figures suggest, Indian bingo, while generically the same, is in another league, with jackpots often in the many thousands of dollars and annual tribal revenues from bingo operations in some cases running into the millions. Table 1 lists bingo revenues for Indian tribes reporting revenues to the BIA for 1986–87, the only year for which aggregate data are available. While this roster of tribes is incomplete and will have changed in subsequent years, as will revenues themselves, the table gives some idea of the sums involved.

As revenues have increased, bingo and other forms of gaming have become increasingly attractive to many tribes as keys to economic development, and the number of tribes involved has rapidly increased. Tribes facing otherwise discouraging economic prospects see in gaming revenues the means of supporting necessary social and governmental services, expanding education, and building economic infrastructure, while gaming operations themselves can employ tribal members.

On the other hand, as Table 1 shows, not all gaming operations are equally successful. Some are extraordinarily prosperous, others make little money, while still others have closed down, some within a short time of inception.

This fact and related aspects of Indian bingo operations raise some important questions. Which gaming operations are working, where, and why? Why is one tribe able to gross $10 million while another makes only $60,000 and others are forced to fold? Are Indians taking money away from their nonprofit competitors? Are gaming profits contributing to the socioeconomic development of the tribe? That is, are gaming revenues directly benefiting tribes—through health care, education, or capital investment—or are profits leaving the reservation and going into the pockets of non-Indian managers? Are Indians being exploited for their legal and regulatory status?

While these questions—and many others—are of substantial interest, the focus of this paper is on the business and economic aspects of bingo. The central question is, What factors appear to contribute to the success or failure of bingo operations?

The paper breaks these factors down into three categories. The first

TABLE 1.
Bingo Revenues for Reporting Tribes July 1986–June 1987
(by BIA Area Office)

TRIBE	LOCATION	REVENUE
Aberdeen Area Office		
Turtle Mountain	Belcourt, ND	$60,000
Flandreau	Flandreau, SD	$474,083
Yankton	Wagner, SD	$800,000
Sisseton	Watertown, SD	$2,648,000
Albuquerque Area Office		
San Juan Pueblo	San Juan Pueblo, NM	$100,000
Isleta Pueblo	Isleta, NM	$100,000
Sandia Pueblo	Bernalillo, NM	$1,000,000
Anadarko Area Office		
Iowa (Oklahoma)	Perkins, OK	$120,000
Kaw	Kaw City, OK	$226,428
Iowa (Kansas)	Hiawatha, KS	$365,000
Cheyenne-Arapaho	Watonga, OK	$376,000
Citizen Band Potawatomi	Shawnee, OK	$600,000
Otoe-Missouria	Red Rock, OK	$1,200,000
Billings Area Office		
Blackfeet	Browning, MT	$150,000
Northern Cheyenne	Lame Deer, MT	$189,381

Eastern Area Office

Pequot	Ledyard, CT	$10,000,000
Cherokee	Cherokee, NC	$10,000,000
Seminole	Brighton, FL	$5,000,000
	Big Cypress, FL	$10,000,000
	Hollywood, FL	$15,000,000
	Tampa, FL	$15,000,000

Minneapolis Area Office

Hannahville Community	Wilson, MI	$250,000
Stockbridge Munsee	Bowler, WI	$250,000
Red Cliff Band	Bayfield, WI	$250,000
Bad River	Odanah, WI	$250,000
Forest Potawatomie	Crandon, WI	$250,000
Bay Mills	Brimley, MI	$1,000,000
Wisconsin Winnebago	Tomah, WI	$1,000,000
Saginaw Chippewa	Mt. Pleasant, MI	$1,000,000
White Earth	White Earth, MN	$1,200,000
Grand Traverse Band	Suttons Bay, MI	$5,000,000
Lac Courte Oreilles	Hayward, WI	$5,000,000
Keweenaw Bay Community	Baraga, MI	$5,000,000
Leech Lake	Cass Lake, MN	$5,000,000
Menominee Indian Tribe	Keshena, WI	$5,000,000
Red Lake Band of Chippewa	Red Lake, MN	$5,000,000
Sault Saint Marie Tribe	Sault Saint Marie, MI	$5,000,000

Muskogee Area Office

United Keetowah	Tahlequah, OK	$100,000
Thlotpthlocco Creek	Clearview, OK	$125,276
Quapaw	Quapaw, OK	$240,000
Chickasaw	Sulphur, OK	$175,598
	Ada, OK	$635,592
Creek	Bristow, OK	$571,352
	Okmulgee, OK	$1,126,088
	Tulsa, OK	$15,802,123

Portland Area Office

Tulalip	Marysville, WA	$15,000,000

Sacramento Area Office

Bishop Tribe	Bishop, CA	$300,000
Hoopa Tribe	Hoopa, CA	$700,000
Robinson Rancheria	Nice, CA	$2,400,000
Barona Band	Lakeside, CA	$3,000,000
Santa Ynez	Santa Ynez, CA	$4,000,000
Santa Rosa Rancheria	Lemoore, CA	$5,300,000
Soboba Band	Hemet, CA	$11,000,000
Morongo Band	Banning, CA	$24,000,000

Source: Bureau of Indian Affairs, "Survey of Indian Bingo Activity,"
  July 1, 1987.

category comprises market variables: population density, income, and related factors which serve to create the supply and demand for a given good, in this case bingo and its payoffs to operators and players. The second category includes organizational factors that influence the type of bingo operation. How, organizationally, do tribes with bingo operations differ? The third category includes tribal capacity variables. These describe different tribes' capabilities in operating businesses, including bingo.

The paper's analytical strategy is to analyze the relationship between these variables and bingo revenues, employing regression analysis to identify key variables and their apparent consequences. The overall purpose is to provide Indian tribes with information useful in making decisions about bingo as a development strategy.

One important caution: good data on bingo or other gaming revenues are extremely difficult to obtain. Few tribes are willing to divulge gaming revenues, and no central source regularly compiles such information. The only significant data set currently available on gaming revenues nation-wide is the 1986-87 BIA survey, which compiled revenue data reported by fifty-four tribes with bingo operations (Table 1). That is the data used in this analysis. It has drawbacks. Not all tribes with bingo operations reported revenues; most of the figures have been variably rounded off; and the survey provides little additional information. While better aggregate data may be forthcoming, as of this writing these are the only data available.

GAMING ON INDIAN RESERVATIONS: AN OVERVIEW

The Oneida tribe of New York State opened what appears to have been the first Indian bingo operation in 1975. In 1979, the Seminole tribe of Florida, backed by a group of non-Indian investors, started the nation's first high-stakes bingo operation in Hollywood, Florida. Gaming has been flourishing in Indian Country ever since.

The primary factor behind the emergence of Indian bingo is tribal sovereignty. Generally speaking, the regulation of gambling in the United States is left up to the governments of individual states. They have the power to decide whether and what kinds of gambling will be permitted within state boundaries, and to regulate gaming operations, including everything from the days of operation to the number of people who can play and the size of the jackpots that can be won. Although in recent years legalized gambling—including lotteries, pari-mutuel betting on horses or dogs, some kinds of card games, and even casino operations—has increased dramatically in the United States, most states continue to forbid most forms of high-stakes gambling.[13] Most states in which bingo is legal limit the awards that can be given out from $100 to $250.

The distinct legal situation of Indian tribes, and in particular their sovereign status vis-à-vis the states, has allowed them to escape, for the most part, these regulations. Indian tribes retain substantial civil regulatory power on their reservations regardless of state law. This power, however, has not been uncontested. As tribes began to assert their sovereignty and initiate gaming operations in the 1970s and 1980s, state governments began to dispute tribal rights to regulate gaming within the reservation. A series of court cases followed, leading eventually to the 1987 United States Supreme Court decision in *State of California v. Cabazon*. Jerome Levine, an attorney specializing in this area of law, summarizes the trend in this series of cases:

> Those decisions analyzed whether a state's gaming laws were truly "criminal/prohibitory" in nature and thus potentially applicable to a tribe under various federal statutes that make some state criminal laws applicable in Indian country, or were merely "civil/ regulatory" and thus could not be imposed upon tribal lands. *Cabazon* summarized the test as holding that a tribe, as a separate government entity, is not bound by a state's gaming rules so long as no violation of the state's public policy is involved.[14]

What this meant, in effect, was that if a particular form of gambling was allowed by the state, tribes could offer that form of gambling within the reservation, free of state interference or regulation. If a state allowed bingo of any kind, a tribe in that state could undertake bingo operations and regulate the operation itself, setting its own schedules, jackpots, and other details.

In 1988, Congress took up the issue. Concerned about the possible influence of organized crime on Indian gaming and about the lack of established federal regulatory authority over gaming on Indian lands, Congress passed the Indian Gaming Regulatory Act (IGRA) in October of that year.[15] This legislation breaks reservation gaming down into three classes. Class I gaming refers to "social games solely for prizes of minimal value or traditional forms of Indian gaming engaged in by individuals as a part of, or in connection with, tribal ceremonies or celebrations." These activities are described as being "within the exclusive jurisdiction of the Indian tribes," and are unregulated by the act. Class II gaming refers to "the game of chance commonly known as bingo" and other, related, specified games. These remain within the jurisdiction of tribes, but are limited by state policy along the lines described by the Court in *Cabazon*. Class III gaming refers to "all forms of gaming that are not Class I gaming or Class II gaming." The legislation requires that a tribe wishing to engage in Class III gaming, which typically includes forms of gaming not at present allowed by the relevant state, enter into a negotiated compact with the state, laying out regulations governing the conduct of such gaming.[16]

Tribes thus retain substantial rights to regulate gaming, including bingo, on Indian lands. For example, a Florida tribe wishing to engage in a full casino operation, with blackjack, roulette, and poker—activities that are not legal in Florida—would require a negotiated compact with the state. However, bingo is legal and regulated by the state, and as a consequence, tribes can operate bingo games and regulate them themselves. Anyone can play bingo at the Seminole tribe's bingo parlor with the hope of winning anywhere from $50 to $2,000 per game, well above what a bingo game is allowed to offer elsewhere in Florida. While some of these winnings may seem trivial, Indian mega-jackpots can reach as high as $250,000 to $1 million.[17]

As a result of the regulatory haven found on the reservations, Indian tribes have realized a comparative advantage in bingo. They have found a niche in the market and have been able to capitalize on it. Given the potential for occasionally enormous winnings, players have flocked to many Indian gaming operations, producing sizeable—sometimes huge— revenues for Indian tribes.

Of course, sovereignty has given Indian tribes regulatory advantages in a number of areas other than gaming, but in some cases it has turned out to be a handicap in attracting private capital from outside the reservation. Development efforts that concentrate on large-scale, capital-intensive investments often accumulate large sunk costs. A tribe's sovereign control over reservation affairs and immunity from suit present investors with the added risk of *ex post* opportunism on the part of the tribe. *Ex post* opportunism describes a supplier's ability to take advantage of investors' sunk costs after the fact.[18] This, combined with the instability of many tribal governments, makes Indian reservations relatively risky places for outsiders to make nonsalvageable investments.

Bingo is less susceptible to this problem—and is therefore a relatively good investment opportunity—for two reasons. First, few sunk costs are involved in a bingo operation, reducing the risk to outside investors of *ex post* opportunism. Although some tribes have built new facilities, other bingo halls are literally converted warehouses. Even new facilities have few of the capital requirements of, say, a manufacturing plant. Indian bingo, then, is more attractive to non-Indian investors because it is less risky.

Furthermore, since bingo operations are not highly capital intensive, tribes often need not worry about attracting outside capital at all. These are development ventures that tribes can (and often do) take on by themselves. The capital investments can come later. The Shakopee Sioux in Minnesota grossed $2.5 million in just one year of operation and as a result were able to build a brand new 1,300-seat auditorium.[19]

The creation of a niche in the marketplace as a result of tribal sovereignty, combined with the noncapital-intensive nature of bingo operations and the potential for major revenues, has fueled the evolution of bingo as a prime development strategy on Indian reservations.

Although bingo has proven its economic value, certain issues continue to be of concern to the federal government and other constituencies, including tribes. Among these is exploitation. Most agreements between tribes and management groups give Indians at least 51 percent of gaming profits, but not much more. While tribes receive a majority of the receipts, in many cases they are paying a great deal of money for management services. In some cases, tribes have been completely dependent on outside managers to calculate revenues and profits, and have seen little of either one.[20]

Another concern is possible destructive competition with traditional bingo: churches and other nonprofit organizations have argued that Indian tribes cut into their proceeds with their more lucrative brand of bingo. In 1983, for example, charitable groups in Tucson, Arizona, argued that a Yaqui bingo operation had taken away a significant chunk of their business in its first three months of operation.[21] Such claims help to make high-stakes

Indian bingo a controversial issue.

A major concern for the federal government has been the role of organized crime in Indian gaming. Solid evidence of organized crime in the Indian bingo industry has been scarce, although rumors and reports have been common.[22] This was one of the issues that prompted Congress to pass the IGRA.

And finally, the move toward gaming as a development strategy has been controversial within tribes themselves, in part for the above reasons, and in part because of concerns over long-term effects on tribal societies and culture. Recently, a group of elders in the Lower Brulé Sioux tribe opposed the tribe's effort to start up casino gambling at Lower Brulé, in South Dakota, because the operation would displace an elders' nutrition center, and because of "the trouble and strife gambling will bring."[23] In 1989 and 1990, trouble and strife turned violent on the St. Regis Indian Reservation, portions of which lie in New York, Ontario, and Quebec, as Mohawk Indians split dramatically over the issue of gambling casinos on the reservation.[24]

Despite these concerns, Indian gaming today is well-established and is supported by a growing body of United States law and case precedent. Indeed, the IGRA explicitly recognizes the value to Indian tribes of gaming as an economic development strategy.

The remainder of this paper analyzes the impact of economic factors on the financial success of Indian bingo.

MODELING SUCCESS IN INDIAN BINGO OPERATIONS

This paper addresses the following issue: Why are some Indian bingo operations more successful than others? In evaluating this question we can employ a framework for analysis using applied microeconomic theory as well as tools developed in the study of industrial organization.

The analysis of the comparative success of Indian bingo operations involves examining the supply and demand for a particular good. In this case, the good at issue is high-stakes bingo. The supply of this good at present is limited. With relatively few exceptions, suppliers of the good are limited to American Indian tribes; they have a virtual monopoly over the market. But what are the elements that influence demand?

In the high-stakes bingo market, at least four main factors affect demand. One factor has to do with the number of potential buyers: How many people are available to purchase the good? The demand for a good is almost unequivocally increased as the population surrounding that good becomes more dense. For example, Indian bingo can be expected to be in greater demand if there are 500,000 people in a given radius of the operation than if there are only 100,000 people in the same radius. Very simply, this holds because a greater number of possible buyers would yield a larger number of actual buyers: people who show up to play the game.

A second factor that might influence the demand for Indian bingo is the amount of money that the people who live within a reasonable proximity of the reservation can afford to spend on the game. In most cases, the demand for a good will rise as people have more money to spend. Since bingo is not a necessity, one might predict that as people had more money to spend on luxuries, the demand for high-stakes bingo would rise.

The price elasticity of demand for bingo is a third element that might affect the revenues of a bingo operation. A good is relatively elastic if it has many substitutes. At a given price, the demand for a particular good will be lower if there are many similar goods in the market that can serve as substitutes. Although there are many forms of gambling in the United States, high-stakes bingo is essentially unique to Indian reservations. Competition, therefore, should be measured against other Indian bingo operations, and not against other forms of gambling or other forms of bingo.

Finally, in analyzing the demand for a good, one must account for the tastes of the consumers. This poses the question: "Given high-stakes bingo, will people be interested in playing?" This depends on people's propensity to play Indian bingo. The propensity to play bingo is a factor that may vary across different regions of the country.

Keeping in mind these four elements that contribute to demand, and the virtual monopoly Indian tribes have over supply, we can construct a model designed to determine those factors that influence the comparative success of Indian bingo operations.

DEFINING SUCCESS

Many indices can be used to measure the success of an Indian bingo operation. One may look at profits, sustainability, job-creation, or size of the operation. In the model introduced below, success is measured by the total revenue of the operation for the one-year period beginning July 1,1986 and ending June 30, 1987, as reported to the BIA (Table 1). This choice is a necessary one; while net revenues (or profits) might be a better indicator of success, such figures are not available for analysis.

In the introduction, I noted some of the weaknesses of this data. I should also note that the BIA survey was conducted through regional BIA offices. Its accuracy and completeness, therefore, depend to a significant degree on the relationships that BIA regional offices had at that time with tribes under their jurisdiction. For example, while six Indian bingo operations are known to operate in the Phoenix area, their revenues are unknown due, apparently, to poor BIA area office relations with the tribes. Conversely, strong tribal relationships with the Sacramento area office have provided a good deal of accurate data on bingo activity among California tribes.[25]

Notwithstanding better indicators of success, such as net revenues, the use of gross revenues is justified in that one would expect these revenues to be positively correlated with other estimators of success such as the size of the operation and increases in employment.

THE MODEL

The model employed here maintains that the gross revenues of bingo operations are dependent upon a series of exogenous variables, that is, upon a series of factors external to bingo operations themselves. These independent variables can be broken down into three categories: market variables, organizational variables, and tribal capacity variables. The regression equation breaks down in the following manner:

Total Revenues $= \alpha + \beta_1$(Market Variables) $+$
β_2(Organizational Variables) $+ \beta_3$(Capacity Variables)

where the alpha term is a constant.

The market variables are those economic factors that contribute to the demand for bingo. One market variable measures the density of the population surrounding the bingo operation. To determine population density, I calculated the numbers of people living within a twenty-five- and a fifty-mile radius of each bingo hall (**POP25** and **POP50**, respectively). To obtain these figures, I drew two circles on a map with the bingo location at the center, and radii of 25 and 50 miles, respectively. Any county whose borders fell within either radius was then included in the respective population figures. I obtained county populations from the Bureau of the Census *County and City Data Book 1988*.[26] While this method does not reveal the exact population within each radius, it at least more or less consistently approximates it across cases.

A second market variable measures the median household incomes of people living within a 25-mile radius (**MINC25**) and a 50-mile radius (**MINC50**) of the bingo operation. This variable assesses how much money people have to spend on bingo. Median household incomes are given in the *County and City Data Book 1988*, so I calculated incomes using the same methodology as I used to compute population figures, weighting the median incomes according to the population of the counties. By weighting these figures, one reduces the risk of misrepresenting the median income of a larger county.

The similarity between **POP25** and **POP50**, and **MINC25** and **MINC50** suggested that a problem of multicollinearity—a high association between two or more independent variables—might arise. A high degree of correlation between two variables can affect the coefficients of these variables, disguising the real effect of each on the dependent variable (bingo revenues). The results of a preliminary regression further suggested multicollinearity. The **POP50** variable proved to be positive and extremely statistically significant at the 99 percent level of confidence. However, the coefficient of **POP25** was negative and statistically insignificant. Similarly, the coefficient of the **MINC50** variable was negative and statistically significant, while the **MINC25** variable proved to be positive and not as significant. To test for multicollinearity, I ran a correlation between the two variables. The test yielded a correlation of 0.854 between the two population variables and a 0.885 correlation between the two median household income variables. Furthermore, I ran both variables separately in the regression equation to check if the difference would be explained by the multicollinearity. The result was that the signs of the **POP50** and the **MINC50** variables remained the same, but the sign of the **POP25** variable changed from negative to positive and became extremely significant. Similarly, the **MINC25** variable also changed signs, from positive to negative, though it still remained statistically insignificant.

Because both variables were essentially measuring the same thing, the regression needed to be run with only one. I chose to use **POP50** since it appears to be a more accurate estimation of the distance people are willing to travel to play bingo. People often travel twenty-five miles daily just in their commute to work. Given that high-stakes bingo is more of a sensational good, people would likely be willing to travel a greater distance to play. In addition, because Indian reservations are not always near large metropolises, and because the good caters mostly to people who live off the reservation, chartered buses often run to and from bingo sites. In one case, the Cherokee Indians of North Carolina attracted at least ninety-four buses one Saturday afternoon from as far away as Washington, D.C., Maryland, and Virginia.[27] Therefore, it seemed logical to use the **POP50** variable instead of **POP25**. Similarly, I kept the **MINC50** variable in place of **MINC25**.

A third possible market factor measures the distance to the nearest alternative high-stakes bingo operation (**DIST**). I use the **DIST** variable to gauge the amount of competition an Indian bingo operation faces. While data do not exist on bingo revenues for all tribes, the names and locations of all 113 tribes operating bingo halls at the time of the BIA survey are available. Therefore, using the same standard road atlas for determining the previous two market variables, it is possible to determine the distance to the nearest Indian bingo halls and to use this as a measure of the nearest competition.

Another economic variable that might affect the demand for high-stakes bingo is the tribe's population (**TPOP**). The tribal population is a useful indication of the tribe's labor force. In addition, many tribal members play the games. Therefore, larger tribal size would give a bingo operation a larger pool of possible players. Tribal populations are listed in the BIA survey of bingo activity, as well as in BIA tribal labor force estimates.[28]

Another variable (**STRTUP**) keeps track of how many months the bingo hall has been in operation. **STRTUP** reveals how much experience the management of the operation has had in running the bingo hall. Data for this variable come from the BIA survey on Indian bingo activity, which provides start-up dates for the operations.

Finally, I introduce the propensity to gamble in a given region of the country with the **PROP** variable. There is no easy or accurate way to measure the propensity to gamble of a region. I first tried to estimate this variable by deriving per capita gambling expenditures for each state. Since lotteries had been legalized in twenty-eight states at the time of the survey, this seemed a promising indicator of gambling activity. However, it turns out that most legal lotteries are in eastern states, while most Indian bingo operations are in the West and Midwest. In addition, where there is overlap, some states had only recently begun lotteries; their revenues were not yet known.

Instead, still relying on data from state lotteries, I created a dummy variable (**PROP**). The theory is that if a state has legalized lotteries, an overall greater propensity to gamble likely exists in that state. If the bingo operation exists in a state where lotteries are legal, it is coded "1." Conversely, if the operation exists in a state where lotteries are not legal, it is coded "0."

Unlike the market variables, organizational variables deal with policy matters that can be influenced by the tribe. The organizational variables describe the different kinds of bingo halls and the ways they are run. Among organizational factors, we might include the size of the halls, the schedule of operation (which ranges from one biweekly session to three sittings per day), and the type of management. Once again, such data are hard to come by. However, the BIA survey includes data on tribal versus nontribal management of bingo operations. I capture this in a dummy variable (**ORGN**), which is coded "1" for a tribally managed bingo operation and "0" for a nontribally managed operation.

Tribal capacity variables attempt to measure the ability of a tribe to operate a bingo hall. A good example of this sort of variable would be one that evaluates civil service stability: how well a specific tribe maintains tribal operations and business under changing conditions. Because some tribes lack the financial or human resources (training, skills, experience) to run efficient tribal bureaucracies, or because of turbulent political conflicts that upset tribal government transitions, many tribes experience difficulty maintaining smooth governmental operations. Such institutional instability often has detrimental impacts on tribal enterprises as bureaucratic personnel turn over and managerial personnel get discouraged and leave. Presumably a tribe with high civil service stability would be more capable of running successful bingo operations.

Unfortunately, few measures of such variables are readily available. The Economic Development Administration has surveyed the Indian tribes that they support, analyzing a number of capacity variables such as civil service stability, capital formation, and financial accounting capabilities.[29] However, there is only a small correlation between the tribes they surveyed and those that run bingo operations.

On the other hand, tribal unemployment figures may offer a proxy for certain tribal capacity variables. While the factors affecting tribal economic conditions are diverse and complex, and many are well outside tribal control, it is possible that unemployment rates indicate, among other things, the tribe's ability to sustain a positive business environment. I therefore created such a proxy variable (**SURATE**) that measures the percent of tribal members unemployed but seeking work, taken from the BIA's *Indian Service Population and Labor Force Estimates*.

These variables and their explanations are given in Table 2.

EXPECTED RESULTS

Before running regressions, we can estimate results—with varying degrees of certainty—in order to see how actual results compare to what one might expect on the basis of the theory alone.

Overall, I expected the market variables to be the most influential of the three categories in determining the success of an Indian bingo operation. This expectation is suggested by the microeconomic theory already discussed in this section; it also gained support from a discussion with the tribal attorney of the Seminole tribe, who argued that location was an essential element in the Seminoles' success.[30] Accordingly, I predicted that the effect of the population test would be both positive and large. The economics of supply and demand anticipate that as an area becomes more densely populated, there will be a greater number of people who will be interested in purchasing the good at issue. Similarly, I predicted that as the distance to the nearest competition increases, so should the revenues of the bingo operation. This follows from the fact that it should be easier to sell a good if there are fewer competitors in the market. I further expected that the variable measuring start-up dates would have a positive coefficient: as a tribe gathers more experience running a bingo operation, its revenues should go up. Additionally, time gives consumers the chance to learn about

TABLE 2.
List of Variables

Variable	Explanation
Independent:	
POP50	Population within a 50-mile radius[a]
MINC50	Median income within a 50-mile radius[a]
TPOP	Tribal population[b]
STRTUP	Number of months in operation[b]
DIST	Distance to nearest competing bingo operation[b]
PROP	Propensity to bingo
	States where lotteries are legalized = 1
	States where lotteries not legalized = 0
ORGN	Type of management[b]
	Tribally managed = 1
	Nontribally managed = 0
SURATE	Percent of tribe unemployed but seeking work[c]
Dependent:	
BREV	Tribal bingo revenues[b]

Sources: a. U. S. Bureau of the Census, *County and City Data Book 1988*
            b. Bureau of Indian Affairs, "Survey of Indian Bingo Activity," July 1, 1987
            c. Bureau of Indian Affairs, *Indian Service Population and Labor Force Estimates*,
            January 1989.

Indian bingo. Finally, I expected that the "propensity to bingo" variable would have a positive effect. States that have a propensity to gamble, as measured by their legalization of lotteries, should yield higher revenues for operators of gambling.

Problems arise in predicting the sign of the income variable. Although this variable is an important part of the model (one needs money to play bingo), it is not clear whether or not bingo can be considered a normal or an inferior good. To some degree bingo is normal, in that the more money one has to spend, the more bingo one is apt to play. Nevertheless, when one reaches a certain level of income, the nature of the game and its promise of instant wealth may lose their attraction. At this point, bingo may become an inferior good. Those with higher incomes may be less likely to purchase the good than those with lower incomes. Consequently, it is difficult to predict the sign of the coefficient of the income variable. (I expect that it will be positive up to a point, and then become negative.) Similarly, it is difficult to predict the magnitude of the variable's influence.

The organizational variable should play an important role in the model; many Indian tribes may lack the education and business experience to run a successful bingo operation. Those that suffer from this problem can make up for it by bringing in experienced outside management. While it is not easy to estimate how many tribes have sufficient human capital to run successful bingo operations, given that, overall, education and business experience on Indian reservations are relatively low, and that a "1" has been assigned to tribally managed bingo halls and a "0" to nontribally managed operations, one would expect the coefficient of this variable to be negative.

Finally, while the tribal capacity variables should play an important role in the analysis, they are extremely difficult to measure with available data. It is difficult to predict the sign of the coefficient of the tribal unemployment rates, which I am using as a proxy. On the one hand, this variable indicates the uncommitted labor resource that a tribe has available to employ in a business; a high unemployment rate would indicate that there are many tribal members who could be employed in the bingo operation. Following this theory, I would predict that the tribal unemployment rate would have a positive effect on bingo revenues. A more realistic way to think about this variable, however, may be that, for present purposes, it gauges a tribe's ability to successfully attract and manage business operations on the reservation. This, admittedly, is a speculative interpretation;

however, if it were the case, we would expect the unemployment rate to have a negative effect on the revenues of the operation. A higher unemployment rate would indicate that a tribe is less capable of managing businesses successfully and, therefore, would be less successful at running a bingo operation. Another reason for predicting a negative effect is that tribal members are themselves potential buyers of the good. If a large proportion are unemployed, fewer will be able to play.

REGRESSION RESULTS

The bar chart in Table 3 summarizes the results of the regression analysis graphically. Each bar represents the impact of a particular exogenous variable (population within the market area, distance to the nearest competition, etc.). One would expect that, given a specific change in the exogenous variable, a bingo operation's revenue would change by the size of the vertical bar for that variable. The key at the bottom of the table explains how much of a change in the exogenous variable is necessary to produce the indicated change in revenue, as well as with what degree of confidence one can predict this change.

Table 4 describes characteristics of the average Indian bingo marketplace.

The results of the regression analysis support at least some of the predictions stated in the previous section. The coefficient of the population variable (**POP50**) proved to be positive and extremely statistically significant at the 99 percent confidence level. This result supports the theory that the demand for a good will rise when there is a greater population density in the area surrounding it. The intuition is that if there are more people near the bingo hall, it is more likely that there will be people who will want to play. A problem facing many tribes is that they are in relatively out-of-the-way places. The coefficient of this variable is relatively small (2.89) with a t-statistic of 5.04. Each additional person within a 50-mile radius of a bingo site yielded an estimated increase of $2.89 in annual revenues for a bingo operation. Although the magnitude of the effect of this variable on gross revenues appears small, one must keep in mind that a third of the populations measured within this radius were in the millions of people. The mean of **POP50** was 1,147,840 with a standard deviation of 1,389,780, and

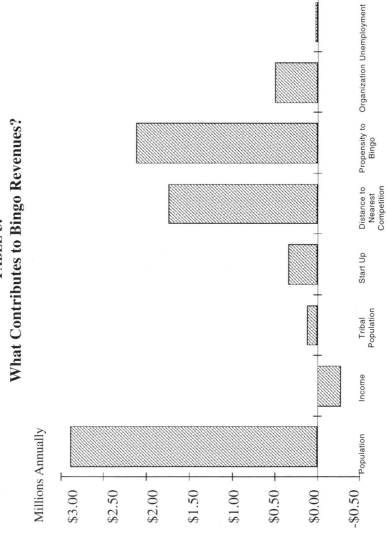

TABLE 3.
What Contributes to Bingo Revenues?

KEY

POPULATION: Each additional 1,000,000 people within the operator's market area (i.e. within 50 miles) adds $2.89 million of revenue (with 99% confidence).

MEDIAN INCOME: Each additional $1,000 in median household income within the operator's market area reduces revenues by $276,676 (but with only 54% confidence).

TRIBAL POPULATION: Each additional 1,000 tribal members increases revenues by $119,202 (with 85% confidence).

START UP: Each additional 10 months of experience adds $334,960 in bingo revenues (with 75% confidence).

DISTANCE: Each additional 100 miles distance from the nearest competing bingo operation adds $1,738,000 of revenue (with 87% confidence).

PROPENSITY: If an operation is located in a state where lotteries are legal, it adds $2,121,180 of revenue (with 86% confidence).

ORGANIZATION: If an organization is tribally managed, it adds $500,475 of revenue (but with only 28% confidence).

"SEEKING" UNEMP. RATE: Each additional 1% of unemployment increases revenues by $29,468 (but with only 67% confidence).

TABLE 4.
Characteristics of the Average Indian Bingo Marketplace

	Average	Range
Population ('88)	1,147,840	45,700–6,639,200
Median Income ('88)	$15,097	$11,472–$19,900
Tribal Population ('86–'87)	5,702	177–25,386
Months of Operation ('86–'87)	42	4–90
Nearest Competitor	54 miles	6.3–235.7 miles
Propensity (State Lottery in '88)	32%	N/A
Tribally Controlled ('86–'87)	68%	N/A
"Seeking" Unemployment Rate ('89)	36%	7%–81%

the observations ranged from 45,700 to a high of 6,369,200. The population variable, then, accounts for a difference of over $18.3 million between counties with the least and the greatest populations.[31]

The tribal population (**TPOP**), the distance to the nearest competition (**DIST**), and the propensity to bingo (**PROP**) all proved to have an effect on total revenues with some statistical significance. The fact that the tribal population coefficient is positive reveals that a larger tribe should expect to make more money running a high-stakes bingo operation than a smaller one. Specifically, a tribe with one more tribal member yielded an estimated $119.20 of additional annual bingo revenues at the 85 percent confidence level.

Why this theory should hold is not obvious, since one does not need many tribal members to run a bingo operation. One possible explanation is that tribal members themselves are playing the games. However, both income and accumulated wealth are very low on Indian reservations, and it seems unlikely that tribal-member playing would significantly boost revenues. A second possible explanation is that tribes can sustain larger populations because they are good economic developers. In other words, size may reflect tribal capacity to some degree. But neither of these, nor any other explanation, is clear from the data.

The coefficient of the competition variable (**DIST**) was also positive and very large, but it too was only somewhat statistically significant (it could only be estimated at the 87 percent confidence level). A tribe should anticipate that with each additional mile that it distances itself from other competing forms of high-stakes bingo, it can expect to take in an estimated $17,380 in revenues each year. This supports the idea that a good will be in higher demand if there are fewer substitutes. The fact that this variable could only be predicted at the 87 percent confidence level might be due to the method of measurement: the distances were measured not in road miles but in straight-line miles from one point on the map to another. If more accurate data were available, it might be possible to predict the influence of competition on Indian bingo with more certainty. Still, it is important to note that the sign of the coefficient is consistent with the economic theory detailed above, and its magnitude was relatively large.

Similarly, the propensity to bingo coefficient (**PROP**) was found to be positive and somewhat statistically significant, being estimated at the 86 percent confidence level. This dummy variable accounted for those bingo operations that were located in states that had legalized state lotteries. The regression result predicts that people will be more likely to play high-stakes bingo in a state where gambling is officially sanctioned. The logic is that states that have passed laws legalizing lotteries have a larger propensity to gamble than those states that had not passed such laws; furthermore, that those states with a greater propensity to gamble are also more likely to play Indian bingo. The coefficient of this variable was also very large. In fact, a tribe should expect to earn an estimated $2,121,180 more each year in bingo revenues in a state where lotteries are legal.

The start-up date of the operation (**STRTUP**) also seems to have some effect on total revenues. The coefficient was very large, but was only statistically significant at the 75 percent confidence level. A bingo operation with one additional month of experience should expect to make an estimated $33,496 in additional bingo revenues per year. I offer three possible explanations for this result. First, over time, management gains experience that is useful in bingo operations: kinks in the business get ironed out and the operation runs more efficiently with lower operational and managerial costs. Second, over time, word about bingo spreads, the number of players increases, and the business grows. Finally, the limitations of the data provide another explanation for this result. The data set includes only tribes that are generating revenues. Tribes that started bingo operations but eventually closed them down are not included. Since business failure rates are highest in the earliest years of operation, it is more likely that an older operation will be a successful one.

The income variable (**MINC50**) was found to be statistically insignificant. The t-statistic was –0.75 and it was only significant at the 54 percent level. While I did not attempt to predict its sign in the previous section, the coefficient is negative. This implies that as the median income of the area surrounding the bingo operation goes up, the tribe should expect to lose bingo revenues. This supports the argument that bingo might be an inferior good and is consistent with evidence that bingo (and noncasino gambling in general) is played by less affluent members of society. Note, however, the low level of confidence with which this was estimated.

Given these results, I introduced another variable to the "market" equation to try to shed light on the "inferior good" theory. The *County and City Data Book* provides information on how many people have incomes below the poverty level in each county. Weighting these percentages for population, I created a "weighted percent below poverty level" variable (**WPBP50**). The intent of this variable was to see if bingo prospers in less affluent regions. Adding this exogenous variable to the regression left the signs and the statistical significance of the variables effectively unchanged. The coefficient of the **WPBP50** variable was negative. However, it proved to be statistically insignificant. While little can be learned from this variable because of its statistical insignificance, the signs indicate that the income level that is most conducive to bingo revenues might be between the median household income and the poverty level.

The results of the organizational variable (**ORGN**) proved statistically insignificant in the analysis. The coefficient of this dummy variable was positive and large, predicting that a tribally managed operation will yield greater profits than a nontribally managed operation. However, these results were very weak, being predicted with only 29 percent confidence. The sign of this variable is the opposite of what I expected.

The other nonmarket variable measured the proportion of the tribe that was unemployed but seeking work (**SURATE**). The idea was that a high unemployment rate might suggest that a tribe had difficulty sustaining businesses, and therefore would do less well with a bingo operation. Although the sign of the coefficient was positive (the opposite of what I expected) and the coefficient was large, it was only statistically significant at the 67 percent confidence level.

ALTERNATIVE ANALYSES

Although the results of the foregoing analysis shed some light on the issue of comparative success among Indian bingo operations, there are still some notable problems. The primary one is the lack of sufficient quantitative data, not only on Indian bingo but on reservation economic development generally.

Of course, quantitative analysis is not the only method of examining the economics of Indian bingo, nor is it necessarily the best. The real world does not always adhere to theoretical models. In their models economists often cite the *ceteris paribus* assumption, which holds all factors not in the model constant: Other things equal, here's what we expect will happen. We know, however, that many factors can affect the market for Indian bingo, and many of these vary across reservations. In trying to account for these, I introduced the nonmarket categories of variables. I had hoped that data unexplained by market variables could be explained by organizational and capacity variables. While I still believe this to be the case, these variables turned out to be impossible to measure with available resources. Riddled with the same data problems that can affect any economic analysis of Native American economic activity, they left me unable to provide quantitative proof that nonmarket variables have an impact on the Indian bingo industry.

With adequate time and other resources, however, one could carry out the kind of research that might solve some of these problems. Here I summarize a few of the things that field-based or other nonquantitative, comparative research might pursue.

The organizational variable (**ORGN**) presented in the model, for example, was a dummy variable that differentiated between tribally managed bingo operations and nontribally managed operations. It is very broad and measures only one aspect of organization. While it distinguishes between different types of management, it does not detect possible differences between these types of management. Two tribally managed bingo operations might still be organized differently from each other. Everything from playing schedules and monetary awards to management techniques may vary. Aggregate data measuring such differences are not readily available.

The Big Cypress bingo hall in Big Cypress, Florida, and the Hollywood bingo hall in Hollywood, Florida, provide an example of two nontribally managed bingo halls that, according to the **ORGN** variable, are the same, but that are actually quite different. As of 1989, the Big Cypress hall had a seating capacity of over 5,000, while the Hollywood hall had a capacity of only 1,200. In addition to the resulting differences in the layout of the floor, the Big Cypress hall ran on a schedule of only one day-long sitting every other week, whereas the Hollywood hall operated three sittings a day, seven days a week. Although the data set represented these two halls as being both nontribally operated (essentially the same in their organization), there were, in fact, important organizational differences that separated the two. This variable proved to be statistically insignificant. A more detailed examination of other organizational factors might well produce significant results.

An even more influential nonmarket variable might be tribal capacity. While the political and social conditions of the tribe surely have some influence on the success of a bingo operation, this category of variables proved equally difficult to measure quantitatively. However, it should be possible to obtain, through tribal enterprise histories and the examination of current business operations, estimates of various tribes' abilities to operate successful tribal enterprises. We know, for example, that some tribes do a very good job of operating such enterprises while others do not.[32] Such data would have to be gathered on a tribe-by-tribe basis and might be difficult to obtain, but as a measure of tribal capacity would probably do a far better job of predicting bingo success than the variables used here.

Another nonmarket variable I was unable to measure that might prove important is the relationship between the tribal government and the management of the bingo operation. Many tribal governments have a history of actively intervening in the day-to-day management of tribal economic enterprises. While tribally owned enterprises obviously are ultimately the responsibility of the tribal government, in many cases political considerations severely undermine good business decision-making and managerial efficiency. Cornell and Kalt argue that the critical point is to separate strategic decision-making, which is properly the task of tribal government, from day-to-day business management, which is properly the task of enterprise managers.[33]

The prosperous bingo operations of the Seminole tribe offer an example of this separation. When the Seminoles moved into high-stakes bingo as a development strategy, Chairman James Billie, realizing that the tribe had accumulated neither the financial nor the human capital sufficient to run a successful bingo operation, concluded that the tribe needed to hire an outside management group. Importantly, in the ten years that the group has managed the bingo operation in Hollywood, neither the tribal chairman nor the tribal council has interfered in management decisions. While some council members have disapproved of certain management decisions, the tribal chairman has held his ground. His philosophy is that the management group was hired to do the job because they knew how to do it best; therefore, they should be allowed to handle day-to-day management of the operation without interference. As long as they remain within the strategic vision set by the council and the chairman and meet overall tribal objectives for the operation, they are largely left alone.[34]

Of course, bingo management covers tricky ground. The history of criminal involvement in gambling operations throughout the United States underscores the importance of good management and adequate oversight. Tribal governments can be so distant from gaming operations that they lose complete track of what is going on. Nonetheless, bingo operations are vulnerable to the same sorts of political interference that undermine other potentially productive economic enterprises, both in Indian Country and elsewhere. Better measures of such government-management relations might help explain the differences in bingo revenues within the sample, but again, they would require different research techniques from those employed in this paper.

CONCLUSIONS

Notwithstanding the difficulty of gathering data on Indian bingo and the existence of extraneous factors that influence bingo revenues, the foregoing analysis suggests several conclusions about the Indian bingo industry. As predicted both by the model and by common sense, market variables proved to be critical factors in determining the success of high-stakes bingo operations. The regression results reveal that the population density of the area surrounding the bingo hall is positive and extremely statistically significant. This appears to be the key variable in the analysis. The results indicate further that the tribal population, the distance to the nearest bingo competitor, and the regional propensity to bingo are also important in determining bingo revenues. Organizational and tribal capacity variables, *as measured here*, have less effect on bingo revenues. More adequate measures of these factors are needed.

The analysis suggests the following. Tribes considering bingo should pay close attention to their own location. Three factors are of primary importance. First, the location should be in an area of relatively high population density. Otherwise, the tribe may end up catering only to the bingo interests of its members, bringing little new income into the tribe. Second, the tribe should be aware of its competition. In regions of the country where there are many Indian reservations, there exists substantial potential competition in high-stakes bingo. The fact that one tribe is running a successful operation does not guarantee that a neighboring or nearby tribe will also profit from bingo; indeed, the analysis suggests the opposite. Third, a tribe that is located in a region that has a higher propensity to gamble may have a better chance of success. Although the propensity to gamble is difficult to measure, the data indicate that those tribes located in states where lotteries are legal display higher bingo revenues.

While tribal population appears to have some effect on bingo revenues, with larger tribes to some degree having greater success, why this is so is not clear, and a tribe may wish to ignore this finding.

The other variables measured were less significant in explaining bingo revenues. There is qualitative evidence, on the other hand, that organizational and capacity variables are important. In particular, it appears that the relationship a tribal government has with bingo management—Indian or non-Indian—can affect success. Exactly how these variables might affect revenues will have to await further research.

Finally, one might ask what relevance this analysis of bingo has for other forms of gaming emerging on Indian reservations, such as casino gambling. While extrapolating from these results to other forms of gaming is risky, there is little reason to believe that those variables that proved most significant in this analysis—market population, competition, and propensity to gamble—would not be significant determinants of success in other gaming operations.

NOTES

1. I would like to thank James T. Hamilton, Ken Hirsh, and the editors of this volume for their assistance and advice.
2. Bureau of Indian Affairs, "Survey of Indian Bingo Activity," Washington, D.C., July 1, 1987.
3. Informal estimate via telephone interview, October 1991.
4. Paul Lieberman, "Lady Luck Turns on Indians," *Los Angeles Times*, October 6, 1991, p. A1.
5. Compiled from Bureau of Indian Affairs, "Survey of Indian Bingo Activity."
6. James McGregor, "High Stakes Bingo Games Flourishing on Reservation." *Las Vegas Review Journal*, November 4, 1984, p. 16E.
7. Ibid.
8. Bureau of Indian Affairs, "Survey of Indian Bingo Activity."
9. "Oneida bingo nets $15 million a year; opens new blackjack tables on Labor Day," *Yakima Nation Review*, September 6, 1991, p. 9.
10. Jerome L. Levine, "More on State Public Policy under the Indian Gaming Regulatory Act: The Lac du Flambeau Decision," *Indian Gaming*, July 1991, p. 16.
11. Lieberman, "Lady Luck Turns on Indians," op cit.
12. Paul Lieberman, "Sycuan Tribe Hits Jackpot with Gambling Operation," *Los Angeles Times*, October 8, 1991, p. A1, A8, A9.
13. For a brief, journalistic overview, see Dirk Johnson, "Gambling's Spread: Gold Rush or Fool's Gold?" *New York Times*, National Edition, October 6, 1991, p. A1, A17. A more detailed but more dated overview is Vicki Abt, James F. Smith, Eugene Martin Christiansen, *The Business of Risk: Commercial Gambling in Mainstream America* (Lawrence: University of Kansas Press, 1985).
14. Jerome L. Levine, "An Update On: Indian Gaming Litigation Developments," *Indian Gaming*, December 1990, p. 4.
15. Public Law 100–497 (1988).
16. See Sections 4 and 11 of the IGRA.
17. McGregor, "High Stakes Bingo Games . . . ," p. 16E.
18. Oliver Williamson offers a detailed explanation of the problems associated with *ex post* opportunism and sunk costs, and the use of hostages to deter opportunistic suppliers. See Oliver E. Williamson,

"Credible Commitments: Using Hostages to Support Exchange," *The American Economic Review* 73, no. 4 (September 1983).

19. Kurt Andersen, "Indian War Cry: Bingo," *Time*, January 2, 1984, p. 58.

20. See, for example, Lieberman, "Sycuan Tribe Hits Jackpot . . . ," op. cit.

21. William E. Schmidt, "Bingo Boom Brings Tribes Profit and Conflict," *New York Times*, March 29, 1983, p. A1; and see, more generally, Art Harris, "Bingo Madness!" *Washington Post*, May 26, 1985, p. G1.

22. See, for example, Bill McAllister, "Mafia Skimming Indian Bingo, Witness Testifies," *Washington Post*, February 9, 1989, p. A3; also Paul Lieberman, "S.D. Tribe's Gambling Business was Mafia Target," *Los Angeles Times*, October 7, 1991, pp. A1, A18, A19, which describes unsuccessful efforts by organized crime to control gaming on the Rincon Reservation in San Diego County, and updates earlier cases; also the summary round-up on "Indian Gambling in California," *Los Angeles Times*, October 8, 1991, p. A8..

23. Avis Little Eagle, "Elders oppose Lower Brulé casino," *Lakota Times*, September 18, 1991, p. A1.

24. Rick Hornung, "One Nation Under the Gun: Inside the Mohawk Civil War," *Village Voice*, May 15, 1990, pp. 22–33.

25. Telephone conversation with Joel Starr, assistant to the Assistant Secretary of the Interior for Indian Affairs, March 1989.

26. U. S. Bureau of the Census, *County and City Data Book 1988* (Washington, DC: Government Printing Office, 1988).

27. Harris, "Bingo Madness," op. cit.

28. Bureau of Indian Affairs, "Indian Service Population and Labor Force Estimates." Washington, D.C., January 1989.

29. Economic Development Administration, "Summary of SSI Indian Grantee Profiles and EDIM's (Matrices)," U. S. Department of Commerce, no date.

30. Interview with Jim Shore, attorney for the Seminole tribe, January 1989.

31. I derived this figure by taking the difference between the counties with the greatest and the least populations and multiplying them by the coefficient of the POP50 variable: $(6,369,200 - 45,700)$ x $2.84 = 18,274,915$.

32. See, for example, Stephen Cornell and Joseph P. Kalt, "Pathways from Poverty: Economic Development and Institution-Building on Ameri-

can Indian Reservations," *American Indian Culture and Research Journal* 14, no. 1 (1990).

33. Ibid., p. 113.
34. This account is based on my interview with tribal counsel Jim Shore, January 1989.

7

THE IMPACT OF WELFARE REFORM IN INDIAN COUNTRY: THE FAMILY SUPPORT ACT OF 1988 AND THE ROSEBUD RESERVATION[1]

Margaret Barnwell Hargreaves and Hedy Nai-Lin Chang

The reservation Indian population today is proportionately among the most welfare-dependent in the United States. In the face of widespread poverty, programs such as Bureau of Indian Affairs-General Assistance and Aid to Families with Dependent Children provide much of the economic foundation of contemporary reservation communities.

In 1988, in an attempt to reduce welfare dependency generally in the United States, Congress passed an ambitious piece of reform legislation called the Family Support Act. One of the primary goals of the Act was to assist families in moving from welfare dependency to self-support through a variety of incentives and employment and training programs..

The Council of Energy Resource Tribes asked the Harvard Project to carry out an analysis of the impact of this legislation in Indian Country. This chapter is a revised version of the 1989 report that Margaret Hargreaves and Hedy Chang wrote in response to that request. The centerpiece of their analysis is an extensive case study of welfare on the Rosebud Sioux Reservation in South Dakota, supplemented with a brief comparative look at the Gila River Reservation in Arizona. Their major finding is that the Family Support Act of 1988 is unlikely to do very much to help reservation families become self-supporting. They make specific recommendations as to how the Rosebud Sioux and other tribes can best respond to the requirements of the Act.

I. INTRODUCTION

Recent welfare reform legislation, known as the Family Support Act of 1988 (PL100-485), represents one of the most significant federal attempts in the last fifty years to reduce dependency on the federal program known as Aid to Families with Dependent Children (AFDC). The new legislation intends to help welfare recipients make the transition from welfare to permanent jobs that provide enough pay to support their families. Implemented under the authority of the United States Department of Health and Human Services (HHS), the reform encourages (1) the improvement of state child support enforcement services, (2) the expansion of AFDC to include unemployed two-parent families, (3) greater transitional child care and Medicaid benefits to individuals who work their way off of welfare, and (4) states and tribes to offer improved employment and training programs through the Jobs Opportunities and Basic Skills (JOBS) Program.

As it stands, however, the Family Support Act will not help many families in Indian Country become self-sufficient. The reform legislation contains the following flaws with respect to its application to Indian Country:

1. Although tribal governments are essential to the development and implementation of policies that effectively reduce welfare dependency, this reform hinders their participation by largely ignoring the civil and legal jurisdiction of tribes over Indian lands.

2. While the reform addresses some of the issues that prevent individuals from leaving welfare, it neglects the primary barriers on many reservations, such as lack of jobs and transportation.

3. By dividing the responsibility for implementing reform between states and tribes, the legislation demands extremely complex coordination between historically hostile governments often inexperienced in working closely together.

4. The tribal JOBS program will probably have minimal effect because of the relatively low level of funding authorized by the reform and the inadequate length of time allotted for program planning.

Tribal government officials who understand the ramifications of the Family Support Act can respond more effectively to the reform and better recognize what further steps are needed to resolve problems of welfare dependency. Based on a case study of the Rosebud Sioux Reservation in South Dakota, this paper illustrates how a tribal government can evaluate welfare reform legislation. In this paper we (1) analyze Rosebud's present welfare system, (2) investigate the difficulties that AFDC recipients currently face when they try to leave welfare, (3) critique how the Family Support Act addresses existing problems, and (4) recommend how the Rosebud tribal government can respond to specific reform provisions. Finally, through a brief comparison with the situation on the Gila River Reservation in Arizona, we assess the broader implications of our Rosebud findings.

Making welfare reform more sensitive to conditions in Indian Country requires an array of tribal government actions. While the unique circumstances of some tribes will dictate reservation-specific responses, certain issues have widespread impact across Indian Country and require unified action among tribal governments. For example, the following actions, which could improve JOBS program provisions, probably could be most effectively pursued via intertribal organizations and multi-tribal campaigns:

1. Lobby the Secretary of the Department of Health and Human Services to establish a reasonable, nonarbitrary set of guidelines that govern the designation of areas as too remote for the administration of state JOBS services.

2. Demand that states furnish equal levels of support services for state and tribal JOBS program participants.

3. Encourage HHS to give reservation-specific waivers for JOBS program requirements.

4. Encourage HHS to develop appropriate performance measures for tribal programs which look at their short-term and long-term effects on individuals as well as community benefits.

5. Lobby the federal government to reduce funding restrictions which inhibit tribes from combining services provided through

employment and training programs such as JTPA, TWEP, Bureau of Indian Affairs (BIA) Employment Assistance, and JOBS.

Even after taking actions such as these, tribal governments will need to address issues beyond the scope of the Family Support Act in order to solve the problems of welfare dependency in Indian Country.

II. A CASE STUDY OF THE ROSEBUD SIOUX RESERVATION

Home to approximately 17,000 enrolled members[2] of the Rosebud Sioux tribe, the Rosebud Reservation is located in a rural area of south-central South Dakota. Until a United States Supreme Court decision greatly reduced its size in 1977, the reservation included nearly one million acres and covered four counties: Mellette, Tripp, Todd, and Gregory. The Court's decision presented the tribe with a difficult situation. While the Court held that the reservation included Todd County alone, the tribe continues to exercise jurisdiction over Sioux communities within the old boundaries.

There are twenty Sioux communities within the pre-1977 reservation boundaries, ranging widely in size and often in other characteristics. In Todd County, the major towns are Antelope, Mission, Parmalee, Rosebud, which is the seat of the tribal government, and St. Francis.[3] The 80 to 85 percent of enrolled members who live in Todd County comprise 79 percent of that county's population.[4]

The Rosebud population differs from the general United States population in several respects. Rosebud residents have a relatively young median age of approximately 19 years, compared to the United States figure of 30. More than 50 percent of those living on Rosebud are less than 20, versus 31.9 percent of the United States population. Only 6.5 percent of the population is over the age of 60.[5]

Relatively few children on Rosebud grow up in two-parent families. Only 46 percent of persons under age 18 live with both their parents. In comparison, the percent of children living in a single-parent home was roughly 20 percent for the nation as a whole in 1985.[6] Moreover, Rosebud children tend to grow up in relatively larger households. In 1987, the average size of Todd County households was 3.8 persons versus 2.6 for the state of South Dakota.[7] This statistic conforms to national findings that American Indian peoples have a greater propensity to form family households than whites.[8]

Educational attainment among Rosebud residents is comparable to that in other impoverished areas of the United States, such as inner-city ghettos, and is somewhat lower than that for the nation as a whole. The secondary educational system on the Rosebud consists of two high schools, the Todd County high school in Mission and a tribally operated high school in St. Francis. Approximately 50 percent of the population over 25 years of age has graduated from high school. Of the persons 16 to 19 years of age at Rosebud, 32.6 percent were neither enrolled in school nor high school graduates in 1980.[9]

Rosebud represents an extreme of national poverty. According to a United Methodist Church study, Todd County was the seventh poorest county in the United States in 1986. In comparison to its neighboring tribes, however, Rosebud's economic situation does not appear unique. Eight of nine South Dakotan American Indian reservations were included within the 25 poorest counties in the country in that year.[10] All are isolated in rural areas.

Although South Dakota claims to have an unemployment rate of only 4.6 percent, the Rosebud rate appears to be far higher.[11] The actual level is difficult to assess. Whereas BIA statistics claim a 1989 Rosebud unemployment rate of 90 percent,[12] the Census Bureau cites 13.9 percent for Todd County in 1982. The disparity between these two figures stems from differences in the definition of the unemployed. The BIA figure is based on the number of nondisabled Indians of working age without a job. Because it does not distinguish those who are seeking work from those who choose not to work, such as some housewives, it overestimates unemployment. The Census Bureau, on the other hand, by only taking into account those who qualify as actively seeking work by applying to area Job Service offices, overlooks discouraged workers or individuals unable to find transportation to these area offices, and thereby underestimates unemployment.

According to the 1980 census, the annual median income for Rosebud residents was $4,518 for men and $3,621 for women, as compared to $9,750 and $4,009 for the South Dakota population as a whole. Inclusion of transfer incomes (welfare, etc.) somewhat raises the level of available income. A 1986 study of sources of nonwage income on the Rosebud Reservation indicates that the combination of land rental, BIA General Assistance, AFDC, and food stamps programs provides, on average, almost $2,000 of each family's annual income.[13]

Like other Indian reservation economies, the Rosebud economy includes an informal sector, an "invisible network of self-employed individuals and families who produce goods and provide services for the benefit of the community."[14] A 1988 study of the neighboring Pine Ridge Sioux Reservation found that households participating in informal economic activities realized a median income of $4,425 from such activities.[15] For those Rosebud households involved in the informal economy—which doesn't include all of them—the figure is probably similar.

THE CURRENT ROSEBUD WELFARE SYSTEM

The impact of federal welfare reform needs to be assessed within the context of the current welfare system. Since AFDC is only one of several income transfer programs, a tribe must evaluate how changes within AFDC affect other programs as well as the AFDC recipients. Furthermore, how welfare reform is received on the reservation depends on how clients currently perceive existing programs.

In addition to BIA General Assistance (BIA-GA) and Aid to Families with Dependent Children (known as ADC in South Dakota), the social welfare programs available to eligible Rosebud Sioux include Social Security, Supplemental Security Income, commodity foods, food stamps, Housing and Urban Development (HUD) programs, and veterans' benefits. ADC and BIA-GA are, however, the largest cash assistance programs in terms of the number of people served and total funds brought on to the reservation. Although an individual cannot simultaneously be eligible for both ADC and BIA-GA, he or she can concurrently receive benefits through other programs such as food stamps, the Commodities program, and HUD housing assistance. Combined, ADC and BIA-GA served at least one-third of all tribal members in 1986.[16]

BUREAU OF INDIAN AFFAIRS-GENERAL ASSISTANCE

BIA-GA provides subsistence level aid to low-income tribal members.[17] The BIA considers General Assistance a program of last resort to be used only when individuals fail to qualify for any other forms of public assistance. Consequently, the extent of BIA-GA programs depends largely on the availability of state assistance for Indians. Theoretically, if state programs exist that provide benefits to all needy Indians on the reservation, the BIA does not furnish General Assistance. Although the BIA traditionally has administered BIA-GA itself, some tribes have used contracting options under Public Law 93-638 to take over program operation.

Because programs such as state General Assistance or Aid to Families with Dependent Children with an Unemployed Parent (AFDC-UP) do not exist in South Dakota, the BIA provides and administers General Assistance on the Rosebud Reservation. Eligibility is extended to enrolled members of the Rosebud Sioux tribe living within the larger former boundaries of the reservation, or to Indians of other tribes residing within Rosebud's current boundaries.

In 1986, total benefits equaled nearly $2 million and the program involved 1509 cases comprising approximately 3,800 individuals. Of the total cases, 59 percent were adults without children; of the cases with children, 84.6 percent were two-parent families. Falling between the ages of 18 and 49, 85.6 percent of all adults served were of working age. A single dependent adult qualified for $57 of GA per month; families of four received on average $300.73 per month. BIA benefits are tied by federal law to the level of ADC benefits. BIA-GA does not appear to be received continuously as only 23 percent received assistance for 11 or 12 months in 1986. However, 66 percent of all cases have been in sporadic contact with the program for six or more years.

One mandatory requirement for BIA-GA is enrollment in Rosebud's Tribal Work Experience Program (TWEP). New BIA-GA recipients must report to the TWEP office for placement in community service projects or in public or nonprofit agencies. If a slot is available, then a participant works 40 hours per week and receives a monthly stipend of $55. At present, funding levels limit the number of program slots to 115. In order to give more tribal members an opportunity to work, in 1988 the BIA limited the length of time that recipients could be in the program to a maximum of two years.[18]

AID TO FAMILIES WITH DEPENDENT CHILDREN

AFDC, a federally mandated program of cash aid to low-income families with children, exists in every state. States play a significant role in determining the program's level of benefits, income cut-offs, and whether two-parent households with an unemployed primary wage earner are eligible. Because AFDC is a matching grant program and funding levels depend upon the willingness of states to allocate their own monies, aid levels can significantly vary between states. For example, in Arizona in 1988 the maximum monthly benefits were $293 for a three-person family, or 38.8 percent of the poverty line, while in South Dakota the same family would have received $366 per month, bringing them to 48 percent of the poverty line.[19]

Our data on the ADC program (South Dakota's version of AFDC) is based on information collected from the Todd County area. In 1986, ADC provided approximately $1.2 million of assistance to a total of 1829 individuals in the county: 506 adults and 1323 children.[20] Seventy-one percent of the total aid went to single-parent families. The average number of children served under ADC was 2.0 per case as compared to the 2.5 per case covered by BIA-GA. In 1986, the average payment for a parent with two children was $357 per month.

CLIENT PERCEPTIONS OF THE WELFARE SYSTEM

The success or failure of a "back-to-work" welfare program, such as the JOBS program initiated under the Family Support Act of 1988, depends in large part on how clients feel about the existing system. Client perceptions of the system evolve from the history of income maintenance programs and are influenced by current program practices.

Rosebud income maintenance programs can be traced back to the Fort Laramie Treaty of 1868 between the United States government and various Sioux Indian tribes. The treaty was designed to induce Sioux warriors to cease recurrent hostilities and agree to live within reservation boundaries. Among other things, it provided certain kinds of assistance to the Sioux:

> And it is hereby expressly stipulated that each Indian over the age of four years, who shall be removed to and settled permanently

upon said reservation and complies with the stipulations of the treaty, shall be entitled to receive from the United States for the period of four years after he had settled upon said reservation, one pound of meat and one pound of flour per day provided the Indians cannot provide their own means of subsistence at an earlier date.[21]

Federal provisions were expanded by an 1876 treaty that stipulated the continuance of 1868 annuities for as long as the need existed:

Also to provide the said Indians with subsistence consisting of a ration for each individual of a pound of beef . . . Such rations, or so much thereof as may be necessary, shall be continued until the Indians are able to support themselves.

Treaty benefits were even expanded to include employment assistance:

The government will aid such Indians as far as possible in finding a market for their surplus productions, and in finding employment and will purchase such surplus as far as may be required for supplying food to those Indians, parties to this agreement who are unable to sustain themselves: and will also employ Indians as far as practicable, in the performance of government work on their reservation.[22]

Although some families may not approve of welfare, many Rosebud Sioux apparently feel little negative stigma in the receipt of public assistance, since federal provision of welfare benefits can be construed as a fulfillment of treaty obligations. Failure of the federal government to provide enough benefits to ensure at least a basic standard of living on the reservation is widely considered unjust. According to a 1985 survey, a majority of Rosebud residents believe that their living conditions would improve if the federal government upheld its treaty agreements.[23]

Recipients also may perceive any welfare programs that encourage them to leave the Rosebud Reservation as breaching treaty agreements. Our interviews with Rosebud residents revealed a high level of resentment against past assimilationist policies, such as BIA relocation programs, which encouraged—some say pressured—25 to 30 percent of the Rosebud Sioux to leave the reservation for educational and vocational opportunities in urban areas.[24] Unless offered viable on-reservation employment or training options, many Rosebud recipients may be reluctant to enter a program just for the sake of getting off welfare. Implementation of welfare reform has to take these historical perspectives into account. It also has to consider the influence of current practices upon client perceptions. The current welfare system on Rosebud has fallen into the trap shared by nearly all welfare programs: although welfare is intended to help people through difficult periods, the need to limit benefits to the truly needy results in elaborate measures to control fraud and abuse.

Getting onto welfare can be a frustrating and confusing process. In order to qualify for ADC benefits, Rosebud Sioux must often travel long distances to apply in person at the Todd County Department of Social Services (DSS) office, complete a twenty-eight-page application, provide substantial amounts of documentation, and typically wait thirty to forty-five days before receiving their first check. Because in Todd County the DSS office relies on the BIA to provide benefits in the interim, clients are shuttled between the two programs. Once on ADC, a client must provide monthly verification of his or her income and dependent status. Clients with children over six years of age are required to sign up for the county's Work Incentive (WIN) program,[25] though few actually participate, due to the small number of available slots.

The intrusive nature of the process in South Dakota is exemplified by its requirement that home visits be completed within ninety days of submitting an application. Home visits can occur unannounced and include verifying the address, substantiating the absence of the father by checking for men's clothing and asking neighbors about his whereabouts, and assessing the value of home assets.[26] Because clients apparently do not usually overtly protest this procedure, caseworkers seem to feel home visits are not an issue.[27] Our interviews with clients suggest, however, that home visits are considered demeaning and that silence stems from the fear of losing benefits. Such practices engender distrust between welfare clients and caseworkers. In the case of the Rosebud Reservation, this situation is even further exacerbated by cultural misunderstandings and underlying racial tensions.

Consequently, when implementing programs intended to encourage recipients to take advantage of opportunities to leave welfare, administrators must be sensitive to the caseworker-client relationship. For example, separating the provision of employment services, such as the JOBS program, from the frustrating and often demeaning process of eligibility determination may help to increase client receptivity and cooperation.

OBSTACLES TO SELF-SUFFICIENCY FOR AFDC RECIPIENTS

Surprisingly, leaving welfare can be an extremely difficult process, even for the many recipients who want to become self-sufficient. Understanding the difficulties such people encounter can provide tribal governments with a basis for assessing the effectiveness of welfare reform.

In late January of 1989, we began an investigation of existing hurdles during a one-week visit to Rosebud. At that time, and in subsequent conversations, we spoke with individuals involved in all aspects of the BIA-GA and ADC system, including current and former recipients of BIA-GA and ADC, clients who were denied benefits, individuals never on public assistance, and officials from the BIA, Indian Health Service (IHS), Todd County Department of Social Services, Tribal Government, Sinte Gleska College, the St. Francis Mission, Dakota Plains Legal Services, Tribal Work Experience Program (TWEP), and tribal Job-Training Partnership Act (JTPA) Program. We also analyzed available statistical information relevant to this issue.

In this section we describe our findings. We divide them into five categories of obstacles to leaving welfare: (1) few local employment opportunities, (2) inadequate transportation and child care, (3) disabling health problems, (4) limited training opportunities, and (5) work disincentives. We consider the lack of jobs and of transportation to be the most crucial issues, although any one of these may be enough to make an individual recipient feel overwhelmed.

1. FEW LOCAL FORMAL EMPLOYMENT OPPORTUNITIES

The number of formal sector jobs available for reservation residents is astonishingly low. According to a Sinte Gleska College survey of jobs, in Todd County as a whole in 1985 there were a total of only 1,406 full-time and 181 part-time positions. Two hundred and fourteen of these positions were in private businesses, while the other 1,192 positions were in the public sector.[28] Thirty-four percent of the public sector full-time positions were managerial or professional positions, while the remainder were para-professional, clerical, or common laborer jobs. Only 8.8 percent of the private full-time positions were managerial or professional in nature.

Barring some major change in the Todd County economy, this small number of jobs leaves most of Rosebud's potential labor force without any hope of local employment. As of January 1989, the labor force of Rosebud Indian residents alone was 7,241 people, more than four-and-a-half times the number of positions in 1985.[29] This lack of jobs was the first explanation most people gave us for the reservation's high level of welfare dependency.

Given the job situation, leaving the reservation becomes one of the only available options. In fact, the Armed Services provide one of the few employment opportunities for young people. Unfortunately, those who return to the reservation from the military still have difficulty locating any jobs, much less jobs in the fields in which they received training. And while leaving the reservation may seem, to an outsider, the most reasonable response to extreme economic conditions, it is the response least favored by the Sioux we talked to for whom kinship relations and historically and culturally rooted attachments to their homeland are profoundly important.

Finding a job appears to be even more difficult for men than for women. As of 1980, American Indian women were more likely to hold managerial or professional positions than American Indian men and to be employed in sales, technical, administrative support, and service occupations.[30] This pattern seems to prevail on Rosebud, where the majority of jobs are positions traditionally filled by females, such as health workers, clerical staff, and teachers. Of the reservation's employment opportunities, 21.9 percent are in public administration, while service occupations comprise another 24.1 percent.

For the individual who wants to stay on the reservation, reliance upon welfare may be virtually his or her only means of survival.

2. INADEQUATE TRANSPORTATION AND CHILD CARE

Finding a job is only a first step in the process of becoming gainfully employed. Keeping a job involves being able to get to work on time every day as well as finding someone to care for children on a consistent full-time basis. Unfortunately, accessible, affordable, reliable forms of transportation and child care are in extremely limited supply on the Rosebud reservation.

Transportation. Transportation represents a serious problem for Indians living on Rosebud. Distances are substantial. Travelling between communities and centers of even minimal economic activity often involves covering more than thirty to forty miles of small, winding country roads, made more dangerous by the severe weather conditions of Northern Plains winters. Since the few jobs that exist tend to be concentrated in the communities of Rosebud and Mission, people who live in any other community must travel significant distances to conduct business or get to work.[31] If a resident has a car, it is typically an older model that consumes large quantities of gas and tends to break down frequently.[32] The many residents who do not possess a functioning vehicle are forced to resort to hitchhiking, walking, or paying exorbitant rates if they cannot catch a ride from a friend.[33] If they do not travel during times when people are driving to or from work, hitchhikers must spend even more time waiting for rides. Minimal public transportation exists through Sinte Gleska College and a van run by the tribal government. Unfortunately, neither of these institutions has adequate resources to run reservation transportation systems; their services go to only a few communities, run infrequently, and are often overcrowded.

The lack of reliable transportation has significant consequences for individuals attempting to leave welfare through employment. It means that they sometimes may not be able to get to work on time, if at all. Even if they have their own car, the costs of transportation may outweigh the monetary benefits of a job. For example, one of our interviewees commuted approximately one hundred miles round trip each day in order to work in the nearest off-reservation town as a cashier for $3.40 per hour. She eventually quit, in large part because most of her income was spent on transportation.

Child Care. If the recipient is on ADC, she (and sometimes he) is by definition a single parent and cannot work or go to school unless child care is provided at least part-time. Organized child care on Rosebud currently consists of ten to twelve Head Start programs and a small day-care center started in December 1988 at the Catholic Mission in St. Francis. Although Head Start programs are sometimes considered a form of child care, in actuality they do not serve this purpose. Because Head Start's programs are only half-day, they do not accommodate the needs of parents who require full-time care. Also, they only serve a preschool population and have long waiting lists.

St. Francis Mission's child care program, run by three Indian women JTPA participants in the On-the-Job-Training program, serves about twelve children, ages one through twelve, is open from 8 A.M. to 5 P.M., and in early 1989 was considering extending hours into the evenings. The daily fee per child is five dollars, not a small sum if a parent has two or more children and earns minimum wage.[34] Father Tillman of the Mission notes that some parents may find this fee too expensive and may not be aware of several kinds of child care subsidies available in the form of tax credits, college stipends, AFDC child care allowances, and job training program allowances.

Although the St. Francis program currently does not meet state licensing requirements, it intends to become a licensed facility in order to qualify for subsidized nutrition programs. Licensing of organized facilities on Rosebud is currently not required, because the tribe maintains civil jurisdiction over the reservation, and tribal licensing ordinances have yet to be developed.

Informal options exist but they can be difficult to find and, because they are not licensed, quality cannot be assured. The extended family acts as a major source of informal child care. However, relatives are not always available, particularly if they are female relatives who work or are engaged in employment and training programs. Babysitters are also a possibility, but it can be difficult to find a reliable caretaker given the high level of alcoholism and substance abuse on the reservation, and again, as with transportation, the cost can consume a large portion of already low wages. Leaving children alone at home under the care of an older sibling, on the other hand, has been used as grounds for charges of child neglect on the part of the Todd County Department of Social Services. In any of these situations, parents can be left without child care if the caretaker gets sick.

When combined with the lack of reliable transportation, child care becomes even more difficult to arrange. If child care arrangements are not located near home or work, they may be completely inaccessible. Even those who find a conveniently located caretaker may not be able to use his or her services because without reliable transportation they are unable to predict when they will return home.

Some parents may be reluctant to work outside the home because of the lack of viable child care options. When Kelly Jones, the Rosebud Tribal Business Manager, attempted to interest women in working in a new doll factory, one group responded by gathering their children in his office. They said they would work if he would be responsible for watching their children.[35]

3. HEALTH PROBLEMS

As is the case on many other reservations, inadequate health care and poor nutrition have led to numerous health problems on Rosebud. Moreover, for many ADC recipients, alcoholism and drug abuse present major barriers to self-sufficiency. Substance abuse problems can interfere with job stability or performance even for those who manage to get a job. Tribal officials estimate that over 60 percent of the adult reservation population experiences problems with alcohol or drug abuse.[36] As anthropologist Elizabeth Grobsmith explains:

> Although unemployment does not by itself cause alcoholism, the mixing of the two ingredients creates a deadly combination— deadly because once one has gotten caught up in the cycle of not having a job and drinking, the two elements work together to perpetuate each other.[37]

Substance abuse creates problems for the addicted individual and others in the community. Such abuse increases the risk of other diseases, raises the incidence of accidental or violence-related injury, and reduces the individual's capacity to work. The behavior of addicted individuals can adversely affect the psychological and social well-being of family and friends. The entire community suffers if employers discriminate against Indian people because they assume that all Indians are alcoholics.

A significant number of people on Rosebud are seeking ways to overcome substance abuse problems. Rosebud currently has a chemical dependency unit at the St. Francis Mission and two tribal programs at the Little Hoop Lodge, one for youths and a transitional/residential program for adults. Including community education, outpatient care, after-care,[38] and other types of services to families and individuals, tribal programs serve roughly 500 people.[39] Those individuals with family circumstances that make on-reservation treatment infeasible have access to off-reservation residential programs. The Indian Health Service covers the cost of substance abuse programs. Nonetheless, people can have difficulty getting help since treatment programs often have long waiting lists and the tribe is having trouble finding enough trained counselors.

4. LIMITED ON-RESERVATION TRAINING OPPORTUNITIES

Training, which we broadly define as activities that improve employment skills, serves both personal and tribal functions. It can: (1) enable recipients to fill existing job openings, (2) prepare them for upcoming employment opportunities, (3) provide recipients with the skills to start their own businesses, and (4) allow the tribe to develop a more qualified workforce that could attract potential employers. Welfare recipients on Rosebud have difficulty getting jobs because they have limited access to both formal and informal types of training. We define formal training as skills gained in the classroom and informal training as skills gained through work experience.

Formal Training. Because adult ADC recipients have children, most who need formal training are limited to on-reservation programs. For them, Sinte Gleska College, the local tribal college, represents their primary opportunity. Sinte Gleska was the first accredited tribal college in the United States, and its presence has significantly expanded reservation educational opportunities.

Located in Mission, Sinte Gleska College currently enrolls approximately 525 students, 60 percent female. The college has experienced some difficulty attracting male students, because the four-year degree programs are for traditionally female-dominated occupations. Primary areas of study include Graduate Equivalency Diploma (GED) preparatory classes; an associate degree in business education composed of clerical, accounting, and bookkeeping courses; and two B.A. programs in human services and education. Rosebud residents lack access to most types of training not offered by the college.

For welfare recipients trying to get an education at Sinte Gleska, completing a degree can be extremely difficult. They must overcome a variety of obstacles simply to get to school: They have to find reliable transportation even in poor weather conditions, locate suitable child care, and find the energy and time to do homework while managing a household. Under such circumstances, many recipients may not be able to complete their courses. If an individual is placed on academic suspension from the college, financial aid is cut off until the individual personally pays for and successfully completes one semester of full-time coursework. Given their lack of financial resources, this is unlikely for most welfare recipients.

Informal Training. Whether a recipient is hired or starts his or her own business, he or she needs skills that are typically gained from work experience. Such skills include knowing about the rights and obligations of employees and employers, learning how to manage credit, and being able to effectively resolve conflicts in the workplace. For people who have relied upon public assistance for prolonged periods of time, have little work experience, and have minimal contact with people who are employed, attaining these skills can be a problem. Such people may not have had the opportunity to learn these skills themselves and may not have friends or relatives to whom they can turn for advice. In fact, interviews suggest that peers may ridicule or resent individuals who appear different because they work or go to school.

Individuals who want to start their own businesses have an even greater difficulty gaining appropriate experience or advice. There are few models or sources of local expertise because of the reservation's extremely small private sector. Public sector experience is not necessarily an appropriate substitute. Whereas profits are the primary motive for private sector operations, the actions of government agencies are guided by the mission of providing services through the administration of public funds. Would-be entrepreneurs have few opportunities to learn.

5. Work Disincentives

The current welfare system creates financial disincentives for recipients to take low-paying jobs or start their own businesses. As soon as an individual begins working, he or she risks losing many of the cash and in-kind benefits received while on welfare. On Rosebud, the largest disincentives seem to be (a) the potential loss of cash benefits, (b) the failure to distinguish between personal and business assets, (c) the reduction in HUD housing subsidies, and (d) the decrease in food stamps.

Loss of Cash Benefits. Earnings reduce cash benefits. Each month ADC recipients must report any income received through a job or self-employment. Because eligibility is based on the previous month's income, occasional or seasonal variation in monthly income is not taken into account. For the first four months that the recipient earns any income, $30 plus one-third of the remainder is "disregarded" in the determination of eligibility. For the next eight months, only $30 is disregarded and after a year, all income is counted. Unless income rises at a rate which more than off-sets the gradually increasing loss of ADC benefits, the recipient loses growing portions of the financial benefit of working.

Business versus Personal Assets. Since AFDC regulations do not differentiate personal from business assets, they inhibit the accumulation of business assets. Countable assets are limited to $1,000 with the exclusion of $1,500 worth of household items such as a vehicle, clothes, and furniture.

> [This] asset limit in combination with other regulations does not allow individuals to purchase equipment for their businesses, maintain inventory and supplies or carry an operating balance to cover operating expenses for future inventory or purchases.[40]

An example: Suppose a female welfare recipient receives a check for the leasing of her land on the reservation.[41] The check is enough to purchase a sewing machine and supplies to start producing star quilts. The woman must declare the receipt of the check to her welfare caseworker, who will add a prorated amount[42] to the level of income used in the calculation of her monthly benefits. The resulting deduction in welfare benefits may mean that she realizes no material benefit from the check. She may decide that she does not have enough money to start her quilting project.

Now suppose this woman manages, nonetheless, to start a business, and sells a quilt for $200. Although she wants to reinvest the sale proceeds for more quilt materials, welfare regulations would allow her to retain only $30 plus an additional $56.60. Such a moderate sum probably would not allow her to repurchase enough materials and pay other costs so as to stay in business and improve her family's well-being.

Reduction in Housing Subsidies. If a welfare recipient acquires a job, he or she generally will pay more for the same housing unit. Most of Rosebud's population lives in the 914 homes (715 rental units and 199 home-ownership units) available through the HUD housing authority. Since the stock of private housing is extremely limited, most have no other option than to live in HUD units. HUD rent is set at 30 percent of household income, which includes nearly all forms of transfer payments and wages with the exception of JTPA training program benefits and food stamps.[43] Because of the relatively high maximum income cut-off, welfare recipients who find work rarely, if ever, lose HUD eligibility.[44] But an individual who gets a job that pays more than his or her previous AFDC benefits loses 30 percent of the increase in income to HUD.

Decreases in Food Stamps. The impact of earned income on the level of food stamps is significant for two reasons. First, most ADC recipients receive food stamps. Second, the cost of food is relatively high on Rosebud. In 1986, an estimated 3,619 individuals living in Todd County received a total of $1,466,313 in food stamps for an average monthly benefit of $33.76 per person. Of the 817 cases, nearly half were also receiving ADC.[45]

Because the Food Stamps program, authorized by the Food Stamp Act of 1977, is based on national guidelines, its benefit levels do not vary with differences in local prices. Our recent informal survey comparing the prices of fifteen food items at major stores in Mission (located on Rosebud), Valentine, Nebraska (one of the nearest off-reservation towns), and Sioux Falls, South Dakota (a large metropolitan area), found that the same grocery items in Mission cost 7 percent more than in Valentine and 18 percent more than in Sioux Falls. A second survey suggests that stores in small, isolated reservation communities, such as Cedar Butte, not only lack certain goods such as fresh fruits and vegetables but also may be charging as much as 19 percent more than stores in Mission (see Appendix B). Consequently, families are extremely sensitive to food stamp decreases.

In order to be eligible for the Food Stamps program, total household income cannot exceed a certain monthly maximum.[46] Until that maximum, every three dollars of additional income causes a one-dollar reduction in food stamps. Since income is counted on a household basis, the income earned by a son or daughter reduces the family's food stamps. During our interviews, we heard of a case where an individual rejected an opportunity to participate in a summer jobs program for youth because his wages would reduce his family's food stamps.

Food stamp disincentives may not, however, be as severe as in nonreservation communities, because many reservation residents can rely upon the Commodities program as a buffer.[47] Unlike the Food Stamps program that uses a cash voucher system, the Commodities program distributes a bundle of food goods including beans, rice, flour, canned meats, and vegetables. As long as an individual falls under the gross income cutoff, he or she receives the same amount of goods. According to South Dakota state director Carol Axtman, the Commodities program has been maintained on reservations because many Indians do not have access to low-cost grocery stores. Unfortunately, the high starch content and limited variety of the foods received make commodity goods less desirable than food stamps. Although a family unit cannot simultaneously qualify for both programs, some families are known to alternate between them.

III. AN EVALUATION OF FEDERAL WELFARE REFORM ON THE ROSEBUD RESERVATION

The Family Support Act of 1988 attempts to increase financial self-sufficiency among AFDC recipients by (1) improving state child support enforcement services, (2) expanding state AFDC programs to include unemployed two-parent families, (3) offering greater transitional child care and Medicaid benefits to individuals who work their way off of welfare, and (4) upgrading state and tribal employment and training programs through Jobs Opportunities and Basic Skills (JOBS) Programs. After describing each major welfare reform provision, we will critique how well each provision meets existing needs and recommend what actions the Rosebud Sioux tribe can take to make welfare reform more responsive to the needs and situation of the Rosebud community. The findings and recommendations offered in this section are relevant to other tribal governments as well, since many of the issues affecting Rosebud are common to the rest of Indian Country.

ESTABLISHMENT OF PATERNITY AND CHILD
SUPPORT ENFORCEMENT

The process of obtaining child support consists of several steps: locating the father, establishing paternity, setting the level of the award, and collecting the payments. Title I of the Family Support Act attempts to prevent single-parent families from relying on welfare by reducing the possibility that an absent parent will fail to provide his or her children with financial support. It does this by (1) mandating better establishment of paternity for children born out of wedlock, (2) increasing state authority to enforce support orders, and (3) requiring stricter enforcement of child support payments by state agencies.[48] The major provisions affecting Rosebud AFDC recipients are outlined below:

*   When a birth certificate is issued, parents are required to provide their social security numbers, unless the state finds a good cause for overlooking the requirement.

*   Beginning in 1992, states must meet federal standards for establishing paternity for children born out of wedlock.

*   Two years after enactment, states are mandated to use automatic wage withholding in all new and modified court-ordered cases regardless of whether they are in arrears. Automatic wage withholding involves the withholding of the child support payment from the absent parent's paycheck.

*   On October 1, 1990, a fifteen-member interstate child support commission appointed by Congress and the Secretary of HHS was established and required to submit recommendations for an improved child-support system by May 1, 1991.

CRITIQUE:

While the reform mandates stricter paternity establishment and child support enforcement by state agencies, it does not enable tribal governments to improve the process of obtaining child support in Indian Country. Nor does it furnish the funds necessary to develop more effective tribal child support systems. With the exception of the few reservations where state jurisdiction was extended through Public Law 280,[49] states do not have jurisdiction over Indian lands. Craig Hathaway of the federal Office of Child Support Enforcement asserts that, because of this, states are not sanctioned for failure to enforce child support collections on Indian lands.[50] Therefore, states have no incentive to use their monies to improve tribal systems. At the same time, because federal funds go only to state child support enforcement agencies created through Section IV-D of the Social Security Act, tribal governments have no direct access to federal matching funds to cover enforcement costs of items such as paternity tests and automated tracking systems.[51]

As in much of Indian Country, Rosebud's present child support process is costly and complex. Without additional funding for Rosebud's tribal court to improve the current system, single mothers are not likely to obtain child support on Rosebud. Nonetheless, with the exception of those mothers who can prove good cause for not cooperating with the state, all ADC recipients are required to file for a child support award.[52]

The complexity of the process stems from the fact that child support cases potentially fall under the jurisdiction of either the state or tribal courts and the two systems do not have well-developed mechanisms for cooperation. The tribe has exclusive jurisdiction if the mother is Rosebud Sioux and the father, regardless of whether he is Indian, also resides on the reservation. If the father is off the reservation, the mother can file a child support order in either the tribal court or in state court. If the father flees the reservation and fails to pay after an award has been established in the tribal system, she must enter her award as a foreign judgment in the state court. The state will not enforce the order until its own courts have recognized the tribal order. Unfortunately, Rosebud does not have reciprocal enforcement agreements with South Dakota or any other state or tribal governments. These issues are further complicated by the fact that relations between the tribe and the state of South Dakota historically have been strained.

Moreover, women who file within the tribal court can incur greater costs. If a mother files in a state court, she is entitled to paternity testing and legal representation. If she files in tribal court, the Indian Health Service, which is held responsible for paying for paternity testing, often does not have the available funds. On Rosebud, testing may be required more often to establish paternity since, for cultural reasons, common law marriages are more prevalent than in white communities.

Once the father is identified, South Dakota does not provide legal counsel. When women pursue their case in the tribal court, they may have trouble establishing an appropriate award. Women who must represent themselves are placed in the uncomfortable position of having to sue their former husbands or boyfriends for just compensation. Consequently, they may not be as successful in arguing for an appropriate award. As in many other court systems, Rosebud's tribal court has not developed standard support award guidelines that can reduce the need for legal representation. The lack of legal representation may also inhibit women from going to court to force fathers to uphold agreements. Automatic withholding of child support payments from paychecks, one way of securing payments, is not practiced by the Rosebud tribal court.

An effective child support system reinforces the importance of fathers taking financial responsibility for their children and is a valuable mechanism for helping many single-parent families avoid or rise out of poverty. Since child support payments, unlike ADC benefits, are not reduced by increased earnings, the addition of child support can help mothers work their way off welfare. However, given Rosebud's current economic conditions, child support may not bring a substantial number of single-parent Rosebud Sioux families off of ADC. While stricter child support enforcement might better tap the resources of a few employed fathers,[53] the high level of unemployment for American Indian men[54] suggests that few fathers have the income to make significant payments.

According to Michael Swallow, Executive Director of Dakota Plains Legal Services, virtually all Rosebud ADC mothers file in tribal court and 80 to 90 percent of the fathers involved in these child support suits are unemployed. If the father is working, income for ADC mothers is only increased up to the $50 that welfare regulations allow to be passed through without being counted as income. Consequently, under the current system, child support becomes more of a bureaucratic hurdle than a benefit for ADC recipients.

Ultimately, the tribe must decide whether or not child support enforcement is a priority. Although child support enforcement may not help many Rosebud families now, it could do so if and when economic conditions improve. Even at this time, the tribe may wish to improve its system for those mothers who would benefit and as a symbolic affirmation of parental responsibility.

RECOMMENDATIONS:

We recommend that the Rosebud Sioux tribe:

1. Develop child support guidelines within the tribal court.

2. Lobby for direct federal funding to tribes to improve the process of obtaining child support.

3. Lobby with the Secretary of Health and Human Services for the appointment of at least one tribal leader with knowledge of this issue to the fifteen-member interstate child support commission.

4. Increase efforts with state agencies and other tribes to establish reciprocal enforcement of child support awards.

AID TO FAMILIES WITH DEPENDENT CHILDREN— UNEMPLOYED PARENT PROGRAM

Although twenty-seven states currently operate welfare programs for impoverished two-parent families where the principal wage-earner is unemployed (AFDC-UP), twenty-three states, including South Dakota, do not. Present law defines unemployment as working fewer than one hundred hours a month unless the hours are of a temporary nature for intermittent work. In addition, the principle wage-earner must have work experience: specifically, within one year of applying for ADC, he or she must have (1) six or more quarters of work in the immediately preceding thirteen-calender-quarter period, or (2) received or been eligible to receive unemployment compensation.[55]

Welfare reform primarily affects the AFDC-UP population through the following measures:

*   Title IV (Related AFDC Amendments) requires the establishment of the unemployed parent program in all states.

*   States required to start AFDC-UP can limit cash benefits to six months per year, but must continue Medicaid coverage even for those months in which the family receives no cash benefits and assure the HHS Secretary that it will help those families obtain

employment.

- Under Title II (JOBS Training Program), states must require at least one parent in an AFDC-UP family to spend at least sixteen hours per week in a work activity. Between 1994 and 1998, states must expand the percent of the AFDC-UP caseload enrolled in work programs from 40 to 75 percent.

- In the case of parents under 25 who failed to complete high school, states are permitted to substitute basic education or courses leading to a high school diploma or the equivalent, for a work program.

- Under Title IV, states are permitted to require full-time participation by either parent in JOBS activities, and cash payments may not be made to AFDC-UP families until after the activities have been performed. If child care arrangements are provided, states can require the participation of both parents (although the caretaker parent would not be required to participate more than twenty hours per week).

CRITIQUE:

The introduction of an AFDC-UP program will have minimal impact on Rosebud. Although many Rosebud families have two parents who are not working, many have been out of work for so long that they fail to meet the AFDC-UP program's eligibility criteria for unemployed status. Consequently, few are likely to qualify for the AFDC-UP program and the BIA-GA program probably will not lose many cases to ADC.

If South Dakota decides that AFDC-UP benefits will be provided on a six-month basis, implementation will be extremely complex. The few families that qualify for AFDC-UP will be shuttled back and forth between the BIA-GA and the AFDC-UP programs. Since BIA-GA already operates a voluntary Tribal Work Experience Program (TWEP), some parents who are participating in the TWEP program will be required to switch to the mandated AFDC-UP work activity. Because the BIA-GA program provides a $55 monthly incentive stipend to TWEP participants, this switch creates program inequities. Ironically, a single man on TWEP would earn more than a father participating in an AFDC-UP work experience program.

The Rosebud TWEP program may have the capacity to provide work experience activities for AFDC-UP parents. In fact, TWEP may be better prepared than the state to operate a work experience program because it has already established ties to local employers and community councils, and has experience working with the clients who will be served. Iver Crow Eagle, TWEP Director, thinks that TWEP could serve more clients if its funding were increased and if it were permitted to place clients with private employers. At present, Crow Eagle cannot fill all the requests for workers received from employers and community leaders.[56]

Lastly, the parents qualifying for AFDC-UP have recently held jobs, and thus, while they might benefit from a JOBS program, are much less likely to gain skills from work experience activities. Such activities are most successful with people who have never worked and need to become acquainted with work environments. In the case of AFDC-UP, the primary benefit of work experience programs seems to be the value they create through community projects.

RECOMMENDATIONS:

In order to make the implementation of AFDC-UP more effective, the state Department of Social Services must work with the BIA Social Services Department and the TWEP program to make the transition between AFDC-UP and BIA-GA as smooth as possible. We recommend that the tribe encourage the formation of a joint committee of county DSS, tribal, and BIA officials to coordinate BIA-GA and AFDC-UP benefits and work activities. In particular, the committee should consider contracting AFDC-UP work activities to the TWEP program, and reducing work program inequities by offering a work stipend to participants in AFDC-UP work experience activities. Costs could be covered by the savings accrued through the transfer of recipients from the BIA-GA program to AFDC-UP.

TRANSITIONAL ASSISTANCE AFTER THE LOSS OF AFDC ELIGIBILITY

Under Title III of the Family Support Act, all recipients, regardless of their involvement in the JOBS program, have greater access to transitional assistance in the form of child care and Medicaid. Child care-related provisions are:

- The new legislation expands the provision of three months of transitional child care for Work Incentive (WIN) participants. Families requiring child care for employment reasons are guaranteed assistance through the state for twelve months after the family becomes ineligible for assistance because of increased income or longer work hours.

- Federal matching for child care is set at the Medicaid rate (50 to 80 percent open entitlement) but funds cannot be used for construction or rehabilitation of facilities.

- Federal matching is available for child care expenditures within established state limits but not in excess of local market rates.

- Child care must meet applicable licensing standards of state and local laws.

- In FY 1990 and FY 1991, the reform authorizes $13 million for grants to states to improve child care licensing and registration requirements and procedures, and to monitor child care provided to AFDC children. States must provide a 10 percent match.

- States can provide child care in a variety of ways, such as providing care directly, supplying cash or vouchers to families, or contracting with providers.

Medicaid-related provisions are:

- As of April 1, 1990, states must provide Medicaid coverage for a total of twelve months to families who received welfare for any three out of the past six months and lost eligibility due to increased hours or earnings.

- States must inform families of their right to extend Medicaid coverage at the time it terminates their cash benefits.

- Instead of Medicaid, during the first six months, the state is permitted to pay a family's expenses for employer-provided insurance and use Medicaid to cover any amounts not covered by the insurance plan.

• During the second six months, states may provide a reduced Medicaid package or enroll families in a group plan or health-maintenance organizations. Benefits can be terminated to families with incomes above 185 percent of the poverty level and states may charge a small fee to those with incomes between 100 and 185 percent.

CRITIQUE:

These child care provisions are utterly inadequate to the task of helping large numbers of Rosebud Sioux move off ADC. The provisions only pay for care in licensed facilities. None currently exist on the reservation, and Rosebud has yet to develop licensing standards. Given that the reform requires states to provide funding for child care, it is unclear whether state or tribal standards should apply. Furthermore, since the funding available through the reform cannot be used to increase supply through the construction or rehabilitation of organized centers or family day care homes, it fails to solve the supply problem. Given the current lack of venture capital on Rosebud, the ability of the private market to respond to increased demand for licensed child care is extremely limited.

Although transitional Medicaid is an important issue for recipients in many communities, on Rosebud it is less significant because the Indian Health Service guarantees at least minimal medical coverage to tribal members. Nonetheless, transitional Medicaid will be of some benefit since the better funded and more extensive Medicaid program provides at least the financial option of seeking care outside IHS.

Most significantly, the transitional benefit provisions neglect key issues. Although South Dakota is required to reimburse state JOBS program participants for transportation costs, this measure is not extended to all recipients attempting to move off ADC. Given the high cost and extremely limited supply of transportation on Rosebud, failure to address this need may mean that a person will spend a high proportion of his or her earnings on getting to work. Unless welfare reform addresses transportation problems and the adverse impact of earnings on food stamps and HUD housing subsidies, ADC recipients will have little monetary incentive to forego ADC benefits for low-wage jobs.

RECOMMENDATIONS:

We recommend that the tribe:

1. Develop acceptable and feasible child care licensing regulations and procedures for child care centers and family day care.

2. Work with the state to explore the feasibility of establishing low-cost community-based family care homes.

3. Contract with the state for the provision of child care required by the reform.

STATE JOBS OPPORTUNITY AND BASIC SKILLS PROGRAMS

An integral part of the Family Support Act is the consolidation of previously existing federal training and employment programs—Work Incentive (WIN), work supplementation, Community Work Experience (CWEP), and job search programs—into a new state-run JOBS program by October 1, 1990. Described in Title II, the JOBS program includes a range of activities including educational programs, job skills training, programs for job readiness, development and placement as well as supportive services in the form of transportation and child care. The major provisions are in three parts: JOBS program components, requirements placed on states, and requirements placed on AFDC recipients.

JOBS program components:

• Welfare agencies must work with each participant to develop an employability plan based on an assessment of his or her education, supportive service needs, work experience, employment skills, and family circumstances.

• Custodial parents under age 20 who have not completed high school or its equivalent must participate in full-time educational activities.

- If individuals are already involved in education or training activities, states may count such activities toward participation requirements, provided they are consistent with the individual's employment goals. The federal government would not, however, pay for costs other than required supportive services.

- Governors must ensure program activities are coordinated with Job Training Partnership Act (JTPA) (PL 97-300) programs.

- States must provide two of the following specific types of programs: (a) group and individual job search, (b) on-the-job training (OJT), (c) work supplementation programs, and (d) community work experience programs (CWEP).

Requirements placed on states:

- Federal matching for the JOBS program is reduced to 50 percent from 90 percent unless 55 percent of the funds are spent on the following target populations:
  (1) families in which the custodial parent is under age 24 and
      (a) has not completed high school or (b) had little or no
      work experience in the preceding year;
  (2) families in which the youngest child is within 2 years of
      being ineligible for assistance because of age;
  (3) families who have received assistance for more than 36
      months during the preceding 60-month period.

- With the appropriate justification, the state will not be required to provide services to those geographic areas where the number of prospective participants, the local economy, or other relevant factors make implementation infeasible.

- Between FY 1990 and FY 1995, states are required to increase participation from 7 to 20 percent of the nonexempt caseload. Failure to comply will result in reductions in federal matching.

Requirements placed on AFDC recipients:

- As long as necessary child care is provided, participation is required for all recipients except for those who are disabled, needed at home to care for a sick family member or child under the age of three, employed 30 or more hours per week, pregnant, under age 16 or attending school full time, or who live where the program is not provided.

• Mandatory recipients who fail to participate without good cause or refuse a bona fide offer of employment in which he or she can engage will be sanctioned.

• The benefit portion of a sanctioned individual will be excluded from the family's AFDC benefits. If a parent is sanctioned, payments will be made to a third party unless such arrangements cannot be made.

CRITIQUE:

South Dakota state JOBS programs will probably not provide any services to Rosebud recipients. The economic circumstances that make training difficult on Rosebud could be sufficient justification for the state to designate the reservation as too remote to implement the JOBS program. We know of no federal or state guidelines governing this decision. In a recent interview, Verne Guericke, Program Administrator of the South Dakota Office of Economic Assistance, stated that South Dakota will not provide JOBS services to Todd County and has yet to decide whether to establish programs in the three adjacent counties. Even if Rosebud or the surrounding counties are not formally designated as "remote," Rosebud Sioux recipients may still not have access to state JOBS services because the programs are placed in inaccessible locations.

Furthermore, given the lack of jobs on Rosebud, the state JOBS program model, which relies heavily upon traditional Job Training Partnership Act (JTPA) approaches such as on-the-job training, job search, and work experience, is not likely to provide ADC recipients with the opportunity to gain permanent on-reservation employment. According to an interview with the Rosebud JTPA program director, Paul Valandra, the limited job market already makes it extremely difficult for him to place current JTPA participants in viable training positions. Most jobs are in the public sector where understaffed and overworked public employees often lack the time to provide adequate supervision.[57] Even those trainees who do upgrade their skills through placement in such agencies are not likely to remain as permanent employees unless the agency's budget increases. Valandra remarked, "Sometimes we feel we are all on welfare. It just so happens that some people are working full time."

RECOMMENDATION:

We recommend that the tribe lobby the Secretary of Health and Human Services to establish a reasonable set of guidelines governing the designation of remote status to ensure against the arbitrary exclusion of reservations from state JOBS programs.

TRIBAL JOBS OPPORTUNITY AND BASIC SKILL (JOBS) PROGRAMS

Recognizing the likelihood of states designating Indian lands as remote areas, Senator Daschle of South Dakota lobbied for the inclusion of the Title II measure which gives tribes a limited opportunity to operate their own work, education, and training programs. Statutory language states that funds will be provided directly through the Department of Health and Human Services and not require matching funds. The amount will be based upon "the ratio of adult recipients in the Tribe relative to the adult recipients in the state multiplied by the state's JOBS program allocation."[58] Tribal allocations will be subtracted from the total capped state allotments. If deemed inappropriate, HHS can also waive JOBS program requirements for tribal programs. According to the Office of Family Assistance, the intent of the legislation is to fund employment and training efforts, not to subsidize directly economic development plans.[59] In order to qualify, a tribe must file a preliminary application by April 13, 1989, but can later rescind the application without any penalty.

CRITIQUE:

This direct funding measure represents a significant step toward recognizing the importance of giving tribal governments a role in the implementation of programs designed to increase self-sufficiency among American Indian welfare recipients. The Rosebud Sioux tribe plans to apply. Unfortunately, this legislation presents implementation problems in the following areas: funding, intergovernmental coordination, program planning, and program evaluation.

Funding. Because determining the ratio of adult American Indian ADC recipients to the adult ADC population is difficult, the exact level of funding for each reservation is somewhat uncertain. Problems arise from two sources: (1) identifying who is Indian and (2) establishing the geographic service area of the tribal JOBS program. The number of recipients who are identified as American Indian can vary with the method (i. e., self-report, tribal enrollment status, or blood quantum) used to establish ethnic identity. Likewise, the number of recipients depends upon the boundaries of the designated service area. If the service area includes all four counties—Todd, Mellette, Tripp, and Gregory—then the greater numbers of recipients raises funding levels, but those recipients living in the outlying areas will probably have decreased access to services. The funding allocation is determined by the number of Indian recipients living within the service area, not by the number actually enrolled in JOBS.

Nonetheless, if Rosebud begins operating its JOBS program on July 1, 1989, Paul Valandra estimates that the tribe will receive an allocation of slightly more than $100,000 for that fiscal year.[60] This estimate is based on self-reports of American Indian ethnicity and includes recipients living in all four counties. Because of Rosebud's large ADC population, this amount is somewhat larger than the allocations other tribes would receive.

Until states determine how much they will allocate to the state JOBS program, it is unclear whether recipients in tribal programs will have access to the same amount of funding available to participants in state programs. If the state provides enough to earn all of the capped federal allocation, then tribal recipients will receive 10 percent less. Ironically, given the high cost of operations in remote areas and the large number of long-term welfare recipients, Rosebud probably requires higher levels of financial support to be able to establish an effective program capable of serving a large proportion of its ADC population.

Intergovernmental Coordination. Despite an antagonistic history of jurisdictional disputes, the tribe must work closely with a variety of state and county agencies in order to successfully operate a JOBS program. First, the tribe will need to coordinate operations with the county DSS office, which will continue to administer the regular ADC program. For example, after recipients are determined eligible by the county, they must be referred to the tribal program. If the recipient fails to comply, then the county must be informed in order to apply appropriate sanctions.

Second, tribal officials must negotiate with the state on the adoption of child care licensing requirements and the provision of support services. The law clearly requires states to provide Indian recipients with transitional child care and medical services. On the other hand, while coverage of the costs of day care, transportation, and other related expenses are legislated components of the state JOBS program, the extent to which states will provide such services to participants in the tribal JOBS programs seems much less certain.

Program Planning. Inadequate planning time and the lack of federal guidance have frustrated the tribal program design process. Tribal governments had only six months after the passage of the Family Support Act to submit preliminary applications for JOBS programs. In large part because of election year changes in leadership, the Office of Family Assistance did not distribute basic program information to tribal governments until December 1988.[61] Regional meetings with tribal social services personnel apparently were not held until March 1989.[62]

Because HHS has yet to complete its regulations, it is unclear what tribes will be required to provide in terms of who should be targeted, how the program should be designed and what should be the program's components. According to the legislation, HHS can waive jobs requirements for tribal programs if appropriate. Given the wide variation among reservation conditions, a standard applicable to one tribal program may be unreasonable for another. To take this into account, HHS may wish to develop minimum standards and grant waivers on a reservation-specific basis rather than develop national requirements.[63]

The lack of clear federal guidance gives Rosebud some flexibility in determining how to design its program even after the April 13 deadline. The Office of Family Assistance states, "Given that Federal policy is still being developed, we recognize that Native American applications will probably need to be supplemented or revised after the initial submittal."[64] We encourage the tribe to take full advantage of this flexibility in designing its

JOBS program.

In the course of developing a JOBS program, Rosebud officials should consider the following factors: the allocated funding level, the tribal government's organizational capacity, the needs of the JOBS clients, and the tribal government's goals. The size of Rosebud's $100,000 allocation suggests that Rosebud must choose between expanding already existing employment and training programs and creating a small, independent program. Tribal JTPA programs in Montana, South Dakota, and North Dakota currently spend approximately $2,400 per enrolled participant,[65] suggesting a service population of thirty to forty clients for Rosebud's JOBS program. But, because the tribal government has the freedom to use existing employment and training programs to lower its costs per participant, or incur greater expense by maintaining a separate program administration, it can choose exactly how many clients to serve.

When planning its JOBS program, Rosebud should assess its present organizational capacity. The JOBS program could draw upon the resources already existing within the reservation community. Potential resources include organizations such as Sinte Gleska College, substance abuse programs, TWEP, JTPA, and vocational education programs. The JOBS program can either refer clients to these organizations or contract with these agencies to provide special services. We recognize, however, that funding restrictions and the regulatory requirements of the existing programs constrain the extent to which different training programs can be creatively integrated. For example, JTPA performance criteria that emphasize short-term job placement limit its ability to work with JOBS in serving traditionally high-risk groups. On the other hand, the JOBS program might try to increase services by looking for outside foundation, state, and federal grants to subsidize administrative costs or to fund an expanded van service. Minimally, the program could encourage individual clients to use outside financial sources, such as BIA scholarship funds.

In order to be effective, the program must both meet the needs of Rosebud ADC recipients and be a more attractive alternative than staying on welfare. Clients enrolled in employment and training programs need a variety of program supports. They must be able to get to the site. They may need help overcoming health problems. All need access to reliable child care. Employment counseling may be crucial to the success of those clients with little work experience. Extremely disadvantaged clients may need more than a short-term program, or may need permission to re-enter training if they fail. Project Match, a Chicago-based employment program that serves clients with very little work experience and low training levels, claims that the possibility of failure must be structured into such programs. Although the majority of Project Match clients lose their first jobs, retention improves dramatically during their second and third placements.[66] Similarly, the Phoenix Indian Center, Inc., operates a successful JTPA program that tracks people for at least one year after they have found jobs, provides counseling if clients have problems at work, and allows those who have lost their jobs to re-enter their program.[67]

Rosebud ADC recipients vary widely in their training needs. While some require remedial education, others would benefit more from advanced technical training. One method of meeting client needs could involve using individualized assessment and case management to guide a small number of participants through a comprehensive training program. Case workers could help clients develop and pursue an employment plan, link them to a variety of services, track their progress, and provide any necessary personal counseling. Such a model could simultaneously address the client's employment needs and problems of substance abuse. The tribal government could also choose to offer a new type of training program, such as community-based adult literacy or GED classes. By holding classes in outlying communities, such a program would alleviate transportation problems. These classes could provide at least some benefit to many recipients, and might encourage some participants to pursue more advanced training.

Tribal goals, particularly tribal economic development strategies, are an important consideration in program design. For example, if the tribal government wants to attract employers by increasing the educational level of Rosebud residents, it may prefer to implement an education-oriented JOBS program. In contrast, if the government intends to promote micro-enterprise development, it could design a program that teaches business skills and provides support services to recipients interested in starting small enterprises. This program would work with county ADC programs to allow recipients to accumulate start-up business capital without losing welfare benefits. Finally, the program might target resources to those people willing to receive training in fields of particular importance to community development at Rosebud. For instance, the tribal government could develop a program to increase the number of trained medical personnel who might find employment in Rosebud's regional IHS hospital.

Program Evaluation. The final issue concerns the design of appropriate program evaluation measurements. According to Norman DeWeaver, an expert on Indian JTPA programs, federal JOBS regulations have yet to be designed, though he fears that, when written, they will inappropriately rely upon current JTPA performance criteria. JTPA evaluates its programs on the basis of outcome measures set according to an equation intended to account for local economic variation. But, as DeWeaver argues, "In Indian Country, the performance standards are mindless."[68]

Particularly in Indian Country, the JTPA methodology is plagued with problems. For example, the unemployment rate is an important variable in the performance formula. But on Rosebud no accurate unemployment statistics exist and current estimates range from 13.9 to 90 percent, depending on what exactly they are counting, who's doing it, and where they get their information. Because high unemployment statistics qualify Rosebud for funding for various training programs, the BIA and the tribal government have a vested interest in obtaining higher figures. On the other hand, the need for an easy method of computation and the competition between states and tribes for federal funding create incentives for states to undercount. JTPA currently bases its estimates upon the lower state figures.

If programs are small, as is likely with tribal JOBS programs, statistical averages do not accurately depict program performance. In this situation, a single individual who does extremely poorly can severely hurt the results for the entire program.[69] This problem is exacerbated by the difficulties of gathering accurate statistics in Indian Country.

Lastly, by emphasizing measures of immediate individual outcome and failing to track clients over time, JTPA does not recognize the importance of process or long-term program effects. Primarily focusing on whether a person was placed in a permanent job overlooks the quality of his or her learning experience, the impact of training on future employment, and the benefit of his or her work to the community. For instance, a trainee working in a public agency probably will not receive a job offer immediately after completing the program, but might have provided invaluable services to the agency, and could be the first person hired when a position eventually opens. In the worst case, an emphasis on placement, regardless of whether a position is located on or off the reservation, can result in a program which indirectly encourages qualified and increasingly skilled individuals to leave the reservation for work.

Alternative measures of evaluation could be developed. Tracking an individual's progress during training and for more than one year after leaving a program is one way to obtain more accurate information about a program's impact. For example, by keeping track of its clients over several years, the previously mentioned Project Match program found that success could not be measured by how well the client kept his or her first job. Performance criteria should also allow JOBS programs to receive credit for community services rendered. The Navajo Nation in Arizona operates work experience programs that consider the benefit to the community as a measure of success.[70]

RECOMMENDATIONS:

We offer two kinds of recommendations: those that can be carried out within the tribal government, and those that require the cooperation of outside organizations. We recommend that the tribe take the following steps internally:

1. When designing the JOBS program, officials should take into account funding levels, organizational capacities, client needs, and the goals of the tribe.

2. When designing the JOBS program, officials should consider a variety of employment and training program models. Such models include:
   a. Adding support services such as employment counseling to existing programs;
   b. Using case management;
   c. Creating a program designed to offer training and educational services which are either under-provided or nonexistent on Rosebud.

3. Track the progress of tribal program participants for the purposes of current and future program evaluation.

We recommend that the tribe take the following steps working with outside agencies:

4. Establish a joint task force consisting of tribal, state, and all four county welfare officials to coordinate activities such as JOBS referrals, sanctions, and support services.

5. Demand that the state furnish equal levels of supportive services for state and tribal JOBS program participants.

6. Encourage HHS to grant reservation-specific waivers for JOBS program requirements.

7. Encourage HHS to develop appropriate performance measures for tribal programs that look at individual short-term and long-term effects as well as community benefits.

8. Lobby the federal government to reduce fund restrictions that inhibit tribal governments from combining services provided through programs such as JTPA, TWEP, BIA, Employment Assistance, and JOBS.

OVERVIEW

As in the rest of Indian Country, the Rosebud Sioux tribe has an active role to play in the implementation of welfare reform. The tribal government can pursue independently many of the actions recommended above. These actions typically involve the development of internal tribal policies, coordination between the tribe and other entities, such as state and county agencies, and negotiations with federal agencies.

On the other hand, some of the actions we recommend would best be taken in conjunction with other tribes. By forming a task force of interested representatives from the nine South Dakota reservations, Rosebud and other tribal governments would be in a better position to influence policy, particularly with respect to issues of child support enforcement and implementation of tribal JOBS programs. The benefits of such a task force are its group strength and its enhanced ability to present the state with cohesive policy positions. Forming such a task force and coming up with reasonable, common policy proposals could be an important step toward increasing tribal control over the welfare process, improving relations with the state, and enhancing the prospects of reducing the overall welfare burden.

IV. BEYOND ROSEBUD: IMPLICATIONS FOR OTHER TRIBES

So far, we have considered the welfare system on the Rosebud Sioux Reservation and the implications of federal welfare reform, as legislated in the Family Support Act of 1988, for the Rosebud Sioux tribe. How applicable is this analysis to other tribes?

A thorough answer to this question is impossible here, but through a brief, comparative study of the Gila River Indian community in Arizona, we have attempted to understand what variables might affect a tribal government's response to the various provisions of the 1988 legislation.

Established in 1859 by an act of Congress rather than through a treaty, the Gila River Indian community in Arizona provides an interesting contrast to the Rosebud Sioux tribe, because of its different economic and geographic conditions and relationship to the Arizona state government. Although there are areas of conflict between the community and the state, such as water rights, tribal social service officials feel that they can work cooperatively with state officials on welfare reform. The community already has a history of working out intergovernmental agreements with the state to provide social services such as child welfare and elderly nutrition programs on the reservation. Establishing such agreements is an integral part of the duties assigned to Michael Hughes, Deputy Assistant Director of Intergovernmental Relations for the Arizona Department of Economic Security (DES). Furthermore, Tribal Governor Thomas White was included in the Arizona Governor's Task Force on Welfare Reform, and chaired an ad-hoc subcommittee specifically addressing the issues on Indian lands.[71]

Gila River Indian community is less isolated and enjoys better economic conditions than Rosebud. Covering 327,000 acres, the long, narrow reservation lies fifteen miles south of the Phoenix metropolitan area, and occupies portions of both Pinal and Maricopa counties. Numbering 11,700 in 1987,[72] Gila River's population includes enrolled members from the Pima and the Maricopa tribes. The reservation's private sector consists of thirty-two industrial operations located in three industrial parks. In 1989, the BIA reported Gila River's unemployment rate at 27 percent.[73] A 1985 evaluation of the tribe's Employment and Training Program and interviews with tribal officials suggested that transportation, the lack of child care, poor health, and job retention problems pose some of the greatest barriers to employment.[74] These geographic and economic factors almost certainly influence the tribal government's response to welfare reform.

CHILD SUPPORT ENFORCEMENT

Because the Family Support Act's child support provisions have practically no impact on Indian lands, the decision to improve on-reservation child support systems is left to the discretion of tribal governments. How a tribal government can upgrade its system depends on several issues:

1. Does the state have civil jurisdiction over the reservation?

2. Does the tribal government have access to internal or external funds to make necessary changes?

3. Does the tribal government need to make paternity testing more accessible?

4. Does the tribal court have standard child support award guidelines?

5. If standard award guidelines do not exist, do parents have access to affordable legal representation?

6. Does the tribal court have reciprocal child support enforcement agreements with other tribes and states?

7. Do tribal wage withholding ordinances already exist?

The Gila River Indian community is currently taking steps to improve its child support system. According to Rod Lewis, tribal attorney, the tribal council is likely to pass a wage garnishment ordinance requiring reservation employers, such as private companies, the tribal government, and the BIA, to withhold wages for child support payments. Such an ordinance might also allow reservation employers to respect garnishment orders from other jurisdictions.[75]

AID TO FAMILIES WITH DEPENDENT CHILDREN— UNEMPLOYED PARENT PROGRAM

If the reservation is in a state that does not already operate an AFDC-UP program,[76] then the tribal government must decide how to respond to the reform's AFDC-UP provisions. An evaluation should include these questions:

1. Will the state offer AFDC-UP on a six-month or twelve-month basis?

2. What percentage of the two-parent families on the BIA-GA caseload will be required to switch to the AFDC-UP program?

3. What is the tribe's TWEP program capacity to serve AFDC-UP parents?

4. Can the tribal government find funds which enable it to offer AFDC-UP participants a work incentive stipend comparable to that provided by TWEP?

Like South Dakota, Arizona does not currently operate an AFDC-UP program and intends to offer only six months of benefits. Although the Governor's Task Force on Welfare Reform has already recommended that HHS "support special projects where tribal governments would plan, organize, and direct the workfare activities of AFDC-UP on Indian lands,"[77] Gila River's plans are yet to be determined.

TRANSITIONAL SERVICES

While transitional child care and Medicaid services will affect all AFDC recipients in Indian Country, the extent to which tribal governments must become involved in ensuring provision of adequate child care can vary. When determining what actions must be taken, tribal governments may need to consider the following questions:

1. How many AFDC recipients will need licensed child care?

2. How much licensed child care is available on the reservation?

    a.   How many organized facilities exist?

    b.   Do these facilities conform to tribal or state licensing standards?

3.   What measures can be taken to ensure an adequate supply of child care?

    a.   Should facilities be upgraded?

    b.   Must new facilities be constructed?

    c.   Can family day care homes be organized?

    d.   Does the tribal government have access to any capacity-building funds?

According to Lewis Lane, Director of Gila River Social Services, the Gila River Indian community does not have any tribal child care licensing standards or any on-reservation facilities that would currently meet state standards. In order to expand organized on-reservation child care services, Lane believes the tribal government will need to develop licensing standards and find funds to construct appropriate facilities. Michael Hughes of the Department of Economic Security (DES) suggests that the child care issue can be resolved through intergovernmental agreements. However, as in the case of the Rosebud Reservation, provision of transitional services fails to address the primary employment barriers on Gila River.

STATE AND TRIBAL JOBS OPPORTUNITIES AND BASIC SKILLS PROGRAMS

Before deciding whether to apply for a tribal JOBS program, tribal governments need to determine whether on-reservation AFDC recipients will receive adequate services through a state JOBS program. Consequently, tribal governments should be concerned about the process through which state governments determine where state JOBS programs are located and what areas are designated as too "remote" for service. When assessing the impact of state JOBS programs, some issues to consider are:

1.   Will the reservation AFDC population have access to state JOBS programs?

    a.   Will the reservation be designated remote?

    b.   How close are reservation communities to potential off-reservation JOBS sites?

c.   Is transportation available to those JOBS sites?

2.   Do state JOBS programs address the needs of the reservation's AFDC recipients?

Until states complete their plans for implementing the Family Support Act, tribal governments will have difficulty finding the answers to these questions.

Those tribes allowed under the legislation to design their own JOBS programs need to consider the following issues:

1.   Given the level of available funding and existing organizational resources, what type of program could meet client needs and complement tribal government goals?

2.   What support services, such as transportation, child care, and other subsidies for work-related expenses, will be available to tribal JOBS participants, either through state or tribal funding?

3.   What is the best way for the tribal government to coordinate its JOBS program services with state welfare authorities?

a.   Can the state contract its support service obligations to tribal governments through intergovernmental agreements?

b.   Can the state contract out the administration of its on-reservation AFDC program to the tribal government through PL 93-638?

c.   Does the tribal government have the will and organizational capacity either to provide the state's support services or to administer the state's entire on-reservation AFDC program?

Gila River tribal officials believe that their reservation, like Rosebud, will be designated remote. Although the reservation is located next to Phoenix, its communities are difficult to serve. Many residents live considerable distances from centers of economic activity and lack access to transportation.

Arizona DES officials estimate that Gila River is eligible for approximately $51,000 in JOBS funding. Alvin Jones, Gila River JTPA Director, believes this level of funding limits his ability to do much more than expand or modestly enhance Gila River's existing employment and training programs. One possible JOBS option augments a current tribal program designed to increase job retention by improving clients' ability to cope with the demands of the workplace. While the tribe's social service officials indicate that they will meet the April 13 deadline, they also expect to revise their application as their plans become more certain.

In order to coordinate the provision of AFDC benefits with the JOBS program, Lewis Lane hopes that the tribal government can take over the on-reservation administration of AFDC benefits. Because Gila River's Social Service Program has experience in successfully operating the BIA-GA program, Lane believes it is feasible to take on this responsibility. The Governor's Task Force on Welfare Reform supports his proposal, recommending that "tribal governments be given the opportunity to receive direct federal funding to operate all programs [including AFDC] under Title IV of the Social Security Act on Indian lands."[78]

V. CONCLUSION

Even if tribal governments respond effectively to the federal welfare reform initiative, problems of welfare dependency in Indian Country will not be solved until tribal governments address issues that lie beyond the limited scope of the Family Support Act of 1988. While the reform legislation recognizes the need for support services, it does not help to create a support system extensive enough to enable large numbers of Native American families to leave welfare.

First, the reform provisions assume that already existing transportation and child care can adequately meet demand. Merely subsidizing recipients' expenses, however, does not enable tribal governments to develop needed services. Second, the Family Support Act does not explicitly acknowledge the importance of other issues such as health problems and counseling needs. Last, although the JOBS program does allow tribal governments to tailor employment and training programs to meet the specific needs of their clients, available funding limits tribal governments' ability to offer comprehensive services to more than a handful of individuals.

The Family Support Act also completely ignores the work disincentives created by the current welfare system. As illustrated by the Rosebud case study, when recipients earn income they face significant losses in welfare benefits, HUD housing subsidies, and food stamps. Eligibility requirements also prevent recipients from attempting to start their own businesses.

Primarily targeting women with children, welfare reform neglects the enormous problem of male unemployment in Indian Country. As the 1980 census indicates, 64 percent of all Native American men, aged 30–54, were not employed. The AFDC-UP program does little to alleviate this problem because few men meet its unemployment criteria, and its mandated work activity is not likely to help those who do participate to find permanent employment. In this era when two incomes are often necessary to lift families out of poverty,[79] welfare dependency will not be solved until both men and women can contribute to the financial well-being of their families.

Finally, any policy intending to reduce the level of welfare dependency must recognize that easy solutions do not exist and that a long-term strategy is essential. Simply training or further educating a welfare recipient accomplishes little if the on-reservation economy cannot offer viable job opportunities. Unless economic development occurs in Indian Country, few American Indian recipients will find the permanent employment they need to achieve financial self-sufficiency.

EPILOGUE: 1991

Despite the lack of clear federal guidelines and the minimal amount of time allowed for planning, the Rosebud Sioux tribe did apply for their own JOBS program. The program began on July 1, 1989, and currently receives $135,000 of federal funding each year. The program is open to eligible tribal members living not only in Todd County but in the other three counties that have been part of the Rosebud Reservation and still have significant Sioux populations: Mellette, Tripp, and Gregory.

Initially, the tribe had difficulty running the program. They were confused by the lack of federal direction and by the Family Support Act mandate that JOBS monies could not be used to fund services already being provided to the general public through other programs. Consequently, for the first year-and-a-half, the tribe had trouble using up its allocation. This situation changed in the fall of 1990 when the tribe hired a tribal member who had been working for the county Department of Social Services to manage the program.

At this time, the program is co-located with JTPA and serves fifty-three clients. Case managers assess clients at the central office as well as in local communities. Once a client is accepted, a case manager helps him or her either enter the Community Work Experience Program, enroll in a GED program, or obtain further education at the local tribal college. JOBS funds are used to arrange and pay for transportation as well as cover the cost of tuition. The state covers child care costs when care is provided in a licensed facility, and the tribe hopes to obtain a block grant to pay for other types of child care. The JOBS program recently hired a second case manager, bringing the total staff to three full-time professionals plus secretarial support. JOBS director Ida Charlee Archambault intends to increase the number of clients served to a couple of hundred per year.

Since October 1990, five clients have successfully completed the program and left welfare. Unfortunately, most clients find it difficult to find work even after they have completed the program. Jobs with adequate pay are simply not available on the Rosebud Reservation.

This year, legislation is being proposed in the United States Congress which could alleviate some of the problems plaguing the implementation of programs designed to help Native American families on reservations become self-sufficient. Senator Tom Daschle (South Dakota) has introduced a bill (S-754) that would allow up to $4,000 received from land lease checks to be excluded from income when determining a person's eligibility for programs like AFDC or social security. In addition, Senator Paul Simon (Illinois) has introduced Senate Bill 1530. If passed, this bill would allow tribal governments to develop integrated employment programs financed by co-mingling funds from a range of employment programs including JOBS, the Carl D. Perkins Vocational Education Act, JTPA, and other BIA employment assistance.

APPENDIX A. GLOSSARY

ADC	South Dakota's version of Aid to Families with Dependent Children
AFDC	Aid to Families with Dependent Children Program
AFDC-UP	Aid to Families with Dependent Children - Unemployed Parent Program
BIA	Bureau of Indian Affairs
BIA-GA	Bureau of Indian Affairs General Assistance Program
DES	Arizona Department of Economic Security
DSS	South Dakota Department of Social Services
HHS	U. S. Department of Health and Human Services
HUD	U. S. Department of Housing and Urban Development
IHS	Indian Health Service
JOBS	Jobs Opportunity and Basic Skills Program
JTPA	Job Training Partnership Act
TWEP	Tribal Work Experience Program
WIN	Work Incentive Program

APPENDIX B. FOOD SURVEY

This survey of selected food items was conducted during the week of January 22, 1989.

ITEM	PRICE (in dollars)		
	Mission	Valentine	SiouxFalls
Cracker Barrel Cheese 10 oz.	2.62	2.63	2.59
Parkay Margarine	.79	.59	.66
Gold Medal Flour	1.63	1.55	1.19
Star Kist Tuna in Water	1.09	.89	.79
Roman Meal Bread	1.33	1.19	1.33
Beef Round Steak (per lb)	2.79	1.99	2.49
80% Lean Gr. Beef (per lb)	1.69	1.49	1.39
Chicken Thighs (per lb)	.99	.79	.69
1/2 Gallon Milk	1.20	1.29	1.14
5 lb. Bag of Oranges	2.69	2.49	2.49
5 lb. Bag of Jonathan Apples	2.98	2.49	1.69
Red Apples (per lb.)	.99	.79	.50
Lettuce	.49	.89	.99
Cornflakes Cereal	2.53	2.79	1.87
Folgers Coffee 14 oz.	3.42	3.35	2.51
TOTAL:	27.23	25.21	22.32
% Different from Mission:		-7.4	-18.0

ITEM	PRICE (in dollars)		
	Cedar Butte	Mission	Sioux Falls
Hormel Canned Beef Stew	2.93	1.95	2.01
Spam	2.59	1.98	1.69
Baking Powder	2.59	1.99	1.93
Cheer Detergent 4 lbs	4.78	4.89	3.95
Star Kist Tuna	1.65	1.09	.79
Total Cereal	3.27	2.89	2.00
Folgers Coffee 48 oz.	8.89	6.59	6.25
Flour	1.59	1.39	1.29
TOTAL:	28.29	22.77	19.91
% Different from Cedar Butte:		-19.5	-29.6

(Note: The smaller sample in the second comparison is owing to the lack of items, including fresh fruits and vegetables, available in the Cedar Butte store.)

APPENDIX C. INTERVIEWS

In the course of this research, we interviewed the following persons, who not only gave us generous amounts of time but provided much of the information on which the paper is based.

Carol Axtman, Program Administrator, South Dakota Commodities Program

Leland Bordeaux, Academic Dean, Sinte Gleska College

Lionel Bordeaux, President, Sinte Gleska College

Joseph Bresette, Executive Director, Great Lakes Inter-tribal Council

Ann Cohloff, Social Services Representative, Bureau of Indian Affairs, Rosebud Reservation

John Cook, Office of Family Assistance, Washington, D.C.

Cheryl Crazy Bull, Director, Institutional Relations, Sinte Gleska College

Iver Crow Eagle, Director, Rosebud Tribal Work Experience Program

Norman DeWeaver, JTPA Specialist, Center for Community Change

Pat Eagle Elk, Director, Rosebud Sioux Alcohol Abuse Programs

Marilyn Gangone, Social Services Committee, Rosebud Sioux Tribal Council

Verne Guericke, Program Administrator, South Dakota Office of Economic Assistance

Dorothy Hallock, Comprehensive Planner, Gila River Indian Community

Craig Hathaway, Office of Child Support Enforcement, Washington, D.C.

Chuck Hill, Director, Lakota Archives and Historical Research Center, Sinte Gleska College

Lena Horselooking, Director, St. Francis Mission Day Care Center

Schuyler Houser, Director, Institutes for Economic Development and Tribal Governance, Sinte Gleska College

Michael Hughes, Deputy Assistant for Intergovernmental Relations, Arizona Department of Economic Security

Irene Ironshell, Social Services Representative, Bureau of Indian Affairs, Rosebud Reservation

Albert Jones, Managing Attorney, Dakota Plains Legal Services

Alvin Jones, Director, JTPA Program, Gila Indian River Community

Calvin Jones, Sr., Business Manager, Rosebud Sioux Tribe

Cora Jones, Acting Superintendent, Bureau of Indian Affairs, Rosebud Reservation

Jerry Killsinwater, Director, St. Francis Artist Cooperative
Cecelia Kitto, Acting Director, Indian Health Service Hospital, Rosebud Reservation
Cheryl Klein, Chair, Human Services Department, Sinte Gleska College
Lewis Lane, Director, Tribal Social Services, Gila River Indian Community
Rodney Lanz, Supervisor, Todd County Department of Social Services
Charlene LaPointe, Archivist/Oral Historian, Sinte Gleska College
Adeline LaPointe, Member, Rosebud Sioux Tribe
Fred Leadercharge, Director, Student Support Services, Sinte Gleska College
John Lewis, President, Inter-tribal Council of Arizona
Rod Lewis, Tribal Attorney, Gila River Indian Community
Alex Lunderman, President, Rosebud Sioux Tribe
Julie Osnes, Program Administrator, South Dakota Food Stamp Program
Amos Prue, Director, HUD Housing Authority, Rosebud Reservation
Robert Purner, Director of Communications, Sinte Gleska College
Fern Schmidt, Supervisor, Todd County Department of Social Services
Jane Shouse, Office of Family Assistance, Washington D.C.
Mike Swallow, Director, Dakota Plains Legal Services
Jim Tail, former Deputy Director, Seattle Indian Health Board
Karen Thorne, Director of Employment and Training, Phoenix Indian Center Inc.
Father Tillman, St. Francis Catholic Mission
Paul Valandra, Director, Rosebud Job Training Partnership Act Program
Thomas White, Governor, Gila River Indian Community
Lila Young, Secretary, Rosebud Sioux Task Force for Tribal Self-Governance

Ten current and past Rosebud Sioux welfare recipients

NOTES

1. Much of this paper is based on interviews. A list of interviewees is given in Appendix C. We are grateful to these persons for their time and their candor. We also would like to thank Schuyler Houser and David Lester for their assistance, encouragement, and sound advice throughout the writing of this paper.

2. Bureau of Indian Affairs, *Indian Service Population and Labor Force Estimates*, January 1989, p. 1.

3. For a concise overview of Rosebud, see Elizabeth S. Grobsmith, *Lakota of the Rosebud: A Contemporary Ethnography* (New York: Holt, Rinehart & Winston, 1981).

4. U. S. Bureau of the Census, *County and City Data Book 1983* (Washington, DC: Government Printing Office, 1983), p. 500; Douglas Johnson, "A Study of the Twenty-Five Poorest Counties in the Continental U. S. A. in 1986," The United Methodist Church, 1987.

5. Donald Arwood, Linda Baer, and Velva-Lu Spencer, "Social Conditions which Influence Development on Native American Reservations in South Dakota," South Dakota State University, 1987, p. 4.

6. David Ellwood, *Poor Support: Poverty in the American Family* (New York: Basic Books, 1988), p. 45.

7. National Planning Data Corporation, 1987, cited in Johnson, "A Study of the Twenty-Five Poorest Counties . . . ," p. 13.

8. Gary Sandefur and Arthur Sakamoto, "American Indian Household Structure and Income," *Demography* 25, no. 1 (February 1988): 73.

9. Velva-Lu Spencer and Donald E. Arwood, *Reservation Data Book*, Department of Rural Sociology, South Dakota State University, February 1987, p. 5.

10. Johnson, "A Study of the Twenty-Five Poorest Counties . . . ," p. 3.

11. Because of how the state defines unemployment, we believe the 4.6 percent does not take into accurate account the unemployment existing on the state's nine Indian reservations.

12. BIA, *Indian Service Populations and Labor Force Estimates,* p. 1.

13. Tony Kaliss, "A Study of Income Received on the Rosebud Sioux Reservation from Land Lease Rentals, the General Assistance Program (BIA), the Food Stamp Program, the Program of Aid to Dependent Children in 1986," Institute for Economic Development, Sinte Gleska College, Rosebud Sioux Reservation, 1988, p. 2.

14. Richard Sherman, "A Study of Traditional and Informal Sector Micro-Enterprise Activity and its Impact on the Pine Ridge Indian Reservation Economy," Aspen Institute for Humanistic Studies, Washington, D.C., September 1988, p. 20.

15. Ibid., p. 49.

16. We computed this figure by dividing the caseload of 4,829 individuals reported by Kaliss ("A Study of Income Received on the Rosebud Sioux Reservation . . .") by the BIA's 10/8/86 estimate of tribal enrollment (15,267).

17. Authorized under the Snyder Act of 1921 (Public Law 67-85; 42 Stat 208; 25 U.S.C. 13; 25 CFR 20). See Richard Jones, *Federal Programs of Assistance to American Indians: A Report Prepared for the Senate Select Committee on Indian Affairs* (Washington, DC: Government Printing Office, 1985), p. 185.

18. Interview with Iver Crow Eagle, Rosebud TWEP Director, April 7, 1989.

19. Isaac Shapiro and Robert Greenstein, *Holes in the Safety Nets: Poverty Programs and Policies in the States,* Center on Budget and Policy Priorities, April 1988, p. 7.

20. According to Fern Schmidt and Rodney Lanz, County ADC program supervisors, an estimated 99 percent of all recipients in Todd County are American Indians.

21. In Roxanne Dunbar Ortiz, *The Great Sioux Nation: Sitting in Judg-*

ment on America (New York and Berkeley, CA: American Indian TreatyCouncil Information Center and Moon Books, 1977), p. 98.

22. In Don C. Klowser, *Dakota Indian Treaties* (Deadwood, SD: published by author, 1974), pp. 229–30.

23. "Rosebud Reservation Demographics Report: Literacy Assessment Adult Educational Services Planning Project," Sinte Gleska College, Rosebud Reservation, 1985–86.

24. On BIA relocation programs, see Elaine M. Neils, *Reservation to City: Indian Migration and Federal Relocation*, Research Paper No. 131 (Chicago: University of Chicago Department of Geography, 1971). On relocation at Rosebud, see an unpublished study by Linda Baer, Department of Rural Sociology, South Dakota State University (unseen by the authors, but cited in conversation by Schuyler Houser, Director, Institutes for Economic Development and Tribal Governance, Sinte Gleska College, Rosebud Reservation, December 1988).

25. WIN is the immediate predecessor to the JOBS program established by the Family Support Act of 1988.

26. The practice of unannounced home visits has already been discontinued in many other states.

27. Interviews with DSS Todd County supervisors, Fern Schmidt and Rodney Lanz, January 26, 1989.

28. Paul Szabo, "Job Survey of Todd County," Sinte Gleska College, Rosebud Reservation, June 12, 1985, p. 1.

29. Bureau of Indian Affairs, *Indian Service Population and Labor Force Estimates*, January 1989, p. 1.

30. U. S. Congress, Office of Technological Assessment, *Indian Health Care* (Washington, DC: Government Printing Office, 1986), p. 70.

31. According to the 1985 Sinte Gleska College job survey, of the 214 private sector jobs, 88 percent were in Mission, 9 percent in Rosebud, and 3 percent in St. Francis.

32. Interview with Father Tillman of the St. Francis Mission, February 17, 1989.

33. According to our interviews, rates in the informal economy can turn transportation into a major purchase for people living on minimal incomes. For example, a ride between Parmalee and Rosebud, a distance of approximately thirty miles, costs $10–15 in cash or twice that in food stamps.

34. Interview with Father Tillman, February 17, 1989.

35. Told to us by Calvin Jones, Sr., Business Manager, Rosebud Sioux tribe.

36. Interviews with Paul Valandra, Director of the Rosebud JTPA program, February 17, 1989, and Pat Eagle Elk, Director of Rosebud Sioux Alcohol Abuse Programs, March 17, 1989.

37. Grobsmith, *Lakota of the Rosebud*, p. 112.

38. The after-care program offers additional support to individuals who have completed a treatment program. On Rosebud, after-care consists of 8–12 weeks of weekly meetings with a support group and then monthly sessions with a counselor for the next two years.

39. Interview with Pat Eagle Elk, March 17, 1989.

40. Kathryn Keeley, "Welfare and Self-Employment," unpublished paper prepared for Wingspread conference on "States in the Lead: Self-Employment for Welfare Recipients," Racine, Wisconsin, July 1986, p. 11.

41. Significant quantities of reservation land are held, in highly fractionated amounts, by multiple heirs to the owners of allotments of tribal land made at the end of the last century or early in this one. Much of this land is leased to cattlemen or others, and the owners receive checks covering lease payments.

42. Land lease checks are prorated on a twelve-month basis.

43. Interview with Amos Prue, Director of Rosebud HUD Housing Assistance Program, March 13, 1989. In contrast, the average portion

of income paid by U. S. metropolitan families is 18.5 percent. "Hub Rent Is Found Worst in Nation," *Boston Globe*, March 19, 1989, p. 82.

44. Maximum income cutoffs range from $24,500 for one person to $43,750 for a family of eight.

45. Kaliss, "A Study of Income Received on the Rosebud Reservation. . . ," p. 45.

46. Gross income eligibility limits range from $596 for one person to $2,037 for a family of eight. See House Ways and Means Committee, United States Congress, "Background Material and Data on Programs within the Jurisdiction of the House Ways and Means Committee," March 24, 1988, p. 787.

47. Authorized under Public Law 95-113, 91 Stat. 958, Sec. 1304, Public Law 97-98. See Jones, *Federal Programs of Assistance to American Indians*, p. 6.

48. Julie Rovner, "Congress Approves Overhaul of Welfare System," *Congressional Quarterly,* October 8, 1988, p. 2825.

49. Passed August 15, 1953, Public Law 280 extends state jurisdiction over criminal offenses and civil causes of action on Indian reservations in California, Minnesota, Nebraska, Oregon, and Wisconsin. See Francis Paul Prucha, *Documents of United States Indian Policy* (Lincoln: University of Nebraska Press, 1975), pp. 233–34.

50. Interview with Craig Hathaway, Office of Child Support Enforcement, Washington, D.C., April 3, 1989.

51. Interviews with Michael Swallow, Executive Director, and Albert C. Jones, Managing Attorney, Dakota Plains Legal Services, February 3, 1989 and January 26, 1989, respectively.

52. Mothers have "good cause" to refuse to cooperate in establishing paternity or collective support when, for example, they are victims of rape and incest, or face threats of violence from the absent parent.

53. Because the majority of absent parents are fathers, we will use father

to denote absent parent and mother to refer to the custodial parent.

54. The Task Force on Indian Economic Development, using 1980 U. S. census data, calculated that 58 percent of all reservation Native American men, as compared to 18 percent of all U. S. men, were not employed in 1980. We should note that these figures include all men, not simply those actually in the labor force. U. S. Department of the Interior, *Report of the Task Force on Indian Economic Development* (Washington, DC: Government Printing Office, 1986), Table 2, p. 6.

55. *Congressional Record*, September 28, 1988, p. 8907.

56. Interview with Iver Crow Eagle, April 7, 1989.

57. Interviews with Sinte Gleska College administrators, 1989.

58. *Congressional Record*, September 28, 1988, p. 8900.

59. Office of Family Assistance, Department of Health and Human Services, "Summary of Family Support Act—JOBS Program Native American Leaders' Meeting," January 11, 1989, p. 3.

60. See the Epilogue to this paper for an update on this process.

61. Catherine Bertini (Director, Office of Family Assistance), letter to officials of federally recognized tribes and Alaska Native organizations, December 13, 1988.

62. According to Michael Hughes of the Arizona Department of Economic Security, HHS regional officials held their first meeting with Arizona tribes on March 24, 1989.

63. Office of Family Assistance, "Summary of Family Support Act . . . ," p. 3.

64. Family Support Administration, U. S. Department of Health and Human Services, "Aid to Families with Dependent Children (AFDC) Action Transmittal," February 24, 1989, p. 5.

65. This figure is for program costs incurred between July 1, 1987 and June 30, 1988, according to Norman DeWeaver, JTPA Specialist,

Center for Community Change, interview March 16, 1989.

66. Lynn Olson and Toby Herr, "Building Opportunity for Disadvantaged Young Families: The Project Match Experience," Northwestern University Center for Urban Affairs and Policy Research, February 1989.

67. Interview with Karen Thorne, Director of Employment and Training, Phoenix Indian Center, Inc., March 30, 1989.

68. Interview with Norman DeWeaver, March 16, 1989.

69. Of course, it may not be the one outlier who is the problem. With a large enough sample size, even trivial differences become statistically significant. Differences of the same magnitude may not be significant for a smaller sample.

70. Interview with Lewis Lane, Director, Gila River Indian Community Social Services, March 27, 1989.

71. Interview with Gila River Indian Community Governor Thomas White, March 27, 1989.

72. Arizona Department of Commerce, "Gila River Indian Community: Community Profile," June 1988.

73. Bureau of Indian Affairs, "Indian Service Population and Labor Force Estimates," January 1989, p. 16.

74. Office of Planning and Evaluation, Gila River Indian Community, "An Evaluation of the Gila River Indian Community Employment and Training Program," November 1985.

75. Interview with Rod Lewis, March 27, 1989.

76. In states which already operate AFDC-UP programs, tribal governments may still need to investigate how the work experience requirement mandated under the Family Support Act affects their BIA-GA recipients.

77. Governor's Task Force on Welfare Reform, Final Reports and Recommendations, *A Family Investment Strategy for Low-Income Families*

in Arizona, January 1989, p. 57.

78. Ibid., p. 53.

79. Ellwood, *Poor Support*, p. 228.

8

MIND SETS AND ECONOMIC DEVELOPMENT ON INDIAN RESERVATIONS[1]

Ronald L. Trosper

A number of key factors in economic development—such as natural resources or financial capital—are relatively easy to measure and analyze. Much more difficult to understand, measure, and plan for is the role in development played by culture, and in particular by the often unarticulated conceptions that people have of themselves and of the world around them.

In the concluding chapter, Ronald Trosper takes up aspects of this issue through an examination of the "mind sets" that Indians and various groups in the larger society bring to the development problem. He analyzes the implications of certain mind sets for economic development policymaking, and closes by relating those implications to some of the recommendations made in the introductory chapter to this volume.

INTRODUCTION

With self-determination moving tribal governments toward control of their economic development, a new range of issues is presented to Indian leadership. Their control, or near control, of economic development challenges tribal leaders to be innovative. Kalt and Cornell point out that proper use of a community's shared ideas can be useful in economic development. They propose that "formal institutions of governance are public goods that are ultimately produced by a society's culture."[2] Economic and political development should be made in ways that do not contradict existing cultural values. But some values seem consistent with economic development and others are not. Is this true, and if so, what can a tribal leader do about it?

In order to understand the role of cultural values, one needs to have ways to compare them. This essay presents a classification of values that assists in such comparisons.[3] The purpose is to assist tribal leaders and their advisors in determining their own community's values. With such an understanding, economic development strategy can be adjusted either to accommodate or to change these values.

This paper presents categories one can use to comprehend another person's perspective. A consultant may wish to understand a tribal leader. A tribal chairman may wish to understand an enterprise manager or a BIA superintendent. A college student may wish to understand a professor. Each person and each culture sees the world slightly differently. Each person has his or her own "mind set." Certain ideas and institutions are consistent with some mind sets and conflict with others. Because of space limitations, the following descriptions of mind sets and their associated ideas about economic development are brief. The goal is to enable the reader to see the mind sets he or she deals with in economic affairs, and to decide what to do about them.

The paper has five parts. The first describes the components of mind sets. The second describes some typical mind sets, particularly those of the dominant society and Indians. The third illustrates differences in economic analysis that correspond to differences in mind sets. The fourth relates mind sets to practical recommendations such as those offered by Cornell and Kalt in their introductory chapter to this volume. A final section offers some process suggestions.

MIND SET COMPONENTS

That American Indians and the dominant society have different mind sets is well known. In order to discuss the differences, and to trace the results of the differences, one needs to have a way to describe the mind sets. One needs dimensions along which to measure them. With the dimensions, one can discuss differences in detail, one can note partial changes, and one can connect the components of the mind sets to the ways people conduct economic action. This essay uses two types of classifications: value orientations and cognitive structures.

Value Orientations. Florence Kluckhohn, working with Fred Strodtbeck, provided a very useful description of mind sets with the concept of "value orientations," which are ordered in four dimensions:[4] (1) Man-nature, (2) Time, (3) Activity, and (4) Relational. Because of constraints of time and resources, they did not study orientations to human nature and to space.[5] Here are brief synopses of the four:

Man/nature: "What is the relation of man to nature (and supernature)?" The answer to this question has three possibilities: subjugation to nature (subj), harmony with nature (with), or mastery over nature (over).

Time: "What is the temporal focus of human life?" In its widest dimension, the orientation to time has three possibilities: past, present, and future.

Activity: "What is the modality of human activity?" Here two possibilities were explored: being, which expresses human personality by spontaneous expression of what is innate; or doing, which expresses human personality through accomplishments.[6]

Relational: "What is the modality of man's relationship to other men?" In a superior's orientation (S), directions and goals for a person are set by elders, and relations are ordered hierarchically. In a group orientation (G), goals for a person are set by the entire group, and relations are ordered with equality. In an individualistic orientation (I), a person's own desires are allowed to determine his or her goals for action, and relations have no particular order, hierarchical or equal.[7]

Kluckhohn and Strodtbeck emphasize that the order of second and third place in each of these orientations matters. In the relational orientation, for instance, the following two differ:

Individuals over Group over Superiors
Individuals over Superiors over Group

While both of these orientations emphasize individualism, the first states that an individual's second duty, after himself or herself, is to attend to the goals of the group. The second states that the individual should attend to the goals of his or her elders or superiors. In comparing two communities or two cultures along these dimensions, the fact that second place differs would mean that a community with the first ordering would appear more democratic.

I was alerted to the importance of taking values seriously by Fremont Lyden's article reporting the results of research by the Values Project Northwest.[8] That article set up two paradigms that appeared to describe the ways of thinking of Indians and non-Indians. Administration of the Kluckhohn questionnaire, however, revealed that individuals in six organizations affecting the Lummi tribe differed and agreed in surprising ways in their value orientations. Each organization had distinctive orientations.

The Kluckhohn questionnaire asks people to select preferred ways of acting in typical situations. The following example illustrates how the questionnaire is set up. Persons are asked about wage work, as follows:

There are three ways in which men who do not themselves hire others may work:

1. One way is working on one's own as an individual. In this case a man is pretty much his own boss. He decides most things himself, and how he gets along is his own business. He only has to take care of himself and he doesn't expect others to look out for him.

2. One way is working in a group of men where all the men work together without there being one main boss. Every man has something to say in the decisions that are made, and all the men can count on one another.

3. One way is working for an owner, a big boss, or a man who has been running things for a long time (a *patron*). In this case,

the men do not take part in deciding how the business will be run, but they know they can depend on the boss to help them out in many ways.

Which of these ways is usually best for a man who does not hire others?

Which of the other two ways is better for a man who does not hire others?

Which of the three ways do you think most other persons in your community would think is best?[9]

If a person selects item 1, he probably has an individualistic orientation. Item 2 indicates a group orientation, and item 3 indicates an orientation to superiors.

Cognitive Structures. Although Kluckhohn and Strodtbeck seem to claim that value orientations are all that we need to use in comparing cultures, and although other people seem to agree, certain dimensions of mind sets are not fully captured by value orientations.[10] Mind sets also include the following two cognitive categories:[11]

Dimensions: "What is truth's structure?" Is knowledge structured in a scheme which has one right answer to most problems—dualism—or are many answers possible, each depending on one's assumptions—relativism?

Unity: "How unified is knowledge?" If it can be broken into pieces without error, and must be to be studied, then knowledge is compartmentalized. If interrelationships are so pervasive that to ignore them creates error, then knowledge is holistic.

These categories present clear differences between the types of mind sets described below.

Organization. Value orientations and cognitive structures are the "deep" or "underlying" aspects of mind sets. Certain other characteristics, however, derive from these and are important. One of these is a culture's approach to organizational issues related to political process. Organizational questions can be addressed by looking at organizational value-sets of a culture. These value-sets may not be as fundamental as are value orientations or cognitive structures. Value orientations and cognitive structures affect everything. Organizational value-sets affect only certain parts of life, but are particularly important when discussing economic activity, which has to be organized in some way. Three aspects allow distinctions that matter regarding Indians:

Leadership: What kind of leadership is preferred? Max Weber suggests three choices: traditional, bureaucratic, and charismatic.[12] A traditional leader gains followers by appealing to shared traditional values from the position of authority defined by these values. A bureaucratic leader's authority rests on apparently "rational," systematic, and explicit rules that are legally enacted. A charismatic leader gains followers because of his or her personality, which may be expressed in one of the ways defined above by the *activity* value orientation.

Autonomy: How independent is the individual or a group of individuals allowed to be from the general organization? Is diversity among departments and individuals allowed, or must everyone conform to one set of standards?

Agreement: In a group or an organization, what is the method of determining the group's goals? Is majority rule sufficient? Is unanimity required? Or is the decision of one person the answer?

These are mostly subcategories under the issue of the relational type of value orientation in a culture, described above.

Some discussion is in order. Suppose a community ranks the group orientation first. The question remains, what rule is used in determining the community's goals? For an individual to submit to the group, is a majority vote sufficient? Or is the person's own vote also required, which means unanimity through consensus?

If a group has an orientation to superiors, the mode of leadership of the person who directs the group still remains an issue: does he or she lead through customary rules (traditional), through the power of personality (charismatic), or through the application of impersonal, legally-enacted rules (bureaucratic)?

The method by which a charismatic leader presents himself or herself depends upon the value orientations and personality structures of potential followers, as well as upon the leader's policies. Indians, having a *doing* activity orientation, look at a leader's accomplishments to determine his or her personal worth. A certain degree of circumspection in conduct may be required. The more usual image of a charismatic leader is one with a *being* orientation, who provides seemingly spontaneous expression of his or her personality.[13]

A better understanding of mind sets could illuminate some of the puzzles encountered as an Indian tribe struggles to adapt institutions from the dominant society to the specific desires of the tribe's members. In order to help in connecting value orientations to economic development, the remainder of this paper proposes some ways in which these categories can illuminate specific types of thinking, and what those different types of thinking mean in terms of economic development strategy.

TYPES OF MIND SETS

In order to contrast the different types of mind sets which underlie analysis of economic development advice, we can observe four mind sets among the teachers, opponents, and allies of Native Americans. The word "paradigm," used loosely, is another way to say "mind set." To distinguish among them, some labels are needed, as follows:

Dominant—the mind set of the powerful people that manage American life, which has three variants:

> **General**—the private business sector

> **Mainstream Academic**—the majority of college professors

> **Federal**—federal bureaucrats, especially those involved in Indian Affairs

Environmental—the leaders of the major environmental groups such as the Sierra Club and the Wilderness Society.

New Left—the emerging group of radical professors on college campuses and writers for magazines such as *The Nation* and *Z*.

Pan-Indian—the views of Indians who try to portray a general "Native American" viewpoint, especially in talking to national media.

Fremont Lyden identified the value orientations of the Dominant Paradigm and the Environmental Paradigm.[14] The current debate on "political correctness" on campus provides two categories, the mainstream academic and the new left. Renato Rosaldo called the mainstream academic attitude the "objectivist-monumentalist coalition" in order to describe it as a combination of scientists and literary scholars who resist change at Stanford and other universities.[15] The "new left" appears on campuses as the opponents to mainstream academic views. Each can be charged with insisting that its point of view, being "correct," is the one that should receive preference in public debate on campus and in the classroom. As we shall see, the new left scholars do not fully agree with the pan-Indian viewpoint. Spelling out the mind sets may help college students in working out the differences.

Table 1 presents a summary of the different stances of each of these mind sets. The following discussion explains the reasons for asserting particular components of each one.

First, the pan-Indian paradigm needs to be contrasted to the dominant paradigm in its general form.

In proposing the existence of a pan-Indian viewpoint, one does not want to assert that it fits exactly with any one tribe. Diversity among American Indian tribes is well known. But if one listens carefully to Indians presenting a "native" viewpoint to non-Indians, certain commonalities can be identified. Generalizing about the dominant culture, while easier, also has risks. One difficulty is that the dominant culture often perceives itself in one way and acts in another. This is particularly true with the orientation to time, in which the perception is future-orientation while the fact is present-orientation. Another difficulty is that considerable variation is possible within a culture.

The difference between American Indians and the dominant culture regarding the man/nature orientation is probably the best known. Most tribes share the idea that man should live in harmony with his surroundings. Indian spirituality demands respect for the natural world. Failure to preserve balance in one's interaction with nature can be dangerous. Christian spirituality, following its early roots in Greece and Judea, allows man to dominate the natural world. The Garden of Eden origin myth justifies man's dominion. The practical consequences of these two different mind sets have been described at great length.[16]

TABLE 1
Mind Sets and Their Characteristics

	DOMINANT			ENVIRONMENTAL	NEW LEFT	PAN-INDIAN
	General	Mainstream Academic	Federal Government			
DIRECTIVE value orientations						
Man/Nature	over > subj > with	over > subj > with	over > subj > with	with > over > subj	with > subj > over	with > subj > over
Time	pres > fut > past	past > pres > fut	pres > fut > past	fut > pres > past	fut > pres > past	pres = fut > past
Activity	doing	doing	being	being	doing	doing
Relational	S > I > G	I > S > G	S > G > I	G > I > S	G > I > S	G > I > S
COGNITIVE Structures						
Dimensions	dualism	dualism	dualism	dualism	relativism	relativism
Degree of Unity	compartments	compartments	compartments	holistic	holistic	holistic
ORGANIZATION value sets						
Leadership	bureaucratic	bureaucratic	bureaucratic	bureaucratic	charismatic	charismatic
Autonomy	conformity	conformity	conformity	conformity	diversity	diversity
Agreement	majority	majority	majority	majority	consensus	consensus

In the time dimension, speakers in the pan-Indian mode like to quote the Iroquois idea that plans should be made with the impacts as far as the seventh generation of descendants taken into account. Tribal leaders worry about the opinion of their grandchildren regarding stewardship decisions made today. The present and the future are seen equally, and are more important than the past.

The dominant culture has a contrast between action and perception. In action, the culture is present oriented. Rates of discount for investment are high, the rate of saving is low. Long-term environmental consequences are usually ignored or given lip service. Ronald Reagan's fiscal policies were allowed to place the entire nation in debt to other countries. But the idea of preparation for the future underlies emphasis on education of youth, on retirement programs, and on the organization of capital markets. This future orientation, however, refers in most cases only to one person's lifetime. Perhaps one's children matter, but grandchildren and later generations are not a major concern.

In orientation to activity, both the pan-Indian viewpoint and the dominant paradigm agree on a *doing* orientation. In the *activity* dimension, Kluckhohn refers to one's "mode of self-expression." Does one express oneself spontaneously (the *being* mode), or does one express oneself through one's accomplishments (the *doing* mode), or does one pursue self-development (the *being in becoming* mode)? Both Indian tribes and the pan-Indians emphasize accomplishment rather than spontaneity. They agree on ranking doing above becoming, and becoming above being.

Generalizations about the ranking of group, superiors, and individualistic relational alternatives among American Indians are difficult. Tribes vary from elder-oriented societies among the Pueblos to the extremely individualistic Sioux. In the pan-Indian synthesis, however, the group relational alternative seems to predominate, with the individualistic alternative in second place. The goals of the group have a greater pull on a modern American Indian than do his or her own personal goals. Since respect for an individual's right to pursue his or her own course is also high, however, one might want to equate the group and individualistic modalities in the pan-Indian synthesis.

The dominant paradigm presents another paradox: Although the perception is that individualism is the primary mode, orientation to superiors in fact dominates. To provide an example, consider the labor market. Most organizations and institutions are highly structured, with the presumption that the boss's orders are to be followed, with little consultation with the workers. The only option a worker has is to move to another organization, where the hierarchy will again dominate. Is this an individualistic or a superior-oriented system in its dominant mode? The superior or hierarchical principle is in first place, governing daily relations, with the individualistic mode in second place, governing job changes.

In comparing the pan-Indian synthesis with the dominant paradigm in relational systems, one can see why misunderstanding in relational matters can be high. Both place respect for individualistic goals in second place. For the dominant society, individuals are expected to subordinate their goals to those set by the top managers of a hierarchy. For a pan-Indian, individuals are expected to moderate their goals according to the goals of the group, which will have set its group goals with individuals' personal goals as one of the factors. Both groups respect individuality in different contexts.

The pan-Indian viewpoint and the dominant paradigm differ on three of Kluckhohn's four operationalized value orientations. The two also disagree on two major cognitive structures. On the dimensionality of knowledge, the dominant paradigm still sees the world in two dimensions, right and wrong, them and us. Proof is given by the popularity of books such as Dinesh D'Souza's *Illiberal Education*, which assumes that there is one right way to understand the world.[17] This is in strong contrast to American Indians' perspective; their own diversity serves as a model for the nature of truth. American Indians ask one another, "What's your origin myth?" Because they accept the idea that there are many truths, the pan-Indian mind set is relativistic. A traditionalist from a particular tribe, however, is likely to defend the correctness of his vision of the nature of knowledge, just as a staunch supporter of the dominant paradigm will defend his belief in just one origin myth.

On the issue of the unity of knowledge, the two disagree again— American Indians tend to see knowledge in a holistic way, while the dominant society tends to break knowledge into compartments. The departmental structure of universities, the federal government, and state governments is an example of this.[18] When tribes assume management of resources, they establish departments of natural resources in an effort to reunify what the dominant culture assigns to separate entities.

If they were not different dimensions of the issue, the relativism-holism versus dualism-compartmentalism of the two mind sets would seem paradoxical. Shouldn't a holistic view also lead to belief in one truth? The solution to this puzzle is that even holistic truth varies with one's perspective; what each person sees can have the shape of a unified whole or the shape of a collection of parts. The dualistic-holism combination would hold that there is only one correct whole truth.

These six dimensions of mind sets have numerous implications and manifestations in the cultures of the dominant society and in pan-Indian events. For the purposes of this paper, the manifestations in organizational patterns are most important. Organizational patterns, or value-sets, depend most heavily on the constellation of relational value orientations and upon the cognitive structures.

For Native Americans, the importance of group relational value orientation means that agreement in a group is by consensus and leadership of the charismatic sort is preferable in most cases to that of a bureaucracy. The relativistic mind set supports the acceptability of diversity within an organization's subunits, while the holistic view would hold the organization as a whole responsible for outcomes. Consensus, which means near-unanimity, determines a group's goals. This means that a charismatic leader, to be successful, must embody goals that nearly everyone agrees to. The leader's charisma, of course, serves to assist achievement of consensus.

For the dominant paradigm, the importance of superiors in relationships matches with acceptance of bureaucratic leadership styles. Leaders are expected to head organizations and to be responsible for the results the organizations attain. The dualistic view leads to an expectation that everyone in an organization will conform to that organization's mind set. Also, if a group uses voting to achieve a group goal, a simple majority is accepted as sufficient to give authority to the group's leadership to proceed with implementation. Because full agreement is not needed, the use of powerfully charismatic persuasion is also not needed. As Lindholm has discussed, however, charisma's occurrence and significance is increasing in the dominant society.[19]

Because the mainstream academic viewpoint on university campuses is representative of the dominant paradigm, most professors agree with it in most dimensions. American Indians seeking education meet the dominant paradigm at college.

Because of the influence of professors of history, English, and other humanities, the mainstream academic viewpoint places much more emphasis on the past than does society at large. Their time orientation, therefore, is considerably different from off campus. What was done in the past is rated above the present as a motivation for decisions, with the future ranked last.

Although the university is also a home of individualists in academic achievement, the tenured staff have more influence than nontenured professors. The importance of tenured professors as a locus of decision-making is great enough to keep the orientation to superiors in first position above individualism as a primary motivation. As in the business sector, the ideology of individualism in academia is overshadowed by hierarchy.

Federal government bureaucrats have another mind set that is a variant of the dominant paradigm. The main documented difference with them is that their activity orientation tends to be being rather than doing.[20] The myriad network of rules and regulations is consistent with an orientation of compliance, which is not easily measured by accomplishment.

The environmental paradigm has some sharp differences in outlook compared to the dominant paradigm.[21] The man/nature orientation is very self-consciously a *harmony with nature* orientation; *subject to nature* is in second place. The use of American Indian images is quite natural because of this orientation. Some Indians have noted that the content of the harmony orientation may differ. The non-Indian justification of a *with nature* orientation is usually based on usefulness rather than upon moral or spiritual ideals. Many environmentalists keep man's needs in first place, justifying good treatment of the environment by its beneficial results in keeping the earth livable.

For environmentalists, the concern about the environment accompanies a future orientation in the time dimension. In the activity dimension, spontaneous enjoyment of the world—being—dominates over the need to accomplish things. In the relational dimension, there is acknowledgment that many users of the environment all need to be consulted and involved in decision-making. The importance of an individual's goals ranks second, however. The orientation to superiors is last.

In the cognitive structures, environmentalism displays a different combination: holism and dualism. Most environmentalists see the holistic viewpoint and emphasize interdependencies in nature. The term "ecology" embodies the holistic viewpoint. But there remains a need to have one right answer, and the dimensional view, while different from the dominant paradigm, still is dualistic, assuming that there is one right answer, rather than a set of possibly right answers.

The national attention focused on critiquing "political correctness" has occurred because a significant minority of scholars have departed radically from the dominant paradigm. The attempts of these new left scholars to assert different viewpoints have been met with considerable resistance. Ironically, adherents of the dominant paradigm project their own intolerance of alternative viewpoints onto the emerging respect for multiculturalism.

The new left shares some orientations with the environmental paradigm. In the orientation of man and nature, they have the *harmony with nature* orientation.[22] The *mastery over nature* orientation is probably still in second place. The activism of this way of thinking assumes some ability to change the way things are, which is an *over nature* orientation. For some on the left, mastery of nature may be in first place.

The new left has a *doing* orientation, or perhaps a *being-in-becoming* orientation. The *being-in-becoming* orientation is part accomplishment and part spontaneity with self-development emphasized. Scholarly accomplishment is still represented by written output. Output in the community is represented by organizational success.

In relational priority, group orientation is on top. In general, the new left are pro-democracy advocates who support empowerment. Empowerment means that everyone participates in decisions. The implications have been worked out in some detail by Albert and Hahnel.[23] Some of the left in academia, however, remain oriented to superiors, and conduct classes in an authoritarian manner.

In cognitive structures, the new left is aggressively relativistic. Beginning in anthropology and spreading to philosophy, literary criticism, and history, the fact of multiple viewpoints is now widely accepted on more than just the left.[24] There is a willingness to cross disciplinary boundaries, although that is not strong enough a movement to satisfy this author.

In the organizational area, the new left support for group relations translates into a set of values that are similar to Indians: tolerance of diversity, a belief that the group is responsible for its members' welfare, and consensus methods of selecting group goals.[25] A consequence is fragmentation in the political sphere, much as there is fragmentation among American Indians along tribal lines and along a variety of national organizational lines. Groups tend to shrink to the size at which consensus is possible.

TYPES OF ECONOMIC DEVELOPMENT ANALYSIS

The four different mind sets, with three variants for the dominant paradigm, lead to very different attitudes about economic development. Because one does not necessarily cure poverty by reversing what caused it, one should separate the analysis of causes of poverty from the prescriptions for curing it. The beliefs about causes and cures are laid out in Table 2.

For purposes of comparison, causes of poverty are divided into economic and political aspects. The economic aspect consists of resource endowment and the organization of firms. The political aspect is simply the nature of government on reservations. For prescriptions, the role of capital is added to resources and organization. The political aspect is divided into the form of government and the type of action government should undertake.

As causes of poverty, American Indians would agree on the expropriation of lands and the governing of reservations by the Bureau of Indian Affairs as the dominant causes. Neither of these positions can be tied directly to American Indian value orientations. They reflect a knowledge of the history of relations between Indians and the dominant society.

The dominant paradigm in its general form, as represented by the movie *Dances with Wolves*, would agree on expropriation as a cause of poverty. But the relevance of the expropriation is different, because the present orientation of the dominant culture is so strong. The dominant mythos seems unaware that the oldest generation alive today on Indian reservations were born during and immediately after the implementation of the allotment policy and directly experienced the loss of wealth it caused. The history is placed in a mythical realm, located in the world of cinema rather than on the ground today.

In debating causes with scholars, one finds a much greater emphasis on cultural differences as an independent cause of poverty: Indians are seen as not wanting development. This results directly from different orientations to nature and different relational orientations. The *with nature* and group

TABLE 2
Mind Sets and Their Economic Development Analyses

	DOMINANT			ENVIRONMENTAL	NEW LEFT	PAN–INDIAN
	General	Mainstream Academic	Federal Government			
CAUSES OF POVERTY						
Economic						
Resources	expropriation	government discrimination	expropriation	expropriation	expropriation	expropriation
Organization	culture	culture	culture	culture	colonialism	colonialism
Political	tribal government	tribal government	tribal government	colonialism	colonialism	colonialism
PRESCRIPTIONS FOR ECONOMIC DEVELOPMENT						
Economic						
Capital	capital	capital	capital	do not develop	capital	capital
Resources	exploit	exploit	exploit	sustainable	sustainable	sustainable
Organization	corporate	private	corporate	corporate	cooperative	tribal or micro
Political						
Gov't Form	hierarchy	hierarchy	hierarchy	sovereignty	sovereignty	sovereignty
Gov't Action	private property	private property	planning	planning	planning	planning

orientations are seen as incompatible with the modern market. Compartmentalizing knowledge and dominating nature, the dominant society can see in a forest only the few useful products—wood fiber, game animals, water—that can be marketed. Oriented to hierarchy, the dominant society sees corporate structures as necessary for proper organization of a business.

Regarding the role of government, the dominant paradigm sees government as a hindrance to economic activity, and accordingly blames tribal leadership for part of the difficulties on their reservations. Much of the focus is on the failure to adopt pure private property systems of land management. This failure is in the first place blamed on tribal government, and in the second place on the federal government in the form of the BIA. Because of historical blinders, the role of the BIA in actually making incorrect development decisions is ignored.

The historical blindness does not connect to value orientations; it is really nothing more than a natural denial of responsibility for what has occurred. It is part of an ideology justifying the status quo.

Adherents to the environmental paradigm agree with American Indians that expropriation played an important role in causing poverty. But they also have a residual suspicion that American Indian culture played a role as well. They themselves are often opponents of development, resulting from their *with nature* and *being* orientations; but "development" is narrowly defined, a result of dualistic thinking. Being less identified with the dominant culture, they are also more willing to see colonial control of reservations as responsible in part for the poverty on the reservations.

The new left would agree with American Indians on every part of the explanation for poverty. They in particular would not agree with culture as an explanation for lack of adopting the proper organizational forms for development, because they are trying to develop new ways of organization themselves.

We see, therefore, considerable disagreement about the causes of poverty, and the disagreements are in part based on different value orientations. Turning to prescriptions for changing things now, given what has happened, what are the different attitudes? Consider five questions:

Is lack of capital a constraint?
How should natural resources be used?
What organizational form should firms have?

What organizational form should tribal government have?
What action should tribal government take?

Answers to these questions do vary, with one exception. Is lack of capital a constraint? All viewpoints seem to agree on this point: it is.

How should natural resources be used? Because of the differences in orientation to nature, the different mind sets have different answers to the use of resources. The *harmony with nature* and future orientations lead one to advocate sustainable management of resources. *Mastery over nature* and present time orientation lead to exploitation of resources. The pan-Indian viewpoint, the environmental paradigm, and the new left all are opposed to the dominant paradigm on the use of resources.

What organizational form should firms have? The form of firm organization is determined by the relational value orientation and the cognitive structure assumptions. The dominant society, with its orientation to superiors and compartmentalized view of knowledge, organizes firms with the corporate structure divided into product-oriented departments. There is one department or one firm for each product.

The pan-Indian synthesis does not have a consensus on the proper organization for economic development. Some advocate tribal enterprise, and some advocate "micro enterprise," which can be either a form of small-scale private firm similar to the small scale firms in the general economy, or small firms organized in traditional ways. One has to be careful in the use of language here, because a "tribal enterprise" may or may not take the form of an independent tribally owned corporation. If it is a corporation, it fits the dominant society's recommendation. If it takes the form of a tribal enterprise, it may be organized on group principles rather than superior-hierarchical principles. The fact that most American Indian nations have group value orientations combined with holistic cognitive views means that the form of organization for firms should be a major issue, in comparison to the general society, and this is indeed the case. Tribal leaders agonize over setting up independent enterprises with hierarchical structures. Once established, tribal enterprises are plagued with the fact that all tribal members and council members consider themselves legitimate authorities on the business, and want to implement their ideas.

What organizational form should tribal government have? The universal support for tribal sovereignty among American Indians is well known.

One reason for the importance of tribal sovereignty is the extensive difference in the mind sets of Indian tribes compared to the dominant paradigm. Without the protections offered by an officially recognized government, a group of Indians faces tremendous difficulties in preserving their identity and their culture. The potential allies of tribal governments, adherents to the environmental paradigm and the new left, support tribal sovereignty: one reason could be that they, too, having large differences from the dominant paradigm, recognize the usefulness of self-government.[26]

Groups of people can defend their ideas better than can isolated individuals.[27] One reason for extensive voluntary associations in the United States is that such organizations can develop their ideas in common. Naturally, given this tradition in the majority society, there is hostility toward the Indians for having the additional advantage of political sovereignty. Voluntary organizations do not have the ability to tax, to pass laws to protect land, and to otherwise promote their way of looking at things within a defined geographic area. Support for sovereignty doesn't follow from the particular values of Indians; it follows from the difference in values and the history of rights based on original residence. Most participants in voluntary associations do not differ in value orientation from the dominant paradigm. The legal possibility of such associations, however, has led to the existence of some which are quite divergent, such as environmentalists, peace activists, and gay rights advocates.

In Table 2, the entry under government form for the dominant paradigm is that tribal governments need hierarchy. The federal government supports training Indians to learn the ways of administration of the dominant society. A tribe needs to appear to have the proper administrative structures in order to receive grants and contracts from the federal government. At the most basic level, tribes need to have accounting systems that can be audited, which is not objectionable. But in setting up programs, such as in environmental management, welfare programs, court systems, and housing, tribes need to proceed with administrative structures that look right to the providers of funds. Organizational charts need to show a hierarchy, even if consensus is used in practice.

What action should tribal government take? The pan-Indian viewpoint, as represented by the agenda of national Indian organizations such as the National Center for American Indian Enterprise, the Council of Energy Resource Tribes, and Americans for Indian Opportunity, is to promote planning. Federal agencies also promote planning, and provide funding for many of the activities of the national Indian organizations. Is there an apparent convergence of prescriptions here? If so, the idea that different mind sets lead to different policy prescriptions is challenged. The answer has two parts. First, both groups favor planning because they have a *doing* orientation. Planning is an expression of doing through accomplishment of particular goals. Second, the *content* of planning differs considerably, reflecting the other value differences.

For an Indian tribe, with its group relational orientation, planning is much less likely to be a top-down activity. Public meetings, discussion with everyone affected, and long periods in the formulation of plans are all typical of planning in Indian Country. Planning in the dominant society is assigned to planners, who report to the top officials. In the interests of efficiency and following the notion of compartmentalized knowledge, planning is assigned to specialists. It is assumed that there exists one right answer that specialists can discover. The form of planning differs, therefore, between Indians and non-Indians.

The content of plans will also differ, at least with respect to land. When a tribe takes over a planning activity, such as a ten-year plan for a forest, or a land-use plan generally, the scope of activities considered in land use expands. The reasons are two: Indians have a *harmony with nature* orientation and they have a holistic view. As a consequence, they consider a wider range of options and activities.

Proponents of the dominant paradigm recommend that tribal governments implement systems of private property. Their arguments for this generally are by analogy; they think that the success of the dominant society is due to the consequences of systems of private property.[28]

Which of the value orientations and cognitive assumptions are linked with the advocacy of private property? The two primary candidates are the individualistic relational orientation and the compartmentalized cognitive structure. The compartmentalized view denies the existence of interdependencies across property lines, or across organizational lines when firms are involved. Once one recognizes the interdependencies, which are clear from a holistic viewpoint, the rationality of a private property system becomes much less clear. The belief in individual liberty and individual rights complements the compartmentalization of knowledge. When *two* fundamental value orientations are involved in a basic organizational idea, it has powerful support.

Even though the superior relational orientation dominates in fact in organizations of the dominant society, in discussing property systems, the fiction of a corporation being an individual supports the private property concept. In fact, the assets of a corporation are common property for the organization, and disposition of those assets is determined by a hierarchical structure. Many corporations own more assets than Indian tribes do, and the efficiency of their use depends upon organizational issues.[29]

In this presentation of the different prescriptions for economic development that result from the different mind sets, no effort has been made to determine which of the prescriptions is *correct*. Readers who believe in one or the other of the mind sets will probably assume that the prescriptions from that mind set are correct.

Are mind sets changeable? Men and women acquire their mind sets in their youth; changing adult mind sets is difficult but not impossible. Parents, elders, teachers, and other authority figures guide the acquisition process. During a person's youth, values and cognitive assumptions change as the person matures.

People maintain their mind sets through interaction with significant people in their lives: coworkers, family, and friends. Change in mind sets can occur when these significant people agree and support the changes.

Some may argue that mind sets can't change in adults. Some Indian communities have changed the role of alcohol through concerted group effort. Individuals who wish to cease dependence on alcohol use the support of others to assist them in abstinence. Certainly a movement to sobriety is a significant change in values: but is it a change in mind set? Alcohol affects self-image and one's sense of well being, issues related to identity. Is its use related to any of the value orientations? Probably only to the human nature orientation.

Another common situation where one observes changes in values is when a person takes a job in a large organization and becomes socialized to the values of that organization. Every organization has a set of ideas about how the external environment is organized and how the organization relates to that environment. Persons who move from the BIA to a tribal government experience a period of transition during which they need to examine certain of the common assumptions of BIA culture. Are these changes in mind sets or ideology? Probably a combination of both.

Individuals find this transition dramatic because of the power of groups of people to influence the beliefs of an individual. Some people can also resist the mind set of an organization, and simply undertake an assigned job. Such people find changing jobs resolves the tension. Such "sorting" helps organizations maintain their mind sets by retaining mutual agreement among employees.

Given that an individual can accommodate himself or herself to new institutional cultures—unless much sorting occurs—we may conclude that some change in mind sets is possible. For a community (or an organization) to change its mind set, however, a great many individuals must change in the same ways. Based on numbers alone, we may say that such changes are unlikely except as generations succeed one another. Strong clear leadership that can persuade people to modify their most basic mind sets is probably rare. Charismatic leadership styles are best able to change mind sets.

Should people's mind sets be changed? How can one agree that a community should change its mind set? Who can make the decision? If one approaches this issue from the pan-Indian respect for diversity, the six factors that form mind sets are very difficult to judge as "right" or "wrong." Support for sovereignty suggests a community should be allowed to adjust as it wishes; the modern market economy provides both pressures to adopt the dominant mind set and opportunities to survive without doing so.

Lyden reports results of interviews in the Pacific Northwest that warn us not to jump to conclusions regarding who holds what mind sets. The Values Project Northwest is sponsored by an Indian tribe that has a man/nature value orientation in which man's domination of nature ranks first, man is subject to nature second, and man should live in harmony with nature third. A timber company working near the tribe placed the *with* relationship in second place.[30] One should expect surprises of this sort.

MIND SETS AND ECONOMIC DEVELOPMENT POLICY TODAY

This collection of articles was assembled by a group of scholars and students interested in suggesting new ideas regarding economic development on Indian reservations. In their introductory chapter to this volume, Cornell and Kalt suggest that a tribe needs institutions that can perform three tasks:

1. Mobilize the community in support of particular strategies;
2. Efficiently carry out strategic choices; and
3. Provide a political environment in which investors—large or small, tribal members or nonmembers—feel secure.[31]

In what ways can the contrasts between mind sets presented above assist in evaluating tribal institutions with regard to these three tasks? Are there conflicts between aspects of Indian mind sets, represented by the pan-Indian viewpoint, and the recommendations offered by Kalt and Cornell?

With regard to the first task, the categories presented in mind sets provide ways to evaluate the match between economic development strategy and culture. For instance, in the use of natural resources for economic development, a harmony with nature orientation, a future time orientation, and a holistic view of knowledge lead to limitations on the rate of exploitation of a tribe's land. Economic development activities which challenge these aspects of a community's mind set will cause dissension and disagreement.

If a community has a group relational orientation, then consensus on economic development policy will be required. Since such consensus takes time to achieve, rapid adoption of an economic development strategy may be unwise. The particular rules and procedures the community has used in achieving consensus need to be respected and utilized.

Some tribes may differ from the pan-Indian consensus on several dimensions. The time orientation may place the present in first place. The man/nature orientation may allow man's domination of nature. These would lead to development policy that would allow a greater rate of consumption of nonrenewable resources than would the pan-Indian combination of ideas.

In carrying out the second task, Cornell and Kalt suggest two actions: formalizing decision rules and procedures and creating professional systems for management of finances, records, and personnel. Are either of these recommendations obviously biased in favor of the dominant paradigm?

Formalized decision rules mean placing the force of law behind the ways in which a community makes major decisions. The rules should be clear and hard to change, as in the example of a constitution. This recommendation has no particular statement about the *content* of the rules: they can vary according to the desires of a community. Each of the components of a mind set can be used to affect the structure of a community's rules. The particular principles that express a community's harmony with nature can determine the environmental laws that the community enacts. Indigenous tribal communities had clear, although unwritten, rules which show that no conflict exists between the recommendation and Indian mind sets.

Where should tribes look to find models for such rules? Their own history and culture is the first place to look. Because of the power of the federal government, tribes are often forced to accept rules from the dominant society. For many of them, the federal government will provide funds only if a tribe adopts rules that comply with federal law. In the area of environmental regulation, for instance, application of money and authority available through the Environmental Protection Agency requires looking at nature as the EPA does. The EPA is not a holistically oriented organization: its targets are *particular* pollutants of water and air. In the management of forests, the dominant society looks only at particular products: wood fiber, certain types of wild game, and endangered species, for instance.

Uncritical adoption of rules from the federal government, or the dominant society generally, may create a conflict between Task 1, achieving community consensus, and Task 2, Action 1, adopting formal rules. Tribes can use their sovereign powers to address this conflict by passing laws that satisfy them, if the federal government will be flexible in application of its laws.

Does a similar problem arise regarding the implementation of financial, record, and personnel systems? Are the commercial financial packages that operate on modern computers biased in their mind sets? Are record systems also biased? The answer to these questions would seem to be no. Keeping track of money and facts is not an issue of people's relationship to nature, or their time orientation, or even their activity orientation.

The structure of a personnel system may be affected by relational orientations. Many mainstream personnel systems may embody more strongly hierarchical relationships than a tribe might be comfortable with.

Individual autonomy may be controlled. Uncritical adoption of models from off the reservation will cause implementation problems. The principle of having a *system*, however, is separate from the particular *content* of the personnel system.

With regard to the two actions recommended for implementing the second task, then, there is no logical conflict between the recommendations and differences in value orientations. Conflicts may arise with regard to particular rules; but such rules can be different from those of the dominant society, if Indian sovereignty is respected.

Task 3 is the provision of a secure environment for investment, for tribal members as well as nonmembers. Cornell and Kalt recommend two actions here: clear separation of powers to create checks and balances on political leadership and the separation of electoral politics from the day-to-day management of business enterprises. Are either of these particularly biased toward one mind set or another?

The principles of separation of powers and checks and balances derive from consensus and rule by unanimous consent. This makes it more closely related to the pan-Indian mind set than that of the dominant society. Evidence for this is that most of the more traditional Indian communities have functioning check and balance systems. The Iroquois system is famous, of course.[32] Cornell and Kalt were impressed by the traditional system at Cochiti. The potlatch in the Northwest, in which a wealthy leader distributes his wealth while enhancing his prestige, is a traditional check-and-balance system that effectively limited the power of governing elders. Tribes that find themselves burdened with a constitution which fails to limit the power of their leaders should be able to find traditions which give ways to limit those powers without compromising tribal mind sets.

Regarding the separation of day-to-day management from electoral politics, the matter may be more complicated. The difficulty arises from a combination of holistic thinking and group relational orientation. From a holistic viewpoint, every decision has broad consequences, through external effects and interactions with the environment around a firm. Drawing a clear line between a business's decisions and the consequences outside of the business is hard to do. The idea that everyone should have a say in political decisions can be extended from issues of policy and direction to minor decisions about day-to-day management.

The intractability of this separation problem would seem to be a consequence of fundamental mind set differences between the dominant paradigm and the pan-Indian paradigm. Unlike the other recommendations of Cornell and Kalt, the advice to separate electoral politics and day-to-day management probably does raise issues related to mind sets that cause the problem to be difficult to solve.

In general, however, the recommendations of Cornell and Kalt do avoid the pitfalls of mind set differences between the general Indian viewpoint and the dominant society. There are possible conflicts if particular models from the dominant society are used which conflict with a particular tribe's mind set. Cornell and Kalt identify some of these in their paper, particularly regarding tribal governmental forms adopted during the implementation of the Indian Reorganizaton Act. For the first three of the four main recommendations, careful interpretation is needed to avoid conflicts.

PROCESS PROPOSAL

One main purpose of this essay has been to provide the reader with some leads on ways to develop self-awareness regarding value orientations and cognitive styles. Because ideas are powerful, one should know what ideas are having influence, and then make conscious decisions about which ones to accept and which ones to modify. Champagne has approached this problem from a related but different perspective, examining the ways in which types of social and political structures limit or allow institutional change. For instance, when the political system is separate from the religious or kinship systems, change in political organization is easier.[33]

Tribal leaders should consider using value-oriented questionnaires such as that developed by Kluckhohn to enable them to see where their people are on these important dimensions, if simple discussion of the ideas is insufficient. Because tribal values have been subject to many influences, each tribe will have its own distinct mind set. Complicated and expensive public administration of questionnaires may not be necessary; discussion of the questionnaires by groups of tribal members may be sufficient to reveal the common attitudes. In fact, the practice of anonymous questionnaires analyzed by experts is probably a thought pattern that is more oriented to superiors than would be comfortable for a group of Indians.

Public discussion by everyone of the values may serve a very useful purpose. Some of the questions needed may not exist, and people interested in developing these ideas should undertake to write and test such questions, to add to the set of questions now in use.

The Lummi tribe established the Values Project Northwest to utilize the Kluckhohn instrument. The Lummi recognized that a questionnaire developed while studying Indians in the Southwest could be very useful in educating themselves and their neighbors about cultural differences. Many conflicts are due to different value orientations and to mistaken assumptions about other groups' attitudes. The Lummi have found study of differences in value orientation to be helpful, particularly when similarities exist that are not recognized. Employees of a bank that works with the Lummi thought the Lummi to be oriented to superiors; but in fact they are group-oriented, as is the majority of the bank's employees. Many believed the Lummi to have a being orientation, when actually they share a doing orientation with their neighbors. Most Lummi even thought other Lummi had a being orientation, when doing was the primary orientation.[34]

The dominance of the group relational value orientation suggests that public processes of decision-making that involve the general Indian public should be used to make the kinds of compromises or innovations that are necessary in order to pursue economic development of the sort that a tribe can undertake successfully. The temptation to utilize the top-down style of decision-making that is prevalent in the dominant society will probably lead to adoption of strategies that are not acceptable to most people in a tribe. They may go along with the strategies as long as sufficient outside support is available; but when and if that support dries up, the project will fail in some manner. Because each tribe's mind set and institutions are a distinctive combination, one cannot provide a simple summary of advice about what solutions will follow from a process of self-evaluation. Such evaluation should lead to selection of new ways of action that are consistent with old ways of thinking and practice.

NOTES

1. I would like to thank Kurt Russo and Stephen Cornell for comments on an earlier version of this paper.

2. Stephen Cornell and Joseph P. Kalt, "Where's the Glue? Institutional Bases of American Indian Economic Development," Project Report Series, Harvard Project on American Indian Economic Development, John F. Kennedy School of Government, Harvard University, February 1991, p. 9.

3. Delores J. Huff undertook a similar project in her article, "The Tribal Ethic, The Protestant Ethic and American Indian Economic Development," *American Indian Policy and Cultural Values: Conflict and Accommodation*, edited by Jennie R. Joe (Los Angeles: American Indian Studies Center, UCLA, 1986), pp. 75–89.

4. Florence Rockwood Kluckhohn and Fred L. Strodtbeck, *Variations in Value Orientations* (Westport, CT: Greenwood Press, 1973), (originally published in 1961 by Row, Peterson and Company, Evanston, Illinois). After having observed value orientations through study of the anthropological literature on culture, Kluckhohn and her colleagues devised a questionnaire and tested the ideas by interviewing members of five communities in the Southwest. The results were that the questionnaire successfully measured the dimensions she had suggested existed, and the results corresponded to what other observers thought about the communities.

5. Ibid., pp. 10–24.

6. For the activity orientation, Kluckhohn and Strodtbeck suggest a third possibility: being-in-becoming, in which human personality is expressed by development of all aspects of the self as an integrated whole. Time did not allow them to develop questions for this orientation; persons in this category fall between being and doing in their responses on the questionnaire.

7. In this paper, I have replaced Kluckhohn's *collateral* with *group,* and *lineal* with *superiors.*

8. Fremont J. Lyden, "Value Orientations in Public Decision-Making," *Policy Studies Journal* 16, no. 4 (Summer 1988): 841–56.

9. Kluckhohn and Strodtbeck, *Variations in Value Orientations*, p. 86. Kluckhohn and Strodtbeck provide an extensive discussion of the origin and meaning of the proposed value orientations (pp. 10–48). They apply the orientations to a discussion of conformity, assimilation, roles, and culture change. The discussion reveals that the value orientations have wide applicability.

10. Ibid., pp. 4–6. As Kluckhohn and Strodtbeck note, value orientations are most strongly influenced by the directive aspect of human judgmental processes. While affected by cognitive and emotional elements, they are oriented toward *action* rather than toward understanding or feeling.

11. This typology has two main sources. The distinction between dualism and relativism comes from William Perry's work describing intellectual development. See William G. Perry, Jr., *Forms of Intellectual and Ethical Development in the College Years* (New York: Holt, Rinehart and Winston, 1970). The distinction between compartmentalized and holistic thinking comes from the literature on American Indian philosophy, summarized in J. Baird Callicott, "American Indian Land Wisdom? Sorting Out the Issues" in Callicott, *In Defense of the Land Ethic* (Albany, NY: State University of New York Press, 1989), pp. 203–22.

12. Max Weber, *Economy and Society*, vol. 1 (Berkeley, CA: University of California Press, 1978), pp. 215–45, 952–54.

13. A recent study of charisma updates Weber's analysis considerably. See Charles Lindholm, *Charisma* (Cambridge: Basil Blackwell, 1990). Lindholm argues (pp. 166–71) that the form and consequences of charisma in modern (capitalist) societies are different from its form and consequences in other societies. Key variables are community support for the leader and the presence of forms which charismatic leadership can use to avoid the dangerous manifestations represented by Hitler and Jim Jones. The dark side of charisma is particularly manifested in "rationalized" society—as Weber describes modern life—rather than

eliminated, as Weber expected. The connection between charisma and personality patterns is also explored by Stephen Ducat, *Taken In: American Gullibility and the Reagan Mythos* (Tacoma, WA: Life Sciences Press, 1988).

14. Lyden, "Value Orientations in Public Decision-Making," p. 848.

15. Renato Rosaldo, *Culture and Truth: The Remaking of Social Analysis* (Boston: Beacon Press, 1989), pp. 218–24.

16. Callicott, "American Indian Land Wisdom," provides some examples. See Peggy V. Beck and Anna L. Walters, *The Sacred: Ways of Knowledge, Sources of Life* (Tsaile, AZ: Navajo Community College Press, 1977) for another survey. The collection of articles in *Teachings from the American Earth: Indian Religion and Philosophy*, ed. Dennis Tedlock and Barbara Tedlock (New York: Liveright, 1975), is also very useful. Eight of the articles document specific world views of cultures such as Ojibwa, Tewa, and Sioux.

17. Dinesh D'Souza, *Illiberal Education: The Politics of Race and Sex on Campus* (New York: The Free Press, 1991). He is especially clear on pages 23 and 251.

18. A test of this would be to see the breakdown of undergraduates regarding choice of major: if more holistically oriented, a higher proportion of American Indians would select multidisciplinary majors.

19. Lindholm, *Charisma*, pp. 175–89.

20. Lyden, "Value Orientations in Public Decision-Making," p. 851.

21. Ibid., p. 848.

22. Robin Hahnel and Michael Albert, *Quiet Revolution in Welfare Economics* (Princeton, NJ: Princeton University Press, 1990), pp. 184–202.

23. Michael Albert and Robin Hahnel, *Looking Forward: Participatory Economics for the Twenty-First Century* (Boston: South End Press, 1991). They provide a clear statement of their value orientations, particularly in the relational dimension, in Hahnel and Albert, *Quiet*

Revolution in Welfare Economics, pp. 184–202.

24. In addition to Rosaldo's *Culture and Truth*, I like Stanley Cavell's *The Claim of Reason* (Oxford: Oxford University Press, 1979), and Ann Garry and Marilyn Pearsall, eds., *Women, Knowledge, and Reality* (Boston: Unwin Hyman, 1989). See also Nancy Fraser and Linda J. Nicholson, "Social Criticism Without Philosophy: An Encounter between Feminism and Postmodernism," in *Feminism/Postmodernism*, ed. Linda J. Nicholson (New York: Routledge, 1990), pp. 19–38.

25. Hahnel and Albert, *Quiet Revolution in Welfare Economics*, pp.184–202; Caroline Whitbeck, "A Different Reality: Feminist Ontology" in Garry and Pearsall, *Women, Knowledge, and Reality*, pp. 51–76; Rosaldo, *Culture and Truth*, pp. 168–217.

26. If a group of environmentalists fears that a tribe may develop a parcel of land, they may oppose tribal sovereignty.

27. An isolated individual has considerable difficulty combatting the persuasive powers of groups, particularly dominant authority. A review of these persuasive techniques is provided by Robert B. Cialdini, *Influence: The New Psychology of Modern Persuasion* (New York: Quill, 1984).

28. In spite of the failures of the allotment policy and termination, proponents of private property systems continue their efforts. The Political Economy Research Center sponsored two conferences and has a book motivated by a desire to promote private property systems for Indians. See Terry Anderson, ed., *Property Rights and Indian Economies* (Lanham, MD: Rowman & Littlefield, 1992).

29. Robert G. Eccles and Harrison C. White, "Price and Authority in Inter-Profit Center Transactions," *American Journal of Sociology* 94, Supplement (1988): pp. 517–51.

30. Lyden, "Value Orientations in Public Decision-Making," p. 851. See also Kurt Russo et al., *Values Project Northwest/XWLEMI* (Bellingham, WA: Lummi Business Council, 1985).

31. See Cornell and Kalt, "Reloading the Dice," in this volume.

32. Bruce E. Johansen and Donald A. Grinde, Jr., "The Debate Regarding Native American Precedents for Democracy: A Recent Historiography," *American Indian Culture and Research Journal*, 14, no. 1 (1990): pp. 61–88, provide, in part, a survey of the evidence regarding the principles of checks and balances of the Iroquois confederacy and their contributions to the American Constitution.

33. Duane Champagne, *American Indian Societies: Strategies and Conditions of Political and Cultural Survival* (Cambridge: Cultural Survival, Inc., 1989), pp. 142–45.

34. Kurt Russo et al., *Values Project Northwest/XWLEMI*. For more information on this project, contact Values Project Northwest, Kurt Russo, Director, 2616 Kwina Road, Bellingham, Washington 98226 (206) 734-8180.

AUTHORS

Michael W. Cameron is a project manager with the Environmental Defense Fund, a nonprofit conservation organization in Oakland, California.

Hedy Nai-Lin Chang is associate director of California Tomorrow, a nonprofit policy research and advocacy organization committed to a fair, working, multicultural, multiracial California.

Eduardo E. Cordeiro is an economic analyst with the Economics Resource Group, Cambridge, Massachusetts.

Stephen Cornell is associate professor of sociology at the University of California, San Diego, and codirector of the Harvard Project on American Indian Economic Development.

Margaret Barnwell Hargreaves is a welfare research analyst at Abt Associates, a Cambridge, Massachusetts-based social policy research and consulting firm.

Joseph P. Kalt is professor of political economy at the John F. Kennedy School of Government, Harvard University, and codirector of the Harvard Project on American Indian Economic Development.

Matthew B. Krepps is a Ph.D. student in business economics at Harvard University.

Paul Nissenbaum is a policy analyst with Apogee Research Inc. in Bethesda, Maryland.

Paul Shadle is a technical analyst at EG&G Dynatrend Inc., working on regional planning issues for the United States Department of Transportation..

Andrea Skari (Turtle Mountain Chippewa) is studying for an MLA degree at the Graduate School of Design at Harvard University.

Ronald L. Trosper (Salish and Kootenai) is associate professor of forestry and director of the Native American Forestry Program at Northern Arizona University and former tribal economist, Confederated Salish and Kootenai Tribes of the Flathead Reservation, Montana.